Hacks and Dunces
Pope, Swift and Grub Street

PAT ROGERS

METHUEN

LONDON and NEW YORK

Grub Street: Studies in a Subculture
first published in 1972
This abridgement first published as a
University Paperback in 1980 by
Methuen & Co. Ltd
11 New Fetter Lane, London EC4P 4EE

Published in the USA by
Methuen & Co.
in association with Methuen, Inc.
733 Third Avenue, New York, NY 10017

© *1972, 1980 Pat Rogers*

Printed in Great Britain by
J. W. Arrowsmith Ltd, Bristol

British Library Cataloguing in Publication Data
Rogers, Pat
Hacks and dunces. – Abridged ed. – (University
paperbacks; 704).
1. *Pope, Alexander – Knowledge – Literature*
2. *Hack writers in literature*
3. *Swift, Jonathan – Knowledge – Literature*
I. *Title*   II. *Grub Street*   III. *Series*
821'.5   PR3637.H/

ISBN 0–416–74240–8

Contents

Preface to the paperback edition

When *Grub Street* was published in 1972, it met with a very generous reception, and some helpful reviews. One criticism made, however, was that the book attempted to cover too much ground. The point was made most forcibly by an anonymous writer in *The Times Literary Supplement*, who exclaimed, 'Is it ungracious to complain at being thus presented with six volumes for the price of one?' The original book has now been out of print for some time, and the opportunity has arisen to meet the point. It was not difficult to take the objection to heart, and to produce a more economical and concentrated version of the work. The present text consists of rather more than half of the original book: that is, a corrected reprint of the Introduction together with Chapters I, II and IV. These are the sections most directly concerned with the literary masterpieces exploring the Grub Street milieu, above all *The Dunciad* and *A Tale of a Tub*. There is therefore a sharper focus on Swift and Pope at the centre of the inquiry. The sections dealing with other topics (Defoe, Fielding, Johnson, and the history of what I term the 'Grub Street myth') have been excluded, on the basis of the *TLS* reviewer's suggestion that they 'belong to another book'.

In other respects I do not see any occasion to alter the substance of what I formerly wrote. The progress of Augustan studies, fortunately, is not so hectic that obsolescence will set in after a decade. I have corrected a few typographical errors, and added a brief passage on page 15 in an attempt to explain more clearly the stance which the book takes on a controversial issue.

1980   P.R.

In Memory of my Mother

Acknowledgements

Most of the work for this book has been undertaken in the Guild-hall Library, the Corporation of London Records Office, the Greater London Council Records Office, Westminster Library, the Public Record Office, the British Museum Library and Cambridge University Library. I am grateful to archivists and librarians who have allowed me access to their collections.

The best way to understand an age, of course, is to read its own books and journals, to look at its own paintings and engravings. But to limit oneself to contemporary sources, when modern scholarship can add so much by way of instruction and delight, is to eat acorn with the swine. Among published writings, the work of these authorities has left me hugely in their debt: Dorothy George, Dorothy Marshall, J. H. Plumb, Sir Leon Radzinowicz, George Rudé, James Sutherland and the late Sir William Holdsworth. Earlier generations of topographical writers, ranging from Strype, Maitland and Malcolm to H. B. Wheatley and Sir Walter Besant, have provided indispensable aid. Nor have I disdained the vast library of popular books on London: the works of E. B. Chancellor furnished a range of usually reliable (if not precisely scholarly) information. Like other commentators on the Plague and the Great Fire, I have found the studies of W. G. Bell still unsupplanted as comprehensive accounts of their subject. Finally, I have relied heavily on the mapmakers of London, especially those of the late seventeenth and early eighteenth centuries. The modern *Survey of London* is alas uncompleted, but the extant volumes in this series, along with certain publications of the London Topographical Society, have always been at hand to consult as informants of the last resort. For a general presentation of the city at the time, Ogilby, Morden and Lea, and Rocque survive without serious challenge from any modern reconstructions.

ix

ACKNOWLEDGEMENTS

When I began on this book, I was lucky to receive the encouragement of Ian Jack, Denis Donoghue and George Watson, whose own distinguished achievements were a stimulus in themselves. Ian Watt kindly read an early draft of the opening sections and made shrewd but charitable criticisms. None of these gentlemen is to be held accountable for the errors and imperfections of the book which has actually emerged.

I have indicated my indebtedness by a specific reference in the footnotes wherever possible. But my enthusiasm for the world delineated in this book was a contagion early succumbed to; and I cannot be sure that I have not on occasions borrowed ideas or emphases unwittingly from previous students of the age.

Abbreviations

Short forms and cue titles are employed for the most frequently consulted printed sources, as follows:

Arbuthnot.	G. A. Aitken, *The Life and Works of John Arbuthnot* (Oxford, 1892).
Baddeley.	J. J. Baddeley, *An Account of the Church and Parish of St Giles, without Cripplegate* (London, 1888).
Bayne-Powell.	Rosamond Bayne-Powell, *Eighteenth-Century London Life* (London, 1937).
Besant.	Sir Walter Besant, *London in the Eighteenth Century* (London, ed. 1925).
Butt.	*The Poems of Alexander Pope*, ed. J. Butt (London, 1963).
Calendar.	*The Newgate Calendar*, ed. G. T. Wilkinson (London, ed. 1963).
Clifford.	J. L. Clifford, *Young Samuel Johnson* (London, 1962).
Cross.	W. L. Cross, *The History of Henry Fielding* (New Haven, 1918).
Defoe, *Letters.*	*The Letters of Daniel Defoe*, ed. G. H. Healey (Oxford, 1955).
Defoe, *Tour.*	Daniel Defoe, *A Tour thro' the Whole Island of Great Britain*, ed. G. D. H. Cole (London, 1927).
Denton.	W. Denton, *Records of St Giles' Cripplegate* (London, 1883).
E/C.	*The Works of Alexander Pope*, ed. W. Elwin, W. J. Courthope (London, 1872–89).
Ehrenpreis.	Irvin Ehrenpreis, *Swift: The Man, the Works and the Age* (London, 1962–).

Faber.	*The Poetical Works of John Gay*, ed. G. C. Faber (London, 1926).
Fielding.	*The Complete Works of Henry Fielding*, ed. W. E. Henley (New York, ed. 1967).
George.	M. Dorothy George, *London Life in the Eighteenth Century* (Harmondsworth, 1966).
Gomme.	*Topographic History of London*, ed. G. L. Gomme (London, 1904).
Harben.	Henry Harben, *A Dictionary of London* (London, 1918).
Holdsworth.	Sir William Holdsworth, *A History of English Law* (London, 1922–38).
Irving.	W. H. Irving, *John Gay's London* (Cambridge, Mass., 1928).
Journal.	Jonathan Swift, *Journal to Stella*, ed. H. Williams (Oxford, 1948).
Lee.	William Lee, *Daniel Defoe : His Life and Recently Discovered Writings* (London, 1869).
London Past & Present.	H. B. Wheatley, P. Cunningham, *London Past and Present* (London, 1891).
Maitland.	William Maitland, *The History and Survey of London* (London, 1756).
Malcolm.	J. P. Malcolm, *Anecdotes of London, during the Eighteenth Century* (London, 1810).
Marshall.	Dorothy Marshall, *Dr Johnson's London* (New York, 1968).
Moore, *Checklist.*	J. R. Moore, *A Checklist of the Writings of Daniel Defoe* (Bloomington, 1960).
Moore, *Citizen.*	J. R. Moore, *Daniel Defoe Citizen of the Modern World* (Chicago, 1958).
New Remarks.	*New Remarks of London . . . Collected by the Company of Parish-Clerks* (London, 1732).
Oldmixon.	John Oldmixon, *The History of England* (London, 1735).
Paulson.	*Hogarth's Graphic Works*, ed. R. Paulson (New Haven, 1965).

Pope,   *The Correspondence of Alexander Pope*, ed. G.
   Correspondence.   Sherburn (Oxford, 1956).

Pope, *Prose Works.* The Prose Works of Alexander Pope, ed. N. Ault (Oxford, 1936), Vol. I (all published).

Radzinowicz.   Leon Radzinowicz, *A History of English Criminal Law* (London, 1948–).

Romances and   *Romances and Narratives by Daniel Defoe*, ed.
   Narratives.   G. A. Aitken (London, 1895).

Sherburn.   George Sherburn, *The Early Career of Alexander Pope* (Oxford, 1934).

Society.   *Memoirs of the Society of Grub-Street* (London, 1737).

Steeves.   Pope, *The Art of Sinking in Poetry*, ed. E. L. Steeves (New York, 1952).

State Trials.   *State Trials*, ed. T. B. Howell (London, 1812).

Stow.   John Stow, *The Survey of London* (London, ed. 1633).

Straus.   Ralph Straus, *The Unspeakable Curll* (London, 1927).

Strype.   John Strype's edn of Stow's *Survey of London* (London, 1720).

Sutherland.   James Sutherland, *Defoe* (London, ed. 1950).

Swift,   *The Prose Works of Jonathan Swift*, ed. H. Davis
   Prose Works.   et. al. (Oxford, 1939–68).

Swift,   *The Correspondence of Jonathan Swift*, ed. H.
   Correspondence. Williams (Oxford, 1963–5).

Swift, *Poems.*   Swift, *Poetical Works*, ed. H. Davis (London, 1967).

Tale.   Swift, *A Tale of a Tub* [etc.], ed. A. C. Guthkelch, D. Nichol Smith (Oxford, ed. 1958).

Thornbury.   Walter Thornbury, *Old and New London* (London, nd.).

TE.   The Twickenham edition of *The Poems of Alexander Pope*, ed. J. Butt (London, 1939–69). *The Dunciad*, ed. J. Sutherland, is quoted from the third edition (1963). For the one-volume text, see Butt.

Trevelyan.   G. M. Trevelyan, *England under Queen Anne* (London, ed. 1965).

Turberville.   *Johnson's England*, ed. A. S. Turberville (Oxford, 1933).

Watt.   Ian Watt, *The Rise of the Novel* (Harmondsworth, 1963).

Webb.   Sidney and Beatrice Webb, *English Local Government* (London, ed. 1963).

Wheatley.   H. B. Wheatley, *Hogarth's London* (London, 1909).

Williams.   Aubrey Williams, *Pope's Dunciad* (London, 1955).

The City of London, Westminster and Southwark in the eighteenth century

Cripplegate Ward in the eighteenth century

Moorfields

Bedlam

Line of City wall
Parish Boundary

Cripplegate Without

Bunhill Fields

FINSBURY

Coleman Street

LITTLE MOORFIELDS
(BACK STREET)

CHISWELL STREET

ROPEMAKERS ALLEY

MOOR LANE

Moorgate

FORE STREET

LONDON-WALL

Guildhall

BASINGHALL STREET

GRUB STREET

Sion College

ALDERMANBURY

WHITE CROSS STREET

Cripplegate

WOOD STREET

BEECH LANE

St Giles

RED CROSS STREET

GOLDEN LANE

JEWEN STREET

BARBICAN

Nursery Theatre

0   100   200 Yards

approximate scale

Introduction
The Topography of Dulness

Thus, *Wit* has its Walks and Purlieus, out of which it may not stray
the breadth of an Hair, upon peril of being lost. The *Moderns* have art-
fully fixed this *Mercury*, and reduced it to the Circumstances of Time,
Place and Person. Such a Jest there is, that will not pass out of *Covent-
Garden*; and such a one, that is nowhere intelligible but at *Hide-Park*
Corner.

Swift, A Tale of a Tub

'Grub Street' entered the language in the seventeenth century, became almost a household phrase in Hanoverian England, and survives
in modern parlance with a rather diminished identity. Its metaphorical sense lives on, although the road itself was renamed Milton
Street in 1830 and has now been swallowed virtually whole in the
immense Barbican building scheme. This loss of physical presence
is a shame. For we can hardly grasp the full force of the metaphor
unless we know something of the literal existence of the place. The
geographical environs of Grub Street were noisy, squalid and
crowded; the moral overtones which the phrase carried in its transferred sense came initially from this fact, and were heightened for
contemporaries by the social character which the district continued
to bear. Hack writers actually did live in Cripplegate Ward Without,
in and around Grub Street. This fact, I believe, gives an added
dimension to the many opprobious references to denizens of the
place which we find in Augustan literature – satire especially.

Yet very little is known about the sociology of the region. The
milieu of Duncehood was, first and foremost, the parish of St Giles',
Cripplegate, in the liberties of the City of London. Now it is not hard
to find out much solid fact concerning the ecology of this parish and
its environs in the early eighteenth century. Surprisingly, no one has

I

ever troubled to do this. The card catalogue of the Guildhall Library, which is perhaps the most compendious reference tool we have to London topography, contains only two entries under the heading 'Grub Street'. In one case, the connection with the street is fortuitous. In the other, we are led to a privately printed monograph of mid-Victorian origin – an amiable and rather desultory work by an antiquarian, very much characteristic of its period, and not very full or rigorous in its scholarship. And that is about all.[1] More recent students have rarely bothered to note, even in passing, the existence of a real place called Grub Street, even though they use the name as a chapter heading and liberally besprinkle their pages with the phrase in its figurative application.[2] One aim of this book is to show that the social conditions in which the hacks lived and worked are not beyond research. Another is to establish the fact that this material, once assembled, can fill out our understanding of eighteenth-century literature at a level deeper than that of mere 'topographic' reference.

If tragedy concerns itself with the insupportable, then satire takes as its province what may just be borne. Augustan satire is peculiarly occupied by that harsh, fetid, oppressively physical world of pain and pestilence which dominates the landscape of Pope, Swift and Hogarth. All satirists need to have enemies. But not all have found it necessary to name names so insistently, to enrol their victims in a society of folly, to stick so closely to topical reality. For these men, the characteristic butt is not a generalised Maevius but an individualised Thomas Wharton. The typical setting is not a vague infernal region but a particular locality such as Covent Garden market or Temple Bar.[3] London, indeed, becomes a central symbol of their work. The city serves as a type of Pandemonium. Its streets, courts and alleys constitute a new map of hell. Its markets, theatres, prisons, hospitals and ditches make up a gazetteer of folly and iniquity. Many critics have supposed that the density of topographic reference in all these artists is a mere trick in the fingers. I think it is less superficial than that. The Augustans use the physical detail of contemporary London to support their fictions, much as Dante used the theological scheme of St Thomas as a poetic framework, or as Blake and Yeats employed an invented mythology. The difference is that Pope did not

2

contrive his own moral universe. His satiric cosmology is based on the geography of the London of his day. He makes topography serve as moral symbolism.

A number of influential recent commentators have argued that we need not concern ourselves unduly with the victims of Augustan satire. No: more than that, they have asserted that it is positively distracting to do so. This book has been actuated by a radically different belief. I shall contend that it *is* profitable to adopt, at least for a moment, the Dunce's eye view.[4] By studying the victim in his natural habitat, we do gain considerable insight into the procedures and motivation of the satirist. By taking seriously the replies which the hack made to Swift, for instance, we may often find out more about the Dean's intentions than if we restricted ourselves to the presuppositions of Renaissance humanism, or the *données* of Anglican rationalism. It is, apart from anything else, a favourite device of the Scriblerian party to beat down an opponent with his own weapon. Footling writers the Dunces may have been – many certainly were – but their existence was no footling thing for the course of English satire.

Bad writing has often been the occasion, or proximate cause, of good – witness *Northanger Abbey*. The great stroke of the Augustan satirists was to make the world of low literature serve as subject and setting of their works. Both Swift's *Tale* and *The Dunciad* reflect in their narrative the buffeting, combative existence of the hacks; their imagery is filled with disease and disaster, as were the seamier parts of London familiar to the hack. This means that the scribbler's environment is as much the satiric target as the writers themselves. Grub Street is the Dunces' milieu; but it is also the expression of their corporate identity. Like so many Scriblerian inventions, it has one foot in the real world, the other in an imaginative realm.

As everybody knows, the subject-matter of Pope, Swift and Hogarth is replete with obnoxious detail. Their recurrent motifs are squalor, pestilence, ordure, poverty: their mode is one of physicality, their tone is often that of outrage or disgust. (Sometimes a hyberbolic outrage for comic ends, but that makes little difference.) I do not think it has been sufficiently realised that this reflects not only a

3

general inheritance, from Juvenal or Bosch, but also a particular response to the conditions of the time. Climatic events of recent history, such as the Plague and the Great Fire, suffuse their imagery and hang over their drama. Once again, we can only come to grips with their richest artistic statements if we desert the overcrowded consulting room of the private pathologist, and follow the satirists to the seething crowd outside Newgate or to the public spectacle which was Bedlam. Theirs was a clamorous, savage, often brutal world. In Professor Plumb's words, it was filled 'with violence and aggression, with coarse language and gross manners, with dirt, disease and lust.'[5] London, especially, was in many parts overcrowded, malodorous, tumultuous: an insecure, neurotic city where King Mob might at any time resume his reign after the briefest interregnum. (Sacheverell, Ormonde, the gin act, the excise crisis – almost anything might be the occasion.) Small wonder that the art of satirist fixes, with hallucinatory clarity, on the here and now. As for the 'now', we may recall how many of the figures portrayed by Hogarth are identifiable individuals, compared with those of Rowlandson. And as for the 'here', there is a further consideration we should keep in mind.

London was then a much smaller place than it is today. The population of the combined metropolis, including Westminster, Southwark and the out-parishes, fell short of 700,000 at the start of the eighteenth century; moreover, these people were herded together appallingly closely in many districts. Most inhabitants of the capital lived near their work. Merchants were beginning to acquire country-boxes at Clapham or Hampstead, but the City was never the ghost-town at the weekends which it is today. Again travel was slow, virtually always on the surface of the earth (rarely subterranean and never superterrene), and often dangerous – it demanded one's full attentiveness. One was, besides, longer about a given journey: 'This Town is grown to such an enormous size,' wrote Mrs Pendarves to Swift in 1736, 'that above half the day must be spent in the streets in going from one place to another.'[6] Places only a few miles distant from the city were regarded as remote: Ward of Hackney could be so identified – as opposed to Ned Ward of Moorfields, say – almost as though he were an ancestral laird. Defoe in Stoke Newington was an early exurbanite. Moreover, it was not yet customary to give numbers to houses, so that a particular coffee-house or bookseller's shop would be located by a physical description, even on the cover of a letter – 'over against Catharine Street' or 'two doors from the Exchange'. Finally, really large buildings were comparatively rare. There were no vast offices, no blocks of flats, no railway termini. Thus, apart from the occasional private mansion such as Montagu House or Marlborough House (and they were mostly on the outskirts), the main public edifices stood out stark and unmistakable. Churches, prisons, hospitals, mercantile centres – this was the kind of landmark which any Londoner would know from childhood. It takes an imaginative effort to put oneself into this visual setting, with its primary horizontal emphasis: but that is the world into which the hacks were born.

It is interesting to note that, at a climatic moment in *Clarissa*, a novel now somewhat overburdened with moral-cum-metaphysical readings, the same particularity reasserts itself. When Clarissa is arrested as she leaves St Paul's, Covent Garden ('at the door fronting Bedford Street'), she is told by the sheriff's officer that she must accompany him to High Holborn. 'I know not where High Holborn is,' is her bewildered response – geographical innocence of the city's thoroughfares portending, of course, much more. Then, 'looking about her, and seeing the three passages, to wit, that leading to Henrietta Street, that to King Street, and the fore-right one, to Bedford Street, crowded, she started. Anywhere – anywhere, said she, but to the woman's!' (Letter CV.) This passage has something of the flavour of a tableau in classical history painting – Hercules at the fork in the road. Something but not all: for the mythological suggestions are severely qualified by the explicitness with which the streets are named. Even at such a fateful moment for the heroine, Richardson keeps his eye on the imaginative geography of the scene. Clarissa's reluctance to go back to Mrs Sinclair's is conveyed by a sort of vertiginous befuddlement, in which the streets appear before her distracted gaze as alarming moral alternatives.[7]

It follows from all these facts, that to contemporaries, the social mode of the satirists was all the more comprehensible because of its ready dependence on topography. In 1730 one navigated not by tube stations or bus routes, but by given features of the landscape, most of which played an obvious part in the religious, legal or commercial life of the city, and dominated a little hinterland of their own. Smithfield, St Paul's and the Fleet River are straightforward examples. Similarly, one navigates the satire of Pope, Gay or Swift with the help of these conspicuous directional aids: now become moral landmarks, they carry special associations – broadly sociological or historical – which help to underpin the satire. In this book I try to provide a sort of gazetteer, to assist the modern reader to pick up these associations with something of the fluency and delight with which men and women of the eighteenth century seized on them. This is a route-map to explore the comedy of Grub Street. For the *zest* with which Pope and Swift, especially, responded to the facts of life around them is not always fully appreciated. In an age when the life of the streets was a standard theme, Swift stands out for the vivid and graphic immediacy of his handling of this topic. The sense of fascinated outrage which penetrates the satire of both men appears with notable force in this area of their response. I shall try in this book to convey something of this energy: an energy often of rejection and contumely, yet an indispensable factor in the concentrated power of their satire. In the imaginatively charted streets of London, Blake – the Londoner born and bred – hears the youthful harlot's curse as a kind of universal malediction. With the Scriblerians, fixing on an external reality somehow alien yet deeply compelling, the harlot becomes a character in a localised drama: her utterance is specified, as it is registered on the mind of the author and reader with the sharpness of outline that belongs to idyll and to nightmare. It is exactly the distinction of Pope and Swift that they are *not* transcendental in Blake's way.

*   *   *

It has, of course, long been recognised that satire in this age is rich in topographic allusion. But this has nearly always been dismissed as a sort of local colour, and not much has been made of this recognition in the service of worthwhile critical ends. In most cases, a little inert social history is dredged out of *Trivia* and poems of that kind, for a section entitled 'The Life of the Streets'.[8] That is, the movement is from literature towards documentation. The author combs satiric literature in order to tell us something about early eighteenth-century life in the capital. This book proceeds in an opposite direction. I hope to show how a knowledge of London topography can inform and enrich a reading of the greatest satire of the period. That is another distinction in passing. Usually critics have found it necessary to engage in London espionage with Ned Ward, and to bring in Pope or Gay only as incidental witnesses from outside, literary daytrippers rather than residents. Here the great writers will be allotted a more central place.

The only serious study of the topography of *The Dunciad*, for example, is that of Aubrey Williams. Excellent as this is, it concentrates entirely on the itinerary of the Dunces' 'progress', and the relation of that to the course followed by the official party on the real-life Lord Mayor's Day.[9] In the context of Williams' immediate purposes, this was an unimpeachable procedure on his part. But there remains a great deal else. For the effective geography of the poem is not confined to the carnival procession of folly to St Mary le Strand and back again. It includes a much denser review of the city, its inhabitants and its institutions; and likewise relies on a far more inward acquaintance with London topography than most of us can hope to possess today. This, of course, is not in order merely to make out the external action of the poem, or the siting of any particular episode. Rather, it is so if we are to understand the imaginative workings of Pope's fiction, and to respond to its underlying human and social implications. On one level, the poem is about the onset/spread/contagious power/epidemic character/low associations of evil. This pestilence may be described as folly, Dulness, modernism, the uncreating word – what you will. About the *content* of Pope's views, if we may distinguish such a thing, I am in almost total agreement with the splendid and authoritative reading provided by Professor Williams. But the *method* of the poem is perhaps even more complex, more fully orchestrated and more effective than he allows. My view of *The Dunciad*, briefly, is that it is a work where human geography becomes symbolism.

The image of the City, in Augustan satire, is a sombre one. Pope, impelled by his 'rage for order', fixes again and again on the thorough-fares of London in order to image disorder. Swift reverts to the dirt and rubble of the streets; his is a world of garrets, night-cellars, prostitutes. John Gay devotes an entire poem to the effective refutation of an ironic thesis:

Happy *Augusta*! law-defended town![10]

Elsewhere Gay composes town eclogues and Newgate pastoral. In each case the point is the same. The unpleasant physical facts of the contemporary town serve as a negative image: an actuality of poverty, confusion and immorality to set against the dream of learning, the vision of heroism, or the pastoral idyll. London, failing to be an Augustan metropolis of epic stature, exposes – as it literally contains – the sordid reality which is the empire of Dulness.

There is a good reason why the satirists should have used geography to make their point. At this time spatial arrangement was still regarded as in some manner symbolic. The self-evident mode of revelation found in a Gothic cathedral was no longer imitated. But the lay-out of a Georgian country-house does, more subtly, affirm a whole hierarchical system of values. To move through such a house is to enact a declaration of assent to the Augustan notions of social living. As one traverses the ground floor, from the imposing central salon, through formal reception-rooms into the library and private apartments, one experiences a sense of public dignity melting into personal amenity. (Sometimes the separation of the parts is more clearcut: but the basic point still holds. At Blenheim, the great hall and the saloon are flanked, in the central block, by state apartments: the private quarters are set at right-angles, in each wing, though this is disguised on the main North front by the curving arcade. But then Blenheim was a monument to official virtue. A house like Stowe is more typical; as well as patriotic zeal, the mansion testifies to the moral value of 'retirement'.)

On occasions, this sense of material symbolism was taken to excess. It was certainly very strong in Horace Walpole, who actually slept with a copy of Magna Carta on one side of his bed and the warrant for the execution of Charles I on the other.[11] Walpole carefully compiled *A Description of . . . Strawberry Hill* (1774), and laid out its separate parts with deliberate artifice: much as he would have adjusted the *disponsibles* of a literary composition. Not all the arrangements were, perhaps, ideal: the pantry was next to the oratory, and the kitchen seems to have been in the opposite corner of the villa from the refectory – which cannot have pleased the servants.[12] But, all in all, it is plain that Walpole did wish to make definite statements about himself and his own mode of living by the way space was allocated. Pope's rhetorical point derives from a similar insight. The way London is laid out testifies to the life which is led there.

The density of topographic allusion, then, in Pope's work is no accident. Places and poems are capable of every kind of mutual relationship. In this case, the social background of a living London goes to inform the whole imaginative construct which Pope has fabricated. A number of factors which contribute to that process are worth brief examination.

Initially, we should remember that on one level *The Dunciad* is a poem about civil dudgeon. From the Restoration onwards an important strand of polite literature takes its origin from what we might call, following the title of a play by John Crowne (1683), city politics. The fervour with which issues were fought out in London a little later has been described by two recent historians: 'A political thermometer would have recorded a constant high temperature in the capital during the reigns of William and Anne . . . Party politics mixed with both the business and pleasure of Londoners. . . . The spirit of party . . . penetrated into the leisure haunts of the capital.' Now, it is true of course that Pope does not directly take up these squabbles in his work: his comments on the attempts to annex *Cato* by the two parties, on its opening night, are detached and amused. But he was after all the son of a London merchant, even though one who had retired to the seclusion of Windsor Forest. He grew up during the time of ferment described in the last quotation. As a result, his work is stuffed with references to aldermen and City magnates – his Horatian poems, perhaps most conspicuously. Just as Swift brought in the famous episode involving Sir Humphrey Edwin into his *Tale*, so Pope never transferred his imaginative gaze from London for very long. Macaulay once observed that in this age 'the influence of the City of London was felt to the remotest corner of the realm.' This is true artistically, as well as politically.[13] The reasons for that lie partly in the sociological character of the place around 1700.

London was then by far the biggest town in the land. The metropolitan area contained about one eighth of the entire population of England and Wales.[14] For this reason alone, civil broils took on microcosmic significance, at the same time as they constituted in sober reality macrocosmic facts. The city as a whole covered a relatively small space by modern standards. Yet within a few square miles there were marked disparities in living standards, whether we interpret that phrase to connote economic levels or *mores*. Restoration London was not much more than a congeries of villages. Hence the readiness with which men and women of the time distinguished between the separate zones of the town, physically adjacent as they were. Steele – to take one example among many – has a character in *The Tender Husband* remark: 'You are so public an envoy, or rather plenipotentiary, from the very different nations of Cheapside, Covent Garden, and St James's: you have, too, the mien and language of each place so naturally . . .' Addison was to use exactly the same significant image ('an aggregate of several nations, distinguished from each other by their respective customs, manners and interests . . .')[15] It was in this way there grew up the situation described by Ian Watt as a typical feature of the new urbanised landscape: 'this combination of physical proximity and vast social distance.'[16] Grub Street was within comfortable walking distance of, say, the new Bank of England. But it was not a very well worn path, for a great dividing line (symbolised neatly by the old walls of the City) stood between the two. Similarly, the slums of St Giles' ran almost up against the opulent new developments to the north of what was beginning to be called Oxford Street: yet their interaction was minimal. In a less sophisticated society, it would seem that visible barriers such as a ditch or a bastion count for more in psychological terms; remarkably often, the parish and ward divisions follow some such obvious feature. The social contours are mapped out by the geographical terrain.

There is an important reason why place names crop up with such remarkable frequency. To the modern city-dweller, the title bestowed on a road or a district is a historical accident – a dead metaphor. To the Augustans, the metaphor was still living, at least in part. If one looks at a contemporary map of London, this becomes clear. Take as a convenient instance the map published by Dodsley in 1761, used for the endpapers of Boswell's *London Journal*.[17] In the borough of Southwark, the following is a complete list of the streets named: The Broad Wall, Angel Street, Melancholy Walk, Gravel Lane, Love Lane, Bankside, Bear Garden, Maid Lane, Clink Street, Dead Man's Place, Red Cross Street, Dirty Lane (twice), Foul Lane. I have set down these names as they came: it would be possible to rearrange them in a more striking, quasi-narrative order. It must be apparent that such titles fulfil more than a narrow attributive role. They are descriptive labels. People of the age still saw symbolic meanings in a name, which in any case was held to be of divine origin and hence magical in quality. A clear case of what happened is provided by the widespread view that the Great Fire was a visitation from the Almighty: a view sanctioned by the erroneous belief that the fire had started in Pudding Lane and ended at Pie Corner – and must consequently have been designed as a warning against gluttony. The same literal-minded concern with nomenclature emerges from one of the many poems written just after the fire, 'London's Remains' (1667):

> *PHYSICIANS COLLEDG* next, its *Seat* did *Fit*,
> Whether by Chance there plac'd or *Wit*.
> It stood at *Amen, Paternoster's* close;
> For he needs pray that takes a *Dose*.

The punning only works because people still took place names seriously, as an indication of what you might expect to find there.[18]

Pope capitalises on this situation, which provided him with a readymade symbolic framework, in a variety of ways. One of his concerns is to suggest that a certain kind of soil breeds and nurtures a certain kind of plant. That is, he takes over from the second *Georgic* the idea that there is a proper habitat for each created thing:

> Nunc locus arvorum ingeniis . . .

It is a long way, perhaps, from willows and vines to starveling writers (that is part of the joke.)[19] But 'the genius of soils' can be applied to human ecology, as well as that of plants. This is one reason why Pope takes such pains to describe 'The cave of Poverty and Poetry' at the outset. 'Th' imperial seat of Fools', whether Rag Fair or Grub Street, is the nerve-centre for Dulness; but in addition it is a type of the social degradation that waits on Dulness ('Emblem of music caus'd by Emptiness . . . The cave of Poverty and Poetry.') Moreover, Pope deliberately selects an image which relates the spiritual squalor of his victims to the actual squalor which he had set out in his 'Further Account of . . . Curll':

> Here in one bed two shiv'ring sisters lye.

In this, they are but avatars of the scapegrace life led by professional hacks: the two translators in bed together in Moorfields, the other pair in the flock-bed at Cursitor's Alley. Both unions, needless to say, are sterile.

Another rhetorical stratagem is to insinuate that literary vice, because it is practised in the same dingy quarters as social wrong-doing, is directly equivalent. Everyone knows the famous couplet about Lady Mary, in the Horatian satire addressed to Fortescue:

> From furious *Sappho* scarce a milder Fate,
> P-x'd by her Love, or libell'd by her Hate . . .[20]

What *The Dunciad* shows is that you got yourself libelled in just the same districts as you got yourself poxed. A topographic identity becomes a moral equivalence. Again, a third device is to deflate grandiose pretensions by reminding the Dunce that his epic ambitions are acted out in downtown slums and suburban alleys. Blackmore's claims as a heroic poet have to withstand a succession of blows in the poem, but few more cutting than the reminder that his effective audience does not extend beyond Tottenham and Hungerford. Pope has dramatised in spatial terms an evaluative critical judgement. We cannot move far in *The Dunciad* without finding this kind of technique. It is an almost topological poem: space and distance are part of its essential mechanics.

The propositions outlined so far may perhaps be corroborated by the insights of the modern study of human ecology. A standard text on *Urban Society*, for instance, described how residential zones follow 'differences of social class, religion, ethnic origin, and race.' And, arguing that 'the division of labour and social differences often reinforce one another', the authors state:

> Social isolationism is reinforced by spatial isolationism; the more people are spatially segregated, the less likely are they to come into intimate contact with each other. At least the possibilities of close relationships on the basis of social equality are greatly reduced. Instead, contacts tend to be formalized, confined principally to the market place or the work situation. People who . . . have contacts of a strictly economic character, may live in entirely different social and ecological worlds.

This is surely apposite to the relations of Pope and his book-sellers. Tonson, alone, had purchased enough respectability at Barn Elms to acquire something approaching friendship, though not equality. Lintot may be used as a subscription agent, but will still be a Dunce. It is much the same with Swift and men like Motte, Barber and Faulkner, whom he genuinely liked (though here London's remoteness from Dublin is a factor). The ease with which the major writers kept themselves at a distance from the trade, except in the purely mercantile role, is symbolised by the fact that Pope scarcely ever went into the City, if his correspondence is any guide, although the trade was increasingly centred there. Nor, of course, did he make many excursions into St Giles' or Cripplegate. His contacts with Drury Lane seem remarkably few, for one who was connected quite closely with the theatre for a number of years. Pope's rejection of the way of life of the city is fitly represented by his withdrawal to Twickenham, whatever the legal basis of that move. Yet he did spend a great deal of time in London, and as we have seen displayed abundant knowledge of the town. It remains true that his first-hand dealings with the enclaves of Dulness must have been fleeting and lacking in intimacy.

The same textbook contains this passage:

> Human ecology goes farther than merely determining where designated groups are localized or where particular functions of these groups are performed. It is also concerned with interactive relationships between individuals and groups and the way these relationships influence, or are influenced by, particular spatial patterns and processes.[21]

13

Now, Pope's treatment of social reality as he saw it makes clear how 'particular spatial patterns and processes' (such as the westward march of the trading class) influences relationships. Augustan society superimposed a spatial segregation on a vertical social hierarchy, and amongst other things *The Dunciad* gives us an imaginative vision of the moral entity which was the city, imaged by its topographic and ecological indentity. The 'map' is finally only a palimpsest. For the Grub Street which shows up there as an outlying enclave is no more than a shadow on the wall of the cave. The real Grub Street is elsewhere: an outlying enclave in the metropolis of letters.

*   *   *

The argument of this book is laid out on a simple plan. Chapter I describes the main centres of Dulness, notably the history and character of Grub Street proper, and locates the Dunces themselves in their particular haunt. The second chapter examines some of the ways in which the 'real life' of London affect Augustan writing. By this I mean not simply the literal occurrence of fire, disease and rioting within eighteenth-century works, but also the imaginative resonance of these motifs in the idiom of satire. The third chapter considers Swift's dealings with Grub Street.

Throughout the book, I have attempted to present a world and not merely to juggle with ideas. First and foremost, this is a history – of words, of places, of feelings. The overriding intent is that of describing how things were, or seemed to people, at a specific moment of time. I do not assert that there is a necessary connection between Grub Street and squalid social conditions: rather, that there was an observable link at this period. It may be that in other ages the hack would stand in a different relationship to the major artist. I have not considered the question, for I am not engaging in the theory of literature. How permanent the conditions that I describe were, is a question which must be left to scholars of other periods, or of all periods, if such there be. In other words, this book starts from and returns to the concrete eighteenth-century setting. It attempts to show what one literary form, satire, took from contemporary life: and how that 'real' world is transfigured by art. It is a study of one aspect of the eighteenth-century mind: its curious loyalty to the actual.

Some users of the original book have expressed surprise that I chose to accept the view of Swift and Pope regarding the status of the Dunces. It has been said that I made a 'tactical mistake' in aligning myself with the great satirists, and not showing the 'tactful generosity' Samuel Johnson displayed towards his former colleagues in the garret. The explanation is that ten years' research convinced me that the gap in talent between, say, Pope and Leonard Welsted was *underestimated* rather than overstated in the received wisdom about the subject. Similarly, I came to feel in writing the book that students of the period made far too little allowance for the huge social and personal disadvantages which Pope had to contend with, and *per contra* that the excellent life-chances available to several of the Dunces were glossed over. Finally, I was unable to take the view that Swift and Pope were secret sharers of the duncely agony, engaged in half-sympathetic recreation of the hack's world, guiltily complicit in the dirty goings-on down Smithfield alleys. Of course, they knew they *could* have ended up in that *galère*, but their writing lives were a prolonged effort to do something else with literature: that is, to enlist the vigour, topicality, raciness and aggression of satire in the creation of works which would outlast the immediate occasion and live beyond the contemporary instance.

Epigraph. *Tale*, p. 43.

1. The only other work dealing directly with this theme is Philip Pinkus's *Grub Street Laid Bare* (London, 1968). This book is about hacks at large, whereas my own study is concerned with the genesis of a metaphor, the name and nature of Grub Street not just in general but in particular. The most interesting recent treatment of Duncehood occurs in an essay by Peter Hughes on 'Allusion and Expression in Eighteenth-Century Literature', *The Author and his Work*, ed. L. L. Martz and A. Williams (New Haven, 1978), pp. 297-317. Hughes relates the opposition of the Scriblerians towards Grub Street to 'their distaste for the printed word' and for 'mechanical replication' (p. 302).

2. See *Grub Street* (1972), pp. 400-3. An interesting case in point is that of Sir Ivor Jennings' section on Grub Street in his *Party Politics*, vol i *The Appeal to the People* (Cambridge, 1960), pp. 134-53. The original Grub Street was

more than a publicity machine: its associations were quite different from those of modern Fleet Street.

3. It should never be forgotten that early editions of *A Tale of a Tub* were garnished with a cut of a wholly unmistakable Bedlam, those of *The Dunciad* with a scene at Bridewell Bridge depicted by no less a hand than Francis Hayman. There is really no possible ambiguity in these cases. Whatever general or symbolic reference we give to these vignettes, it remains a fact that the narrative prescribes a definite locality which the illustrator has no qualms in setting down with the careless fidelity that goes with utter familiarity. It has been pointed out that T. S. Eliot used as the basis of a scene in the *Four Quartets* a recollection of Gloucester Road underground station; and it is argued that in a novel he would probably have named the location quite openly. I am not entirely sure about this; but that the Augustan satirists would have done as much, I am quite certain. See Graham Hough, *An Essay in Criticism* (London, 1966), p. 117. The fact is that most present-day critics are insufficiently literal-minded when it comes to Scriblerian comedy.

4. By this I do not mean that we should take the hacks' word for everything. Pinkus's intention to present 'the story of the Grub Street hacks through their own writings' seems a curious undertaking. 'What evolves from this,' he says, 'will not be pure, laboratory-tested historical truth, but the usual amalgam of fact and fiction that contemporary writers create of their own world. Where it is not history it becomes legend, and legend has its own validity. Surely the legend that the hack writers created of themselves is as much a picture of Grub Street as any so-called objective study.' Yes; but a different kind of picture. The validity of legend is one thing, the rejection of historical evidence quite another. Pinkus concludes, 'The final effect, at least, is immediate, and what the reader cannot see he should be able to smell' (pp. xi–xii). We may hope to achieve this immediacy without sacrificing objectivity quite so shamelessly.

5. For the views of J. H. Plumb on violence and aggression in the eighteenth century, cf. the following: *England in the Eighteenth Century* (Harmondsworth, 1950), pp. 2–4; *The First Four Georges* (London, 1956), pp. 14–20; *Sir Robert Walpole: The Making of a Statesman* (London, 1956), pp. 30–4; *Men and Places* (Harmondsworth, 1966), pp. 19–21.

6. Swift, *Correspondence*, IV, 475.

7. Incidentally, we know a good deal about Clarissa's movements around London – which churches she attended on which occasion, the address of Lovelace's wigmaker, and so on. One recalls that another cockney, Defoe, built up his plague-ravaged London from contemporary observation and from childhood memories, notably of St Botolph's, Aldgate and St Stephen's, Coleman Street. See an excellent article by Manuel Schonhorn, 'Defoe's

Journal of the Plague Year: Topography and Intention', *RES* XIX (1968), 387–402.

8. Irving, pp. 150–222. It should be added that Irving's book is well written and makes no bones about its real aims. There are other less distinguished examples in this genre.

9. See Williams, esp. pp. 29–41.

10. Faber, p. 81.

11. W. S. Lewis, *Horace Walpole* (London, 1961), p. 73.

12. See Austin Dobson, *Horace Walpole: A Memoir* (London, 1910), map opp. p. 212.

13. G. S. Holmes and W. A. Speck, *The Divided Society* (London, 1967), pp. 40–1, 132: cf. Macaulay, I, 274.

14. George, p. 319: cf. Watt, p. 184, and authorities cited there.

15. *The Tender Husband*, ed. C. Winton (London, 1967), p. 14: Watt, p. 184, citing *Spectator*, no. 403. See also George, p. 91, for Jack Ketch's Warren as constituting 'a separate town.'

16. Watt, p. 185.

17. I refer to the Yale edition, ed. F. A. Pottle (London, 1950).

18. *London in Flames, London in Glory*, ed. R. A. Aubin (New York, 1943), p. 97.

19. *Georgics*, II. 177: translated by Dryden, 'The nature of the several soils now see . . .'

20. *Imitations of Horace*, Sat II. i. 83–4 (Butt, p. 616).

21. N. P. Gist and Silvia F. Fara, *Urban Society* (New York, 5th edn, 1964), pp. 96, 118–46. See also sections on 'City versus the Country', pp. 528–30: 'The City in Literature', pp. 530–1: and Ch. XXIII, 'The Image of the City'. Relevant to any consideration of eighteenth-century London, as regards the siting of various political, cultural, religious, recreational and other socially important localities, is Robert E. Dickenson, *The West European City* (London, 1951), pp. 254–8.

In emphasising the spatial drama which underlines the moral dialectic of Pope's poem, I do not wish to suggest a one-for-one correspondence between the two. It is of course true that the broad social character of a given area might be qualified by a number of factors, which could affect its imaginative availability for Pope. None the less, one would be hard put to if one were to seek a Dunce resident in Cavendish Square (erected in the early 1720's) or, a member of the literary aristocracy who openly frequented Jack Ketch's Warren.

I

The Suburban Muse

> But as it is fatall to the Suburbs of every great Citie, to be infected with some foule and unclean Birds, that there build their nests, although not with professed and ignominious staine of lewd life; because (within the limits of *Houns-ditch*) dwell many a good and honest Citizen, that will never endure such scandalous neighbourhood: yet there are crept in among them a base kinde of vermine, wel-deserving to bee ranked and numbred with them, who, our old Prophet and Countryman *Gyldas*, called *Aetatis atramentum*, the black discredit of the Age, and of place where they are suffered to live.
>
> *Stow, Survey of London*

> *O Grub Street!* thou fruitful Nursery of tow'ring Genius's! How do I lament thy downfal? Thy Ruin could never be meditated by any who meant well to *English Liberty*: No modern *Lycaeum* will ever equal thy Glory . . .
>
> *Arbuthnot, Preface to John Bull*

Where was Grub Street? The question is not just rhetorical. I have borrowed the formula from B. H. Bronson, whose essay 'When was Neo-classicism?' offers a new perspective on the eighteenth century by regarding the age 'as if it were a spatial rather than a temporal panorama.'[1] My intention is broadly analogous. I wish to consider the lexical space occupied by the term 'Grub Street', along with its derivatives: and to do that, I shall start from geography. The panorama we shall be looking at is that of the real city of London.

A recent work on the politics of the age of Anne suggests that party writing occupied 'most of the rank and file of what came to be known, half-affectionately, half-contemptuously as "Grub Street" '. It is not beyond argument that a hack author would have readily detected any affection in the way this expression was used. Still, the

18

more interesting point is the way in which Grub Street is safely distanced by the quotation marks that encompass it. So it is no surprise to find the same distinguished historian (this time as co-author) writing elsewhere:

> For politics as for journalism, the end of the Stuart censorship of the press, with the lapse of the Licensing Act in 1695, proved a seminal event. To it can be traced the spectacular rise of 'Grub Street', that fictitious abode of a new generation of political writers whose many different talents . . . were recruited by the Whig and Tory parties.[2]

Now the truth is that the phrase we are considering incorporates not a fiction, but synecdoche. And contemporary usage – as opposed to nineteenth-century misapplication of the term – reflects more than a fabulous existence. Grub Street was, as Ian Watt accurately describes it, a legend.[3] That is to say, the figurative meaning was based on a vestigial historical truth. This germ of reality became increasingly remote and spectral, but it was there all the same.

The clue to this situation was provided forty years ago by A. S. Turberville, though no one seems to have taken the hint:

> The original and actual Grub Street, as distinct from the Grub Street of metaphor, acquired its notoriety in the seventeenth century and is thus described in Johnson's *Dictionary* – 'a street near Moorfields, much inhabited by writers of small histories, dictionaries, and temporary poems.' Hence the term Grub Street came to be used in reference to the essentially ephemeral production of the literary hack.

Perhaps this is to imply a readier distinction between tenor and vehicle of the metaphor than can always be made; but otherwise it is an excellent statement of the position. Turberville does two things. He lends the expression a historical dimension and makes it clear that the figurative sense postdated a specific and literal usage. Secondly, he quotes Johnson's significant definition virtually in full (barring the examples provided). Now the first few words of that entry are usually slid over without much thought. In fact, the propinquity to Moorfields which Johnson remarks on at the outset was of the utmost significance in the development of the term and the concept, 'Grub Street'. On his own admission Johnson did not frequent the street – he had perhaps never been there as late as 1783, when he facetiously suggested dining there with the miscellaneous writer Hoole, who had been brought up in Grub Street. But everyone knew the whereabouts of the street; and Johnson not the least, as St John's Gate was a bare half-mile away (Ch. II).

Presently, Turberville supplies another pointer. He writes:

> Defoe is indeed the great exemplar of the literary Jack of all Trades, and as such he is one of the greatest citizens in the Grub Street republic. The author of Robinson Crusoe came of humble parentage, his father being a butcher in the parish of St Giles, Cripplegate . . .

Later on, I shall set out Defoe's credentials for recognition as a Dunce, and assess his place in the 'Grub Street republic' (as Turberville, with an unconscious Augustanism, puts it). Here it is enough to note that the truth extends well beyond the facts mentioned. For instance, James Foe was a resident of Fore Street – the very centre of the duncely parish of St Giles', on one side of which the church itself stood, whose eastern end adjoined Moorfields, and into which debouched a road of moderate size called – Grub Street! Moreover, Defoe died in an alley a matter of yards away from this same street.[4]

The essence of the matter is there. Grub Street acquired its notoriety for a combination of reasons. These included the fact that it lay at the heart of a district long in ill repute on account of its poverty and unhealthy character. In addition, there were specific places in its immediate vicinity, such as Moorfields and Bedlam, with which Grub Street could easily be connected: a circumstance which played straight into the hands of those consummate allegorisers, Pope and Swift. Again, it was the case that writers actually were domiciled in this region; and there were further historical links (Cromwell, Milton and John Foxe were all associated with the church of St Giles'). Moreover, looking at the relation of the district to the City and other wards such as Farringdon Without, we can see that the parish occupied a special position in the overall geography of London. In particular, St Giles' figured itself to Pope as one of the 'liberties' of the City – the twilight areas surrounding the rich and powerful centre administered by the ancient corporation. In other words, the region was uniquely suited to the symbolic role cast for it by the satirists. It was the earlier practitioners of this genre, Marvell and Oldham for example, who had established the usage. But it was the great Augustan satirists who first saw the moral, comic and artistic possibilities offered up to them by the accidents of urban ecology.

The rest of this chapter takes the form of a review of these factors. I shall consider first the physical location of Grub Street, its history, its social character, and its environmental status. It is not necessary to show that all the facts mentioned would be known to Pope and his friends. The broad picture was assuredly available to them. They could gauge both the 'physical proximity' and the 'vast social distance' noted by Watt as endemic to the city, so conspicuous were these in early eighteenth-century London.[5] The ward and parish of Cripplegate (their boundaries were coextensive) provide a remarkably good case in point. Grub Street was a mere stone's throw from the City within the walls: but in sociological terms it was light-years distant.

Meridian of Grub Street

The district had enjoyed what is usually called a chequered history. That means, as it usually does, a history of pretty well unmixed gloom and murk. The tenebrosity of the place started generations before the obscure writers came to hide there from the ravages of bailiffs, creditors, and better poets – all of whom located their quarry without difficulty. The rise in the currency of 'Grub Street', as a literary expression, came at a time when hackney authors inhabited the region. But it was not these men who gave the street its bad name. *That* it had from the start.

I know of only one, very brief, attempt to relate the social history of Grub Street to the acceptation of this term in literary usage. Ronald Paulson writes in his study of *A Tale of a Tub*:

> The Hack's milieu, Grub Street, would have had certain connotations for a contemporary. The street, whose name came from a refuse ditch (grub) which ran alongside it, lay outside the old walls, in Cripplegate, and like other of the areas lying outside the immediate jurisdiction of

the city became a haven for wanted men. Through the seventeenth century it carried a reputation for harbouring dissenters, who took their printing presses there to escape more active surveillance; and, in fact, both Cromwell and Milton lived there. All sorts of scurrilous writing, pornographic as well as seditious, was spawned in Cripplegate and along its main street. It had already passed its peak of prosperity by 1700, and by the time Pope attacked it, and the *Grub Street Journal* flourished, and Samuel Johnson lived there, its population of hacks had dwindled to only a fraction of its former size. Thus, to a Londoner, Grub Street would have suggested dissenting and scurrilous literature; and the word Grub might have further suggested a refuse ditch and a verb meaning 'to dig up, to destroy by digging', as well as 'a small worm that eats holes in bodies' (Johnson) – all connotations which Swift exploits in the course of the *Tale*.[6]

Taken as a whole, this is a most valuable lead: though there is a nice symbolism in the fact that it occurs in a foot-note! Nevertheless, many reservations have to be made as to detail. I shall list these as briefly as possible.

(1) Paulson does not seem clear as to whether he is talking about the literal street itself, the ward of Cripplegate or indeed that gateway, so called. This leads to confusion in places. (2) The liberties of the City were *not* 'outside the immediate jurisdiction' of the city courts. They were physically a little removed, and so 'active' surveillance may have been harder. It is certainly true that the wards surrounding the city, outside the walls, did become known as refuges for the outcast: but from a judicial and administrative standpoint they were part of the City. (3) There is no evidence that Cromwell lived in the ward, so far as I am aware, although he married at St Giles'. Milton did live in the parish but not (as Paulson's phrasing might suggest) in Grub Street. (4) Grub Street had been the main street in earlier centuries. By the time we are considering it was possibly less important than Fore Street, and certainly less imposing socially than White Cross Street and other parts of the ward. (5) Paulson cites no evidence for his statement that the street 'had passed its peak of prosperity' by 1700; and I believe this would be hard to come by. It can be shown that Grub Street had not been a prosperous place in the early part of the seventeenth century. (6) Similarly,

Paulson provides no backing for his very strange assertion regarding the 'population of hacks'. Since no-one has ever actually *named* a scribbler living there, and since the primitive population returns of the age do not recognise the sociological category 'Hack', it is difficult to imagine on what Paulson has based his statement. One of my aims, indeed, is to indicate some of the evidence which might affect the contentions discussed under this and the previous heading. (7) Johnson is not known to have lived in the ward at all, let alone the literal Grub Street. It is possible that Paulson is shifting into the metaphoric application here (as with the title of Bloom's book, *Samuel Johnson in Grub Street*).[7] In the context, such a procedure on his part is either unguarded or disingenuous.

Grub Street had to overcome the initial handicap of a poor site. Originally an extensive marsh occupied the land eastward from the Fleet Ditch as far as Bishopsgate. On the eastern side of this tract lay Moorfields, 'the great fen', of which more presently. The ground to the west of Moorfields was scarcely less swampy, though it did not function as a refuse-tip. The proximity of so much by way of 'noise-some waters' inevitably had its effect.[8] Cripplegate parish became notorious for the ague in winter and fever or the black death in the summer. The land commanded a poor price and by course of nature the inhabitants of the ward tended to be paupers or little better. In 1635 the Lord Mayor and Council appointed the Commissioners of Sewers, along with Inigo Jones (then Surveyor-General), to look into the annoyance caused by the over-charging of the main sewer, which had been flooded out by the unspeakable Moorditch. As one might expect, infection had been rife in the area. The plague raged there the following year too. When the Great Plague was at its height, thirty years later, nearly eight thousand people of the parish were buried, most of these as a result of the disease. By the early eighteenth century, the region was overburdened with poor people once more. In addition, Cripplegate had for some time been known as a haunt of counterfeiters, receivers, beggars, foreigners and houses of ill repute. As the historian of St Giles' parish says, the poor were always in evidence: but so, too, were the idle and feckless.[9] Stow is clear on the point. It is possible also to trace in extant parish records the social disrepute into which Cripplegate fell. For example, a list of tithes and rentals in 1638, covering the whole city, makes dispiriting reading when we get to St Giles'.[10] Here the average valuations were notably low. One or two streets are not too bad. But for the most part we read of tenements rated at no more than 30s. or £1, and properties at £3 or £4, especially in the side-alleys. (In the West End, valuations of £20 and more were commonplace.) It can be said with certainty that it was not the influx of hack writers later in the century which induced a loss of caste in Grub Street. It was already a depressed area.

The etymology of the name accords with this picture. As Paulson suggests, the most widely accepted view is that the derivation is from 'grube', a drain or ditch. Forms which are found in early records are 'Grobstrat' and 'Grubbestrate' (twelfth century).[11] The name therefore carried overtones of refuse-disposal; and suited the satirists' rhetorical aim of connecting vice and squalor with the sewerage of the town. From this point of view Grub Street conveniently linked up with Fleet Ditch, the main artery of disease and Dulness (Ch. II). 'Grub' was also defined by Nathan Bailey as a maggot and as 'a dwarf or short fellow' – the puny stature of a mediocre writer.

As regards nomenclature, there was an appropriate irony, too, in the fact that the parish church should have been dedicated to St Giles, in Cripplegate. Modern scholars doubt whether cripples really did congregate around the postern at this point,[12] but to Pope or Swift that would not reduce the availability of the notion. Equally, St Giles was peculiarly well cast as the special protector of Dunces. As Thomas Fuller had written, in his *Worthies of London*:

> St Giles is accompted the patron of creeples; and whereas churches dedicated to other saints of better footmanship get the speed of him and come into the city, generally lame St Giles *laggeth* behind in the suburbs, as in London, Cambridge, &c.[13]

This, then, was the saint of the halt and the lame, the feeble and those with impaired faculties. He was the protector of beggars, as well as cripples. Pope's victims bear the mark of Cain – Dulness, a sort of hereditary and quasi-syphilitic condition – and their proper place of sojourn is the precincts of St Giles' church. They belong to the suburbs: and this connotes, in 1720, not the comfortable place of retirement, but the 'scandalous neighbourhood[s]' to which Stow had referred.[14] A Dunce is a pariah who has been driven outside the City walls. St Giles' is thus a refuge in more than a literal sense. It serves as a topographic metaphor, to suggest the outcast and enfeebled state of Duncehood.

The population supported in these areas is hard to assess accurately. Hatton in 1708 gives a figure of four thousand houses (this includes both the London liberty and the Middlesex portion).[15] Demographers are nct entirely agreed on the population which this would indicate when applied to individual residents. It seems reasonable, however, to take the mean figure which obtained at the 1801 census, i.e. six to seven persons per dwelling.[16] This would yield a total of about twenty-five thousand. The parish clerks' survey of 1732 yields a gross figure of 4910 houses, of which 1800 only lay in the London segment.[17] Clearly it was the Middlesex part which was developing most quickly at this period, a fact recognised by the creation of the parish of St Luke's, Old Street in 1733 (6 Geo.II.c. 28).[18] Maitland's figures confirm the accuracy of this assessment. By the end of the century St Giles' alone was shrinking; St Luke's continued to grow but not at the spectacular rate of parishes farther out from the city. Not long afterwards Grub Street itself lost its identity; but we know that Milton Street quite failed to change its black spots. A writer of the 1850's remarks that the street is 'noted for its great number of alleys, courts, and back-ways, and old inn-yards'.[19] If the density of population had declined, that was partly a matter of residential property giving way to commercial buildings, partly the disappearance of the worst of the rickety seventeenth-century housing – but scarcely at all an index of a better social character for the area. The old City chapel, briefly a theatre, had however become a bath-house, which suggests some amelioration in living conditions.

By far the fullest account of Cripplegate is to be found in the nineteenth-century history by Rev. W. Denton, incumbent of St Bartholomew's, Moor Lane (erected in 1850).[20] This is reliable on most points of fact, amply documented, and forms an unpretentious but worthy monument to the historical zeal which augmented local piety in so many Victorian clerics. Nor is his social and economic history altogether betrayed by a picturesque style:

> Gradually there grew up in the early part of the middle ages a population of tanners and skinners, catgut makers, tallow melters, dealers in old clothes, receivers of stolen goods, charcoal sellers, makers of sham jewellery, coiners, clippers of coin and silver refiners, who kept their melting-pot ready day and night for any silver plate that might come to hand, toilers in noisesome trades and dishonest dealers. Down to later times ale and beer houses of the worst reputation, and yet even worse than such reputation, stood at the edge of the moor, where, despite the City authorities, gambling was always going on. . . . Even murder was not infrequent, and was seldom enquired into and punished. Forgers of seals, of bills, of writs, professional pick-purses, sharpers and other thieves, conjurors, wizards and fortune tellers, beggars and harlots found a refuge here.

Sharpers, thieves, beggars and harlots – it sounds like a recipe for the hack author, as the Scriblerians present that class. Denton goes on to describe various forging offences. He points out, too, that 'perhaps because of the lawless character of the moor outside Cripplegate . . . executions frequently took place there,' with thieves and murderers left dangling in their chains on Moorfields. He then refers to the dismal housing conditions prevailing in this kind of area: an aspect of the Middle Ages which waned all too slowly in Cripplegate.[21]

As Denton's study brings out, the area remained a blighted one. The parish was forced to maintain at least four 'cages' for the purpose of housing two main groups: the unfortunate poor and idle imposters. Such places were also the refuge for destitute women at the time of lying-in, and for homeless persons generally. One such cage stood 'at Grub Street end'. Quackery continued to hold Cripplegate dear: 'it was the outskirts of the town', Denton writes, 'and . . . a favourite retreat for fortune-tellers, astrologers, coiners, pick-pockets, *et hoc genus omne* . . . The gibbets on the moor and the grave yards near, the memorials of times of pestilence, yielded a supply of the horrid materials popularly supposed to be used by these diviners.' To the pagan imagination, Cripplegate Without was a locality instinct with memories from its troubled past. As for the burial grounds, there were six at least: St Giles' own churchyard, the so-called Upper

Churchyard in White Cross Street, the Pesthouse ground, Tindal's (in Bunhill Fields), the Quaker cemetery and the Bedlam ground. The poor, as well as suicides, were buried near the Pest House in the north-eastern corner of the parish. At times of plague these places came into special prominence; but their presence was always felt. Apt, then, that the first book of *The Dunciad* should fashion a grave-yard for obscure literary names.

All the hereditary taints of Dulness were thickly in evidence here during the seventeenth century. The quarrels of the age were acted out in the forty-three acres of St Giles' as warmly as anywhere. Religious dispute, inevitably, headed the list; and equally inevitably, politics followed on that. So we find Ned Ward writing:

> O bury not my peaceful corpse
> In Cripplegate, where discord dwells
> And wrangling parties jangle worse,
> Than alley's scolds or Sunday's bell.

There is nice irony that Ward, Dunce and alley-cat of the literary world, should offer up this cry. Cripplegate knew more of corpses than peace. At the time of the Civil War, a large section of the population were zealous Parliamentarians. The Vicar of St Giles' was a strong loyalist. He was eventually deprived, despoiled of his goods and imprisoned: an item in the loyalist martyrology that befitted such a parish. Subsequently, a Presbyterian lectureship was instituted during the 1640's and 1650's; four volumes of sermons delivered on the foundation were published (1661-90) by Samuel Annesley. Annesley had been presented to the living by Richard Cromwell in 1659; he was predictably ejected soon' after the Restoration. He is most relevant to this history, perhaps, as an early mentor of Defoe; but any such unquenchably dissident spirit would be typical of Cripplegate at this period.

Parliamentarians or independents were one thing: anabaptists or fifth-monarchy men a different proposition. Fanatical republicans were believed to have made the parish their sheltering-place after Charles II had returned: but this may only be rumour. More firmly established is an affray of January 1661, when the Saints rose and began rioting through the city. The hard core of fanatics ultimately entrenched themselves in the Blue Anchor alehouse near Moor-fields, and set up a protracted defence. At least twenty men were killed before the fifth-monarchist leader, Venner, and nine other survivors could be captured. All were executed: one in White Cross Street, one in Red Cross Street. The head of every rioter was set up on London Bridge. Then, a generation later, popular discontent again inflamed the brittle emotions of the inhabitants. In 1695 the gaol of Finsbury Manor (near modern Finsbury Pavement, at its junction with Chiswell Street) was burnt to the ground. The mob had been incensed by alleged corruption in official places, as well as by a periodic fit of xenophobia against the Huguenot refugees. The militia was called into service to quell the disturbance. As we shall see, destructive rioting was a hallmark of Dulness in action. And the mode of demolition is just as indicative. Fire had long ravaged Cripplegate, along with other rickety and densely-peopled quarters of London. In FitzStephen's time drunkenness and frequent fires had been accounted the two chief inconveniences; with the Dunces, inebriation and incendiary urges came together. In fact St Giles' church itself had been partially destroyed by fire in 1545, when most of the tower perished: a calamity rather greater than that suffered in the bombing of 1940, so far as one can judge. Likewise the Fortune Theatre, between Golden Lane and White Cross Street was burnt down one Sunday in 1621. It was rebuilt in brick, but the interior was once again ravaged in 1649 – not through divine visitation, some thought, or even through common arson: the intervention of the puritan conscience was suspected. Whatever the cause, fire was a constant threat in the parish. The bonfires set up in White Street and in Moorfields during the Gordon riots serve as a convenient emblem of the destructive energy common to Duncehood and to fire (see Ch. II).

Another of the plagues of Dulness, as I have called them, was the pestilential fever itself. As indicated, the parish was particularly badly hit. In 1603, that onset of the disease which used to be put among the contributory causes of Jacobean melancholy (when *that* ailment was recognised) coursed through St Giles'. Not far short of three thousand people died that year from plague. And of course in

1665 the district again suffered appallingly – part of Moorfields was still a city laystall and refuse tip. Tillotson wrote to Sancroft, 'I am sure that the miserable condition of St Giles' Cripplegate is more to be pitied than any other parish in or about London, where all have liberty, the parish not being able to relieve their necessities.' Burial places understandably grew hard to come by; as early as June 1664, a year before, the White Cross Street graveyard had been closed for fresh burials by order of the vestry. The most famous cemetery, however, was the 'Parish Field' up against Old Street – the Pesthouse Burying Ground. Here the destitute were brought to be interred. During the Great Plague it became hopelessly oversubscribed, if one may put it that way: large numbers of victims had been removed to the pest house, as Defoe's *Journal* tells us,[22] and inevitably many of them died in a short space of time. As a result the burial ground was closed for seven years.[23] When it reopened, the northern part of the parish was once again provided with its most fitting emblem: the resting-place of those hapless men and women who were the incurable victims of contagious disease. It should be added that in 1699 proposals were made to make a burial place in some waste ground at Butler's Alley, off Grub Street itself. Nothing came of the suggestion, but it indicates the status of the neighbourhood. Incidentally, the 'Parish Field' should not be confused with Bunhill Fields. The latter, originally known as Tindall's, was the place of burial for Defoe, Bunyan and many other dissenters. St Giles' parish was indeed a harbinger of mortality – its very name must have served as a *memento mori* to contemporary Londoners.[24] The most symptomatic of all the observations which Denton makes regarding this parish of misfortune is the following:

> The mental strain and terror which people were under in this dreadful time were evinced in the numbers who are recorded to have lost their reason during this visitation of the plague. In parish account-books side by side are notices of sums paid for the removal of the plague-stricken to the Pest House, and of moneys given for the conveyance of the insane to Bedlam.

The felicitous, if cruel, touch by which Pope places the breeding ground of Dulness, with all its spawning 'nameless Somethings', its maggots and its 'craw[ing] . . . feet' (B.I.56ff), close to the walls of Folly, stands revealed and explained. Each onslaught of the plague brings new inmates to Bedlam; and each fit of Dulness does the same.

From the 1720s there was, too, a workhouse in Sugar Loaf Court, off Moor Lane (next adjoining Grub Street). This was additional to that founded in Beech Lane around 1700, the first in the City. As befitted a parish named after the patron saint of cripples and beggars, a notable mental hospital was later sited there: St Luke's, in Old Street, on the west side of City Road. In 1733 a church was erected in the same street and a separate parish formed, also dedicated to St Luke. Both survived into the nineteenth century. For the rest, Cripplegate Ward was chiefly noteworthy for its complement of breweries, taverns, almshouses and Jewish enclaves. The northern part of the ward, outside the liberties of the City, was no better. The 1638 assessment recorded the fact that this region 'consist[ed] of a multitude of poor people'. For the parish as a whole there are references such as, 'Lost per annum in tithes by reason of the extreme poverty of the place, £100.' Let no one suppose that it was the literary imagination which brought disgrace to Grub Street.[25] The historian Oldmixon (himself a Dunce) records a Tory riot, set up by the rabble of Cripplegate in 1723.[26] Dissenting houses and conventicles abounded in this vicinity. There had long been trouble with the municipal plumbing: apart from the episode of the sewers in 1635 the water-course of the Company of Barber-Surgeons ran into St Giles' churchyard, with baneful results, and had to be diverted. Plague, as we have seen, was rife; and fire almost as destructive. The parish church just escaped in 1666, though some of its windows appear to have been damaged; later on, the primitive fire-fighting equipment which the ward possessed became a cause for concern. There was a high concentration of foreigners in the population. Even in Elizabethan times, a perceptible number of aliens were recorded in the region of Grub Street and Golden Lane. After the revocation of the Edict of Nantes, in 1685, a flood of French protestants took refuge in Cripplegate. The Irish also settled in large numbers. Not surprisingly, Grub Street, Golden Lane and Moor Lane headed the list of the 'dirtiest and meanest parts of the town' where cheap lodgings were to be had.[27]

What of Grub Street *per se*? In the seventeenth century, Denton states, it was 'going down in the world'. Surrounded by conventicles, and housing the single openly proclaimed popish meeting house in London,[28] its condition was assuredly no better in the early years of the next century. One or two 'spacious or handsome houses', such as those known – however unreliably – as Dick Whittington's and as General Monk's, did survive:[29] it was Victorian commerce, rather than the disgrace suffered at the wits' hands, which killed these places. But there were exceptions in the street. Denton relates this loss of caste to its environs, and cites a seventeenth-century writer: 'a nasty stinking lodging in jayle is sweeter land than any garden-house about Bunhill.'[30] Yet the truth is that Grub Street contaminated its surroundings quite as much as the reverse; and the residents who thought that things would get better if the name were changed were not altogether naïve. Grub Street had been picked out for notoriety among a score of such extramural blackspots. The choice was arbitrary but it was not unfair.

Denton writes of the old walled city:

> The suburbs of London – and when this term suburb is used in old writers, the city parishes immediately lying without the gates were meant – abounded with the most lawless classes of the community. Little Moorfields was dangerous to the unwary, with its small low alehouses and tenements of a still more disreputable kind. Grub Street, which at best was never a safe place, had become in the time of the Tudors . . . in a great measure deserted except for low gambling houses and bowling alleys . . . The 'Harrow' in Moorfields was well-known to the City authorities as one of the 'harbouring houses for masterless men, and for such as live by theft and other such like shifts.'

The historical associations remain encrusted on to the name. Grub Street in Pope's poem is a harbouring house for those who live by literary theft and other such shifts. It is the proper home, topographically and morally, of the suburban muse.

This, then, is the typical pattern of a twilight zone. Contemporary descriptions provide further evidence of the social character of Grub

Street proper. Stow has little to say of the street itself, but he does describe the shortcomings of the parts about Moorfields, and mentions the ditches and lay-stalls scattered about the parish. (He also alludes with some misdirection to the prostitutes around Wood Street, in the ward of Cripplegate Within.)[31] It has been stated that, in the sixteenth century, Grub Street was full of 'small and mean domiciles, good enough for beggars and literary men, but too bad for any more self-respecting class.'[32] Certainly, when Lancelot Andrewes was incumbent of St Giles', from 1589 to 1604, and Thomas Morley served as church organist, the parish had names on which to pride itself: John Foxe, the Martyrologist, Martin Frobisher and John Speed were buried here between 1587 and 1629. It was at the church that Oliver Cromwell married Elizabeth Bourchier on 22 August 1620. Then, later in the century, Milton was to occupy various addresses in this part of London: Jewen Street and Artillery Walk, off Bunhill Row, and was to be buried at St Giles' in 1674. But these substantial men are the exception. It was chiefly the submerged elements of the population that came to Cripplegate. The most notable literary men to emerge from the region in later years were Defoe (the son of a butcher and presbyterian) and Bernard Mandeville, who was domiciled there in 1700 along with many other emigrés.[33] A few years later the parish received a less welcome immigrant.

Around 1713–14 Jonathan Wild, recently of the Wood Street Compter in Cripplegate Within, took a house in Cock Alley, right up against St Giles', on the corner of Fore Street and White Cross Street. Here Wild and Mary Milliner set up their first thriving establishment. The house became a favourite haunt of thieves, prostitutes, highwaymen and gamblers; more importantly, it was the centre of Wild's initial ventures as a receiver of stolen property and 'thief catcher'. Pope seems to have known about Wild's association with Lewkner's Lane; it is possible that he was also aware of the fact that Wild had started off in the immediate environs of Grub Street. Incidentally, Wild himself referred in a published pamphlet to 'a bucklemaker near Cripplegate': this might mean himself, but more likely it is Edward Burnworth, alias 'Young Frazier', a notorious rogue who ended up in Newgate.[34] Once again we find that poverty and disease anticipate a more serious charge – that association with crime which pervades so much of the topography of Duncehood.

The best contemporary account is that of Strype, in his rescension of Stow's *Survey of London* (1720). The maps prepared for this edition, incidentally, are of great independent interest;[35] and Strype's descriptions are exceedingly valuable, not least the following:

> *Grubstreet*, very long, coming out of *Forestreet*, and running Northwards, into *Chiswell Street*; but some small part, to wit, from *Sun Alley* to *Chiswell Street* is not in the Ward, but in the Liberty of *Finsbury*. This *Street*, taking in the whole, is but indifferent, as to its Houses and Inhabitants; and sufficiently pestered with Courts and Alleys, the Names of which are as follows . . .

This might serve as an epigraph to *The Dunciad*. The haunts of Dulness, taking them in the whole, are distinctly indifferent as to locale and personal composition. *Their* quarters of London are pestered with courts and alleys. Translating this ecological metaphor, we may say that morally, for Pope, contemporary culture is riddled with the mean, the devious, the soiled, the gimcrack constructions of Dulness. Eighteenth-century writers, as Paul Fussell has shown, often use the image of a stately mansion or keep to body forth their sense of achieved stability (Burke's use of Windsor Castle is the most famous example). The flimsy, verminous structures of Grub Street were therefore fit emblems to convey an antithetical order of things.[36]

Strype then goes on to describe certain of these side-alleys. It is enough to mention these in summary form. Lund Alley is 'long and ordinary' (the sense of the latter word, in Strype's usage, is roughly that of 'mediocre'). Honeysuckle Court is, surprisingly, 'pretty good, with new built Houses'. But Flower de Lis Court is 'very small and ordinary'; Flying Horse Court, 'long, but ordinary built; and by consequence, the Inhabitants answerable'. Likewise for Pope, the inhabitants of a district are 'answerable' to the character of that district in terms of housing, social standards, occupational structure, and so on. The Nags Head Inn has been recently rebuilt 'out of a Place called *Soldiers Court*, which was before old and decayed'. Next comes Oakley Court, 'large and open; the greatest part, at present, unbuilt and lying wast'. Butlers Alley is 'narrow and ordinary'; whilst Cross Keys Court is 'indifferent large, and old built'. Maidenhead Court and Great Bell Alley are little better. Uniquely, Haberdashers Court, at the upper end of the street, is 'very genteel, with new well built Houses . . . This Court was made out of two old ones, *viz. Paviers Court and Robin Hood Court.*' Next to it, Sun Court is 'but small'. How long this privileged enclave of Grub Street survived, I do not know. Assuredly the street as a whole was anything but genteel. In another passage Strype follows Stow's account:

> . . . *Grub Street*, of late Years inhabited (for the most part) by Bowyers, Fletchers, Bowstring Makers and such like Occupations; now little occupied; Archery gives place to a Number of Bowling Allies, and Dicing Houses, which in all Places are increased, and too much frequented.

Both the vices and the homily look more Elizabethan than Georgian; but at all events Grub Street had been known as a place of idleness long before Queen Dulness let out her infectious yawn over it.[37]

Maitland a few years later was to elaborate on this description in certain particulars. He glosses the ward of Cripplegate Without in these terms:

> A large Tract of Ground, containing several Streets, and all crowded with Courts and Alleys; the chief are *Fore-street*, the *Postern-street*, *Back-street* in *Little-Moorfields*, *Moor-lane*, *Grub-street*, *Whitecross-Street*, *Redcross-street*, *Beech-Lane*, *Golden-lane*, *Barbican*, and *Jewen-Street*. . . .

This is a veritable gazetteer of duncely localities. Fore Street, the birthplace of Defoe, is described as 'broad, and inhabited by Butchers, Smiths, Turners, &c. runs from the North End of *St Giles's Cripplegate* Church to *Moor-Lane*, Eastward, and then falls into *Postern street*, which leads to *Little Moorfields*, against *New Bethlehem* . . .' The propinquity of Bedlam is thus stressed yet again. Maitland speaks of the many courts and alleys around St Giles's, and lists both Little Cock Alley ('ordinary') and Great Cock Alley, which is Jonathan Wild's ('a large Place, indifferently built, and has a passage into *Whitecross-street* . . .'). The words 'indifferent, mean, narrow' recur in these descriptions. For instance, Moor Lane, directly along-side Grub Street, is termed 'for the Generality, but meanly built and inhabited, especially the upper End, which is narrow', and which leads incidentally through Ropemakers Alley (where Defoe died) and Butlers Alley to Grub Street. Maitland's description of Grub Street and its 'mean, small and ordinary' courts (excepting Haberdashers Square) is taken from Strype more or less verbatim. White Cross Street and Red Cross Street come off a little better, but Golden Lane is 'of no great Account either for Buildings or In-habitants'. The Barbican is notable chiefly because old clothes are sold there, a doubtful distinction when one thinks of Rag Fair.[38]

To the west of Cripplegate lay Jewen or Jewin Street, which en-tered Red Cross Street just beyond the churchyard of St Giles's. This was the route to Aldersgate, and beyond that to Smithfield – a district abutting on the westernmost fringe of the parish, so that the 'Smithfield Muses' might almost be said to occupy the next 'apartment' (Swift's word) to those of Grub Street. Jewen Street was situated on the site of the former Jews' Garden, which according to Stow was at first the only place in England appointed for the burial of Jewish citizens. It later became a pleasure garden, and ac-quired a cockpit.[39] However, this indignity did not last – the cockpit disappeared, only to be replaced by a conventicle, which would hardly have raised the street in Pope's estimation.[40] Contemporary descriptions of the district are usually quite favourable: the street is said to be 'well built and inhabited, except at the West End, of some Trade for *Button-Mould-Makers*'.[41] But it had certain disagreeable connotations, cockpit and conventicle apart, and leaving aside the brewhouse which had been set up in the sixteenth century.[42] The first prominent literary resident was John Milton, from 1661–2. Here a good part of *Paradise Lost* was written, and Marvell visited the poet. But the standard was not maintained. John Dunton, eccentric pub-lisher and author, who duly achieved a niche in *The Dunciad* ('a broken Bookseller and abusive scribler' – note to A.II.136), sent out his works to the world from this address at one period. Again, that archetypal Dunce Charles Gildon was lodged there shortly before his death. We learn this from two rather pathetic letters he wrote to

35

Matthew Prior in 1721. Blind and feeble, he had evidently left his garret in Chancery Lane, and moved into the purlieus of Grub Street. His letters are headed 'Bull Head Court', which Maitland describes as 'old Buildings, but well inhabited'. Prior died a matter of weeks later, and there is no more extant correspondence between Pope and himself – but it is quite likely that Pope would have known, by one means or another, where his favourite victim spent his latter days. Another connection with the book trade was provided by John Leake, father-in-law of Samuel Richardson, who was a printer in Jewen Street following his move from Aldersgate. Subsequently Leake went the way of several other members of his profession and took up business in the vicinity of St Paul's.[43] Incidentally, Jewen Street has suffered the same fate as Grub Street itself: the Barbican project has swallowed it without trace.

By 1867 the formerly genteel Haberdashers Square had become 'a squalid quadrangle'. Houses on both sides of Grub Street had been levelled during construction work for the Metropolitan Railway. Today the line from Moorgate to Aldersgate station runs under what was Grub Street and became in 1830 Milton Street[44] (commemorating, most probably, not the poet, but a builder who owned the lease).[45] However, there is scarcely any of Milton Street surviving. The upper stretch of about eighty yards, near the junction with Chiswell Street, alone remains. Whitbread's brewery is all that has managed to resist the huge Barbican development. Fore Street now contains, not butchers and turners, but the National Telephone Exchange. One can walk on a raised pedestrian footway above the street, and gaze down on Defoe's (probable) birthplace and Milton's place of rest from a modernistic complex of shops, restaurants and offices. Destruction continues to attend the region, centuries after the Plague. It was in Fore Street that the first bombs fell during the blitz, in August 1940. There is an irony, too, in the fact that eschatology continues a visible presence with the London Mortuary, on the junction of Ropemaker Street and Moor Lane. But finally the impression left by the redevelopment programme is more positive than that. Stage 3 of the Barbican scheme is without doubt the most imaginative and happy transformation the region has ever known. It is interesting that as late as 1953 the Cripplegate region was described by a land economist as 'a muddled area', with depressed hinterland areas, 'some of them around Jewen Street'. From the 'value contour map' appended, it emerges that troughs of low-valuation in market terms existed on the west side of Milton Street and in the vicinity of a goods station between White Cross Street and Red Cross Street. The new pattern, as determined by the Barbican scheme, shows a quite different set of 'value contours'. Incidentally, the district was chosen for study as 'the largest single devastated area in the City of London' after the war.[46] But at long last the Cripplegate region has outlived its poverty and ugliness. It has taken a couple of centuries longer to do so, than Grub Street did to lay its own, metaphoric, ghost.

The Caves of Poverty and Poetry

Dulness is specifically linked with a number of parts of London. These include references to 'the Smithfield Muses'; the 'bleak recess' of the Goddess, at first Rag Fair and then near Bedlam; and the area around the Strand. I shall consider each of these, not just as a 'venue' of *The Dunciad*, but as poetic and dramatic counters: they operate much as do the sustained patterns of imagery in Shakespeare, or the symbolic figures in the Jamesian carpet.

Take the relatively simple case of Smithfield. As all commentators have noted, from Martinus Scriblerus onwards, this was the scene of Bartholomew Fair. It was a district thereby associated with raree-shows and low farces. Williams is accordingly justified in seeing its presence as connoting a degree of theatricality – a low pantomimic quality in Dulness.[47] But there is more to it than that. In the first place, as Swift's 'City Shower' reminds us, a tributary stream ran from Smithfield to the Fleet Ditch near Holborn Bridge, adding its quota of dogs, cats, 'Dung, Guts, and Blood' to the foul drain as it crept sluggishly to the Thames. As a matter of fact, the bed of such a stream was found by archaeologists in 1924, running along what is now Cowcross Street – a matter of fifty yards north of the modern

Smithfield market, near Farringdon tube station. The district thus contributed its own share of pollution to the City, and indeed was responsible for some of that oozing, evil-smelling water in which the Dunces were pleased to hold their high heroic games of mud-diving. The area drained by this stream, in addition, would include the notorious bog of Moorfield, the pleasure-ground for the stately residences of Grub Street.

Secondly, the area immediately surrounding Smithfield had an infamous reputation as a haunt of the dissolute. The *Newgate Calendar* reported the existence of a house here which sheltered 'all sorts of burglars, footpads, fences and other villains'. It is said that this house 'stood alongside the brook, whose rapid torrent was well adapted to convey away everything that might be evidence of crime . . . Once a sailor was decoyed there, robbed and thrown naked out of a window into the stream, and was taken up at Blackfriars Bridge a corpse.' This account dates from later in the century, when Robert Mylne (despite Dr Johnson's efforts) had been allowed to site his bridge almost at the precise venue of the Dunces' acquatic sports. Nevertheless it indicates the general notoriety of the Smithfield area. Even before the Restoration 'every street between Golden Lane [in Cripplegate] and Smithfield' was regarded as a place of ill fame. Early in the nineteenth century, this was one of the districts where typhus raged most strongly. The historical reasons for this state of affairs have been explained by Dorothy George, who notes that the liberty of West Smithfield, just outside the walls to the north-west of the City, was soon inhabited by a depressed population, forbidden by guild regulations to exercise their trade within the City itself.[48] When, therefore, Pope conjured up the name at the very start of his poem:

> Books and the Man I sing, the first who brings
> The Smithfield Muses to the Ear of Kings . . . (A.I.1)

and moreover kept the basic reference in his revised *Dunciad*,[49] a whole constellation of associations was set twinkling. As early as this, the notions of plague, poverty and pollution, which are to serve as a leitmotif throughout, are called up .

Consider another example. In the first version, at A.I.27, Pope names for the headquarters of Dulness, the honour he subsequently transfers to the neighbourhood of Bedlam, a locality known as 'Rag Fair'. He supplies the curt note, '*Rag-fair* is a place near the *Tower of London*, where old cloaths and frippery are sold.'[50] The text itself is a little more communicative:

> Where wave the tatter'd ensigns of Rag-Fair,
> A yawning ruin hangs and nods in air;
> Keen, hollow winds howl thro' the bleak recess,
> Emblem of Music caus'd by Emptiness:
> Here in one bed two shiv'ring sisters lye,
> The cave of Poverty and Poetry.
> This, the Great Mother dearer held than all
> The clubs of Quidnunc's, or her own Guild-hall.
> Here stood her Opium, here she nurs'd her Owls,
> And destin'd here th' imperial seat of Fools.
> Hence springs each weekly Muse, the living boast
> Of Curll's chaste press, and Lintot's rubric post,
> Hence hymning Tyburn's elegiac lay,
> Hence the soft sing-song on Cecilia's day,
> Sepulcral lyes our holy walls to grace,
> And New-year Odes, and all the Grubstreet race.
>
> (A.I.27–42)

One might assume that Pope is invoking the propinquity of the Tower so that it may serve as a symbol of historic endurance, as (just off-stage) the Castle had done in *Windsor Forest*. The truth is almost the opposite. The Tower provides an ironic contrast to the squalid neighbourhood surroundings; the main point of the note is to localise Dulness. 'Th' imperial seat of Fools' is set up, in fact, at the heart of a notorious hotbed of vice and penury. The wider poetic purpose which sustains the joke here is a familiar one in Pope. He wishes (and this is what *The Dunciad* is largely about) to associate his literary victims with *acknowledged* lowlife haunts. In this passage Pope explicitly states that the City connections of which Aubrey Williams makes so much ('her own Guildhall') are secondary. Dulness is identified by the range of its productions (cheap weekly journalism; the dying confessions of highwaymen; annual poems to order, beautifully caught in a line of clashing sibilants and dribbling expectoration;

commissioned epitaphs; celebratory odes by the Laureate, and so on.) The last line quoted draws these ideas together and links them firmly with Grub Street. Hardly anyone seems to have thought it worthy of notice that the venue of the poem should have been shifted across London between the two versions. This radical change was made easier for Pope because he had already identified Grub Street – the 'Cell' of B.I.33, as I shall argue – with the cave of poverty and poetry. Some of the work had already been done for him, in fact. Hard actuality once again came to the rescue of poetic invention.

In order to understand this point, we shall have to look briefly at the known facts with regard to Rag Fair. The fair itself is best known to us through eighteenth-century prints. One, called 'High Change, or Rag Fair', was published by Thomas Bowles (1795). It shows the eastern part of Rosemary Lane near Well Close Square on the edge of Stepney. More familiar is Rowlandson's water-colour of the same scene, 'The Rag Fair'. Both these views show a teeming, pullulating world full of sharpers and hucksters. They portray, in fact, what is now the inmost part of Cable Street: that is, the City end. But Rag Fair took place all down the middle of Rosemary Lane; it extended the length of modern Royal Mint Street to the very edge of the Tower itself. In this respect Pope's note is not at all misleading.

Nor, granted his disparaging intent, is the phrase concerning 'old cloaths and frippery'. A modern writer has stated that Rag Fair was more squalid even than Petticoat Lane. 'Much of the clothing that was sold there was stolen; the market was also the final destination of all cast-off rags, in an epoch notorious for its careless habits and for seldom or never changing its linen.'[51] If one substitutes 'poems' for 'clothes' here, one can see what Pope is implying. The sale of old clothes, incidentally, went on here until the second quarter of the nineteenth century. At this time the region was transformed, successively by the moving of the Mint from the precints of the Tower to the new building in Royal Mint Street (as Rosemary Lane became in due course), and by the carving out of St Katharine's Docks just to the south, with attendant work on rail depots.[52] It was only at this time that 'Rag Fair' lost its strong pejorative overtones.

In any list of black spots drawn up from the seventeenth to the nineteenth century, the name of Rosemary Lane, with its environs, is sure to figure. Strype, in 1720, describes the mean alleys in the district, as well as the 'small, nasty and beggarly' streets around the Minories, just to the north. He tells of the fair held on Little Tower Hill.[53] Goodman's Fields, whose insalubrious reputation was not improved by the coming of the theatre in 1728, lay immediately adjacent. Sir John Hawkins was particularly severe on the matter:

> . . . What was apprehended from the advertisement of plays to be exhibited in that quarter of the town, soon followed: the adjacent houses became taverns in name, but in truth they were houses of lewd resort; and the former occupiers of them, useful manufacturers and industrious artificers, were driven to seek elsewhere for a residence.[54]

This process was beginning, we should note, in the very year during which the first version of *The Dunciad* appeared. But it is doubtful if Rosemary Lane itself had ever harboured many 'useful manufacturers and industrious artificers.' As late as Mayhew, indeed, we find the Irish community singled out for comment in this locality – always the sign of a depressed area. For the earlier period, however, Mrs George provides abundant evidence of the standing of this quarter. Rosemary Lane is named along with East Smithfield, Hounsditch, Petticoat Lane and Goodman's Fields as 'a deplorable district', and a 'dangerous neighbourhood'. In the late eighteenth century, we find an account isolating the most unhealthy regions of London. The writer speaks of

> the wretched inhabitants of some streets in St Giles' [in the Fields] parish, of the courts and alleys adjoining to Liquor Pond Street, Hog Island, Turnmill Street, Old Street, Whitecross Street, Grub Street, Golden Lane, the two Brook Lanes, Rosemary Lane, Petticoat Lane, Lower East Smithfield, some parts of upper Westminster, and several streets of Rotherhithe, etc.

These are the districts we shall come on repeatedly, the purlieus of Dulness. The high concentration of streets listed in and around Cripplegate Ward will be apparent.[55] Nor is this the only occasion on which Rag Fair is aligned with the Grub Street area – most conveniently, from the point of view of Pope. A seventeenth-century source names as centres of prostitution

> St Giles [in the Fields], Turnbul Street . . . Long Acre near the Mews, Drury Lane, Sodom and all her painted drabs, . . . Ratclife Highway, Rosemary-lane, Shore-ditch, Morefields, White-crosse-street, Golden-lane, every street twixt that and Clarken-well, Cow-crosse, Smith-field . . . and all the country girls.[56]

Even more apposite is a pamphlet of 1767, which refers to the 'cheap lodging' (only, at present, not so cheap) to be found in the 'dirtiest and meanest parts of the town'. These latter are, predictably, named as 'Grub Street, Golden Lane, Moor Lane, Fee Lane, Rag Fair or the Mint'.[57] Three of these are Cripplegate addresses: one is the refuge in Southwark to which a recent poet laureate, Nahum Tate, had been obliged to flee, and where Pope locates one of Curll's authors in 1716: and another is Rag Fair. The associations which the place would call up in the mind of a reader, when *The Dunciad* first came before the public, can scarcely be doubted.

Only six years before, Defoe, who must have known the district well, had brought out *Colonel Jack*. In the first two pages Jack tells us that he 'had [his] Breeding, *viz.* near *Goodman's-fields*'. His youth was spent in such activities as 'rambling about' Rosemary Lane and Ratcliff. After his nurse died, Jack and his companions lived for some years each winter in the glasshouse near Rosemary Lane. On one occasion he went to Rag Fair and bought two pairs of shoes and stockings there for fivepence. He then visited a 'boiling Cook's in *Rosemary-Lane*' and found almost equally cheap fare.[58]

In 1724, two years later, a book came out under the title of *The History of the Remarkable Life of John Sheppard*. This has been reprinted as Defoe's, and may well be his. But the point is immaterial. There are several references to Rosemary Lane in this short essay in the rogue's biography. Together with *A Narrative of all the Robberies, Escapes, &c. of John Sheppard*, another work attributed to Defoe, it provides further revidence of the social image which Rag Fair had acquired. On one occasion Sheppard was taken, following a

tip-off by his mistress Edgworth Bess, in Rosemary Lane itself. He
had been lodging there with the mother of his associate, Joseph Blake
or 'Blueskin' – a highwayman almost as well-known at the time as
Sheppard himself. Perhaps more interesting is a passage in the *History*,
describing the reactions of the populace after Sheppard had
been caught for the last time: 'Newgate night and day [was] surrounded with the curious from St Giles's and Rag-Fair, and Tyburn
Road daily lined with women and children, and the gallows as carefully watched by night lest he should be hanged incog., for a report
of that nature obtained much upon the rabble.'[59] Rag Fair, it is safe
to conclude, was peopled by 'the rabble'. Its links with the criminal
class made it the more suitable for Pope's purposes. (Incidentally the
hangman who had executed both Strafford and Charles I lived and
died in the street, a further blemish on its name.)

It is not only chapbooks and popular novels which supply testimony to the standing of Rag Fair. Sober annals of criminal justice
show us a murderer pursued by the mob to the Fair (that was in 1760).
Sir Alan Herbert's researches have dredged up the story of a draper
in Great Turnstile, Holborn, who lost forty-three pairs of stockings
in the year 1733; he instantly (as the court deposition reveals) sent a
boy to look for them in Mr Hancock's, of Rosemary Lane, opposite
the Chequer alehouse. The eighteenth-century idea of the place is
well conveyed in an account which mentions 'lawless Petticoat Lane
and Rosemary Lane', where 'thieves run from side to side eluding
officers'. And as always prostitution went along with crime, indicated by Tom Durfey's reference to the 'sisterhood of Nightingale
Lane', adjoining the Fair, and a long list of other quarters of London
including Rosemary Lane, Saffron Hill, Whetstone Park and Lute-
nor's Lane. There was one fairly pleasant residential district in the
vicinity, near Well Close Square; but even this had been less salubrious at one time, as a paragraph in Defoe's *Tour* makes apparent:

On the more *Eastern* Part, the same Increase [in building] goes on in
Proportion, namely, all *Goodman's Fields* . . . and the many Streets
between *White-Chapel* and *Rosemary Lane*, all built since the Year
1678. *Well Close*, now called *Marine Square*, was so remote from Houses,
that it used to be a very dangerous Place to go over after it was dark,

and many People have been robbed and abused in passing it; a Well standing in the middle, just where the *Danish* Church is now built, there the Mischief was generally done.

It had been, in short, a Moorfields of the East End. The 'many streets' which had been developed now constituted a different sort of blot on the landscape. In the words of a modern historian, the region – which made up the northern fringe of Wapping – contained 'small houses, chandler's shops, brothels, cheap lodging houses, alehouses, taverns . . .' Grub Street itself had nothing more to offer. A final link was with Execution Dock, 'so call'd, because it is the only Place where Pirates and Sea-robbers are executed'.[60] This Tyburn of the river lay at the southernmost extent of East Smithfield, a region which Rag Fair typified.

It can be seen, then, that it was no casual or arbitrary choice by which Pope first assigned 'th' imperial seat of Fools' to Rosemary Lane. Economic and social history had already underwritten this imaginative stroke. Rag Fair, a place infamous for crime, prostitution, poverty and cheap secondhand trading, makes an exact emblem for Pope's artistic point. Grub Street, likewise, is a place notable for literary crime, for poverty of invention, for the prostitution of poetry, and for the retailing of shoddy stolen goods. It was perhaps chance that the literal Grub Street had often been linked with Rosemary Lane under the first set of headings. It was no accident that Pope introduced Grub Street into his own description of Rag Fair. With a kind of prevenient grace, the instincts of a great artist led Pope to incorporate in his first version of *The Dunciad* the hint of his recast poem. What had been simile, then evolved into metaphor. *The Dunciad* of 1743 has become, quite openly, the epic of Grub Street; the cave of poverty and poetry has moved from the neighbourhood of the Tower to the neighbourhood of Bedlam. Cripplegate replaces Port-soken Ward: but the character of the district is changed not a whit.

I turn now to this second home of Queen Dulness, set in the vicinity of Bedlam. The meridian of Grub Street (as Dr Arbuthnot called it),[61] was not a state of mind but an actuality. By a species of metonymy, the literal environment of the street came to colour the figurative sense of the term. In the work of Pope and Swift, above all, Grub Street is regularly associated with Moorfields, and implicitly or explicitly with Bedlam. Indeed the entire *Dunciad* serves to enforce this connection: that is, to show Grub Street and Bedlam as coeval 'colleges' in the vicinity of Moorfields. Now the latter district had long enjoyed an unhealthy reputation on several accounts: while Bedlam – as is well known – had served writers for some time as a type of frenzied or deluded behaviour. The manner in which the Augustan satirists develop this connection will repay study.

As often, Dr Johnson gives us the clue: or at least Boswell. In 1783 the biographer reports the following conversation:

> Mrs. Burney wondered that some very beautiful new buildings should be erected in Moorfields, in so shocking a situation as between Bedlam and St Luke's Hospital; and she said she could not live there.
> JOHNSON. 'Nay, Madam, you see nothing there to hurt you. You no more think of madness by having windows that look to Bedlam, than you think of death by having windows that look to a church-yard.'[62]

Grub Street, to the eighteenth-century observer, had windows that looked out both on Bedlam and on to a churchyard – on a madhouse and a burial ground. As it happened, no beautiful buildings *were* erected in Moorfields in the first half of the century.[63] The only important construction (after Hooke's new hospital) was the imaginary college set up on the spot in the revised *Dunciad*. Nevertheless, the associations were the same.

The clearest instance of the mental trick to which I have alluded comes in a letter from Pope to Broome of 16 February 1719. The poet looks forward to the 'day of [his] deliverance' when the *Iliad* should be off his hands. He writes:

> I shall retire a *miles emeritus*, and pity the poets militant who are to succeed me. I really wish them so well, that if my gains by Homer were sufficient, I would gladly found an hospital, like that of Chelsea, for such of my tribe as are disabled in the muses' service, or whose years require a dismissal from the unnatural task of rhyming themselves, and others, to death. Poor Gildon should have his itch and – cured together, and old Dennis not want good looking after, and better accommodation than poets usually meet with in Moorfields.[64]

George Sherburn glosses the last word 'the site of Bedlam'. Yes: that is the main point; but there is a submerged joke in the fact that the natural habitat of the active 'poets militant' was just over the way, the other end of Fore Street. The kind office referred to – that of setting up a hospital for incurable hacks – was ironically carried out by Pope and Swift more than once; again, *The Dunciad in Four Books* may be seen as the execution of this early hint. It should also be re-called that Swift speaks of '*Moor-Fields*', i.e. Bedlam, as one of the institutions to which the author of the *Tale of a Tub* is most indebted for assistance. Swift's *Serious and Useful Scheme, to make an Hospital for Incurables* is headed 'from my garret in Moorfields'. Nor was this collocation made only by the major satirists. Henry Carey, who often employs such Swiftian themes as the Smithfield shows and the juggler Fawkes, tells the story of an apprentice who treated his girl 'with a sight of Bedlam, the puppet-shews, the flying chairs, and all the elegancies of Moorfields'.[65] The irony of this latter phrase may require some elucidation .

As a historian of London writes, 'This "Moorfields" was orig-inally a swamp into which much of the City refuse was thrown. Little by little it was raised and attempts made to drain it . . .' The place became in time the first of London's recreation grounds, much fav-oured by the beau monde and frequented by Pepys among others. Stow was lyrical about the improvement which had been effected: at the start of his chapter on Cripplegate, he described Fore Street and the Postern, and then proceeded:

> Of these More-fields you have formerly read, what a moorish rotten ground they were, unpassable, but for Cawswaies purposely made to that intent; what they were also in our owne neerer times of memory, even till Sir *Leonard Hallyday* was Lord Maior of *London* . . . And what they are now at this instant, by the honourable cost and care of this City . . . For the Walkes themselves, and continual care of the City, to have them in that comely and worthy maner maintained: I am certainly perswaded, that our thankfulnesse to God being first truely performed, they are no meane cause of preserving health and whole-some ayre to the City, and such an eternal honour thereto, as no iniquity of time shall ever be able to deface.

Thus complacently Stow moves on in his next sentence to Moor

Lane and Grub Street. Later on, in treating of the suburbs without the walls, he includes a fuller description of the fen, 'a waste and unprofitable ground a long time', and the ditching operations carried out there to make it more habitable (and, doubtless, profitable).[66] Such pious genuflexions before the idol of civic thrift would have greatly amused Pope. He had, however, a better reason for his scepticism.

The point is that Moorfields served as something more than a pleasure ground, or than a site for military exercises. The 'walks' were, quite simply, the haunts of prostitutes of either sex. A pamphlet by Jonathan Wild, in reply to one by Charles Hitchen, appearing in 1718, contains the following:

> Not long after this a gentleman in liquor, dropping into the Blew Boar near Morefields with a woman of the town immediate lost his watch. He applied himself to the M[arshal] [Hitchen], desiring his assistance, but the man being well acquainted with the walk between Cripplegate and Morefields had the good fortune to find out the women.[67]

There is other evidence that the walk dividing upper and lower Moorfields was traditionally allocated to homosexuals. Add to these the fact that the games played on Moorfields were not always innocent (we find contemporary references to such 'Moorfield exercises as qualify a man first for the road and then for the gallows'); that suicides were buried in the ditches there; that the homeless fled to the spot and camped there after the Great Fire; that the function of a refuse tip did not entirely die out even when the district had become 'a patchwork of haphazard new building';[68] that dissenters and later Wesleyan preachers set up their pulpit in this locality; that neighbouring parishes sent their dead to the new burial ground at Moorfields when the Plague had overtaxed their own facilities for interment; add all these, and it is not surprising that Moorfields should have held on to its former reputation long after Stow had rhapsodised over its transformation. Defoe knew the district well: as his biographer has said, if he had run hard from his father's house in Fore Street he could have reached Moorfields in less than five minutes.[69] So could any child brought up in Grub Street: comfortably so. We find that Colonel Jack in making his escape from a robbery in the City went 'down old *Bedlam*, into *Moorfields*', where it was at last safe to pause for breath. On a second occasion, after a daylight raid in the region of Smithfield, Jack and his accomplice Will meet up at their 'old agreed Rendezvous' in Moorfields. To get there, Jack has to run like the wind 'thro' innumerable Alleys' and 'cross all the streets' – and that includes Grub Street.[70]

The delinquency sheet for Moorfields is a long one, and it will be enough to mention a few representative items in a broadly chrono-logical order. The historian of St Giles' parish has described the general trend:

> For a century and a half these fields presented a scene of great liveli-ness, and became a proverb for a riotous assemblage. Instead of round-about phrases about 'hubbub and confusion,' men said of any great tumult, 'It's as bad as Moorfields.' Thus a royalist writer, speaking of the Parliament, in King Charles I's time, says, 'By the noise they made at every factious resolve, you would take it to be a Moorfields tumult at a wrestling, rather than a sober council at a debate'.

The implications of this for *The Dunciad* are obvious. A Grub Street tumult, one might say, was a Moorfields tumult in its hack-literary aspect. As for particular affrays, one can point to an affair in 1664 (of which more in a moment), an occasion around 1720 when the watch-house was attacked by forty toughs, and an episode in 1764 when a sodomite arrested in the Mall (a gravel walk running east-west across the fields) was snatched away by a large gang who beat off the constables.[71]

Denton goes on to observe that

> The fields were the meeting ground of the apprentices, the place where workmen met to discuss the fall of wages and the rise in price[s] . . . the spot used for political gatherings of all kinds when folk-motes had ceased, and discontent or patriotism could find no sufficient outlet in the Common Hall.

The first function was illustrated by the 'great tumult' in 1664, when two apprentices had been put in the pillory. Their fellows took a number of retaliatory measures, including breaking the pillory to pieces and 'deforcing' the house of the apprentices' master. On the

Sunday following some four or five thousand apprentices met together, with the largest gathering in Moorfields.[72] Later in the eighteenth century the venue for such gatherings was more often St
George's Fields in Southwark – perhaps because building was going
on steadily in the parish of St Luke's (formerly the northern part of
St Giles'), and only the Fields themselves remained unoccupied. As
to the other gatherings, we find records of the Spitalfields weavers
assembling in Moorfields in 1765. They were 'accompanied by drums'
and arrayed in a kind of symbolic uniform. In this manner they
marched to St James's and Westminster Hall, which they surrounded :
a ritual progress the Dunces had enacted a generation earlier. In
1773 the same body of men again used Moorfields as a setting to vent
industrial grievances. The Spitalfields Act (13 Geo.III.c.68) was
a direct outcome of the discontent expressed on this occasion; patrio-
tism was less obviously at stake.[73] However, the use made of the
adjoining (New) Artillery Ground by the Company of that name
supplies that deficiency. The residents of Bunhill Row, who did not
yet include Milton, drew up a list of complaints when the Company
were granted this lease in 1641, specifying a number of evils which
would be attendant on the exercises of 'the military gentlemen of
London'.[74] However, the more prim inhabitants of Cripplegate seem
to have been markedly unsuccessful in keeping their parish free from
these indignities. Whatever the grounds of their objection, the playhouse or hospital or artillery ground duly appeared in the ward;
probably because the City authorities wanted such things kept well
away from the historic capital.

Some of the other uses to which Moorfields was put are thus
described by Denton:

> A more motley assemblage . . . than that which thronged Moorfields
> can hardly be imagined. The small penthouse shops which soon after
> 1600 began to spring up on the outskirts of the Moor, were tenanted by
> botchers . . . jobbing tailors, and renovators of old clothes, always
> ready to leave their shop boards and to join in the scuffles which went
> on before their doors. Under trees planted across the lower [southern]
> part of the Moor were stalls of second-hand booksellers, where anti-
> quaries rummaged for black-letter tracts . . . On lines stretched from
> tree to tree, slips of ballads fluttered in the breeze . . . In one corner

of the ground or another, wrestling matches gathered crowds of spectators for three or four centuries, and boxing and cudgel playing went on continually for the amusement of loiterers, and the advantage of the thieves who frequented these fields. Here, too, the place where the thief plied his vocation witnessed his punishment; for . . . Moorfields was chosen as the proper spot for publicly whipping the thief. A lock-up house for rioters, felons and other offenders . . . stood in these fields . . . Punch with his unfailing attractions, jugglers with their tricks of dexterity, and merry-andrews with their ready gibes, collect little crowds of idlers. Here, again, were ballad singers, sturdy beggars, and cripples, and at night . . . the prowling footpad and the burglar. . . .[75]

It is apparent that Pope knew what he was doing when he transferred the nerve-centre of the Dull from Rag Fair to a spot near Bedlam. The overtones are the same; a place of vagrancy, dissolute behaviour and crude physical action. Moreover, it is a simple metaphoric process to convert these ecological features into a critique of low professional scribbling. Writers (like the cheapjacks) deal in the second-hand; they are thieves; they are literary contortionists. At Moorfields (and, as we shall see, along the railings of Bedlam itself) lines of mean poetasters' wares were hung up like washing. The means of distribution – the 'point of sale' methods in use – reinforced Pope's point. Cheap literature was a commodity which had to be flaunted before the buyer's eyes like so much greengrocery. Its primary existence was one of visible, external substance;[76] as opposed to the inner life of true literature. The physicalities and literary fisticuffs of Pope's satire (e.g. in his prose pamphlets against Curll) are an image of Moorfields tumult, built into the artistic mode.

It is not hard to provide documentation of all the activities mentioned in Denton's account. The cheap stalls of Moorfields were mentioned by Garth; cheap meals were spoken of in 1755 as 'Farthing fries at Moorfields'.[77] (The Farthing Pye House, on the northern extremities of the region, will reappear presently.) Pepys describes the wrestling in 1661.[78] The cudgel players are mentioned by Shadwell. Throwing at cocks was another popular pastime, which thieves seem to have taken to around the turn of the century. Thirty years later we hear of strange wagers which were laid here.[79] As for the sturdy beggars to whom Denton refers, *A Trip through London*

(1728) has a phrase relating to 'the honest *Beggar* upon his *Truss of Straw* in *Moor-fields* . . .'[80] Again, the presence of low theatrical shows of one kind or another is attested by a number of sources. In 1739 the Grand Jury of Middlesex issued a presentment against the builders of booths erected in Moorfields, to which idle and disorderly people resorted to the disturbance of the peace. The constables of the Finsbury division were instructed to apprehend offenders. Similarly, in 1748 players were said to infest Moorfields daily.[81] The text of *The Dunciad* gives eloquent proof of what Pope thought about such Smithfield drolls (e.g. B.III.285ff.) Settle's prophecy envisages a day when

> . . . rais'd from booths, to Theatre, to Court,
> Her seat imperial Dulness shall transport. (B.III.299)

The movement of the poem, then, is from suburban fastnesses like Moorfields to the newly colonised areas of the West End.

The most direct link with literary topics, however, resides in the book trade. For example, the stalls which were cleared away from St Paul's Churchyard soon found a home elsewhere: 'by 1750 they seem to have congregated especially in Moorfields.'[82] About this time Gray wrote to Warton of the penny histories 'that hang upon the rails in Moorfields'. In Smyth's *Obituary*, an invaluable source for any student of Grub Street and its environs, we come on a bookseller at Bedlam who died in 1671; besides a variety of Moorfields residents in occupations ranging from hemp-beater to 'Ye City Painter'.[83] In *Trivia* the 'copious' stock market of Newgate is ranged with the fruit emporium of Covent Garden, whilst '*Moor-fields* [gives] old books; and *Monmouth-street* old suits.'

To these associations might be added such Moorfields specialities as itinerant preachers (Wesley and Whitefield used a shed in the old Canon Foundry on Windmill Hill, north of the fields towards the pest-house); brothels;[84] a dissenting academy which produced some of Samuel Johnson's early contacts in metaphoric Grub Street;[85] and the alehouses and singing-rooms which Pepys visited.[86] The stage of the Windmill tavern, opposite Bedlam, was used for strongman acts, whilst the Flying Horse in Little Moorfields was celebrated for music, merry andrews and cudgel play.[87] Finally there was a sad historical link with murder: in 1718 the public executioner, John Price, alias Jack Ketch, was hanged in Bunhill Fields for the brutal homicide of an old woman in Moorfields.[88]

This then was Moorfields in itself. That Dunces such as Ned Ward should have seen fit to set up their own taverns in the district was a further proof of that urban blight which Pope marked out as his special subject.[89] Again, it was more convenient than essential to the satirist's purposes that the disreputable Calves-Head Club, 'which caused scandal by celebrating the anniversary of Charles I's execution with ghoulish rites', should have been stated by a contemporary to have assembled 'in a blind alley about Moorfields'.[90] It all helped. But the major blot on this particular scutcheon was the existence of Bedlam.

Bethlehem Hospital had been founded in the thirteenth century, and stood originally near St Helen's, Bishopsgate. In 1675–6 a new building was erected by Robert Hooke, a short distance to the west. Stow refers to the narrow alleys surrounding the first hospital, 'of late time too much pesterd with people (a great cause of infection) up to the Bars'. Strype calls the original site an 'obscure and close Place, near unto many common Sewers'.[91] The new situation was generally considered to be better. James Ralph wrote in 1734, '*Bedlam* is very well situated in point of view and is laid out in a very elegant taste', although he deplored the 'near neighbourhood' of Moorgate as 'something of a blemish to this pile, because 'tis built in the same stile with it'.[92] The view from Bedlam was in essence the view from Grub Street. For completeness, it may be added that the hospital moved to St George's Fields, Southwark, in 1812–15, and occupied what is now the Imperial War Museum. The Bethlehem Hospital has since amalgamated with the Maudsley and has moved to Kent.

One striking visual aspect of Hooke's building was not precisely architectural at all; the two massive figures of Dementia and Mania (or 'Melancholy Madness' and 'Raving Madness') erected by Caius Gabriel Cibber, father of Colley Cibber, over the hospital gates. Pope, with his customary economy, utilised this feature of Bedlam in his revised *Dunciad*; whilst Hogarth is supposed to have parodied the figures in the background of his Bedlam scene in the *Rake's Progress*. This is a good clue to the importance of Bedlam in Augustan contexts. The significance it has in earlier literature has long been recognised; a monograph, indeed, called *Bedlam on the Jacobean Stage* contains useful information for our present purposes.[93] But there are several new components when we turn to Pope and Swift. Some of these relate to changing views of abnormal psychology, and to different provision for mentally sick persons. But other factors are connected with the new hospital itself, and its part in London life. There is a grim irony in the fact that a stately baroque mansion should have been dedicated to the task of housing the mad. According to Strype, 'Now those are judged the fittest Objects for this Hospital that are raving and furious, and are capable of cure . . . or if not, yet are likely to do mischief to themselves or others; and are Poor, and cannot be otherwise provided for.'[94] There was, as a matter of fact, a ward for incurables added, and this is shown in Hogarth's picture of Tom Rakewell. In general, however, Strype's account of the earlier dispensation fits the plan Pope had set out in his letter to Broome. He had stressed the age and penury of the 'tribe' of hack authors, and their claim to enjoy 'good looking after', Gildon and Dennis are to go out to stud, like Chelsea pensioners: their 'accommodation' is to be better than that experienced in Bedlam, by poets and others – but the implication is that the service will be of the same order.

In speaking of the treatment 'poets usually meet with in Moorfields', Pope undoubtedly had in mind the case of Nathaniel Lee,[95] who had been confined in the hospital from 1684 to 1688. This celebrated item of Grub Street mythology was of course as familiar to Pope as to anyone else. He seems, however, to have made only one explicit reference in an Horatian imitation (Sat.II.i):

> Whether the darkn'd Room to muse invite,
> Or whiten'd Wall provoke the Skew'r to write,
> In Durance, Exile, Bedlam, or the Mint,
> Like *Lee* or *Budgell*, I will Rhyme and Print.

The canard (retailed in the Twickenham edition, most recently) that Lee had written a twenty-five act drama in Bedlam serves to give added point. Pope often links madness with poetry in his Horatian essays, but nowhere else is certified lunacy tied so inextricably to the production of mindless, unwanted verses. One more indirect allusion comes in Ep.I.i, where Pope addresses Bolingbroke:

> You never change one muscle of your face,
> You think this Madness but a common case,
> Nor once to Chanc'ry, nor to Hales apply . . .[96]

Dr Hales is glossed simply as 'The Doctor of Bedlam' in Pope's note.

There had been one development, associated with the new building, which had brought Bedlam and literary production further together since the time of the Jacobean dramatists. This was the practice of using the long railings fronting the hospital on the south side as a publisher's billboard. Here books were advertised by the simple expedient of displaying the title-page (a habit which Gay describes at the end of *Trivia*).[97] Unlike St Paul's Churchyard, Bedlam seems to have been a market chiefly for second-hand works. Throughout the period from 1710 to 1786, books lined the perimeter of the hospital. On the wooden palings outside, broadsheets were displayed, whilst next to the wall second-hand bookstalls were set up. Pope himself alludes to this practice in the closing lines of his epistle to Augustus:

> And when I flatter, let my dirty leaves
> (Like Journals, Odes, and such forgotten things,
> As Eusden, Philips, Settle, writ of Kings)
> Cloath spice, line trunks, or flutt'ring in a row,
> Befringe the rails of Bedlam and Sohoe.[98]

It was yet another way in which the Dunces' hide-out could be associated with the shabby and the second-hand. In the first version of Pope's poem, the cell of Dulness is situated near a well-known mart for cast-off clothing. In the revised version, the Cave of Poverty and Poetry is found near the bastions of Bedlam – indeed, the actual walls (where the unwanted products of the duncely imagination were on show) are mentioned at the outset:

> Close to those walls where Folly holds her throne . . .
> One Cell there is, conceal'd from vulgar eye . . .
>
> (B.I.29)

Characteristically, Pope has made dreary quotidinial reality foster the creative ends of satire. In the words of the poem he addressed to Fortescue, he has chosen to 'Publish the present Age'.[99] But ironically: the literal facts are drawn on, only in order to add weight to a grotesque fiction.

The singular preference Swift exhibits for the Bedlamite theme has not, I think, been sufficiently regarded. The biographic facts are plainly on record. We know that the Dean caused some consternation by his generous endowment of St Patrick's Hospital. It is also a matter of historical certainty that Swift (like his friend Atterbury) was appointed a governor of Bethlehem Hospital on 26 February 1714.[100] He is not recorded as having attended any meeting of the governors, which is accountable in view of his permanent departure for Ireland shortly afterwards. But again, in 1732, Swift received in a letter from Sir William Fownes detailed proposals for the establishment of a Bedlam Hospital in the city of Dublin, containing the interesting passage:

> I own to you I was for some time averse to our having a public Bedlam, apprehending we should be overloaded with numbers under the name of the mad. Nay I was apprehensive our Case would soon be like that in England.[101]

In other words, there can be no doubt that Swift was seriously interested in the problem of dealing with mentally sick patients.

But even without this documentation, there is plenty of literary evidence. In section IX–X of the *Tale*, Swift's obsession with this particular *topos* shines out very clearly. The '*Academy of Modern Bedlam*' is singled out in the Digression on Madness, and a description of an enquiry into the present state of Bedlam provided later. (In early editions this was garnished with a graphic illustration opposite the text.)[102] I shall return to this section subsequently (Ch. III). More briefly, mention may be made here of the running conceit in the poem on 'The Legion Club', which identifies the Irish parliament with a madhouse, and the reference at the end of the 'Verses on the Death of Dr. Swift':

> He gave the little Wealth he had,
> To build a House for Fools and Mad . . .[103]

55

It is a familiar piece of social history that eighteenth-century men and women went along to Bedlam as to any other cheap pantomimic entertainment. Ned Ward described the scene in Part III of his *London Spy* (1698–9). As J. H. Plumb has written:

> Such strong passions could only flourish amidst a callous people, and it is not surprising that the popular sights of London were the lunatics in Bedlam, the whipping of half-naked women at Bridewell, the stoning to death of pilloried men and women, or the hangings at Tyburn, where a girl and a boy might be seen dangling between a highwayman and a murderer.[104]

Some of these occurrences were rare, as a matter of fact, but the show at Bedlam virtually never closed. It is also to the point that in one way or another the Dunces were connected with all four activities named. Bedlam it was, however, which was most conspicuously linked with literary folly. That was already true in 1742. The splendid imaginative stroke by which Pope made this connection actual in his *Dunciad in Four Books* has not had the critical recognition it deserves. To make Bedlam operative on the fringes of the actual plot was delicately arranged: for Grub Street, as the poem tells us, was itself flanked by that hospital.

Epic of Grub Street

One of the major changes in the revised *Dunciad*, as we have seen, is the shift of the centre of duncely operations from a spot near Rag Fair to one near Bedlam. I do not believe that the meaning of this alteration has been properly understood. Pope does not make such radical transformations idly. It is my view that the aim of this procedure is nothing less than the localisation of folly in Grub Street itself. What had been in the first version mere innuendo becomes finite, stated, *placed*.

The critical passage must be quoted in full if we are to understand the nature of this change:

> Close to those walls where Folly holds her throne,
> And laughs to think Monroe would take her down,

Where o'er the gates, by his fam'd father father's hand
Great Cibber's brazen, brainless brothers stand;
One Cell there is, conceal'd from vulgar eye,
The Cave of Poverty and Poetry.
Keen, hollow winds howl thro' the bleak recess,
Emblem of Music caus'd by Emptiness.
Hence Bards, like Proteus long in vain ty'd down,
Escape in Monsters, and amaze the town.
Hence Miscellanies spring, the weekly boast
Of Curl's chaste press, and Lintot's rubric post:
Hence hymning Tyburn's elegiac lines,
Hence Journals, Medleys, Merc'ries, Magazines:
Sepulcral Lyes, our holy walls to grace,
And New-year Odes, and all the Grub-street race. (B.I.29)

There are several important differences from the earlier version (quoted above, p. 39), apart from the shift of location. Pope has moved to a later position the reference to 'the imperial seat of Fools'; his note had suggested a parallel with the *Aeneid*, I.15–18. Literally this would have equated the cave of Dulness with Carthage, a somewhat distracting association as the poem develops. Secondly, the poet introduces mention of 'Bards' at the outset; this is to form an important part of his presentation of Duncehood. Thirdly, Pope has dropped the reference to the Quidnuncs, to the Guildhall and to Saint Cecilia's Day odes. (The first two are found at B.I.270.) He has substituted increased emphasis on the productions of folly ('Journals, Medleys . . .').

On the line 'One Cell there is . . .', the Twickenham edition has the following note, quoting at the start Warburton's gloss:

The cell of poor Poetry is here very properly represented as a little *unendowed Hall* in the neighbourhood of the Magnific *College* of *Bedlam*; and as the surest Seminary to supply those learned walls with Professors. For there cannot be a plainer indication of madness than in men's persisting to starve themselves and offend the public by scribling,
　　Escape in Monsters and amaze the town.
when they might have benefited themselves and others in profitable and honest employments. The *Qualities* and *Productions* of the students of this private Academy are afterwards described in this first book; as are also their *Actions* throughout the second; by which it appears, how near allied Dulness is to Madness. This naturally prepares us for the subject

of the third book, where we find them in union, and acting in conjunction to produce the Catastrophe of the fourth; a mad poetical Sybil leading our Hero through the Regions of Vision, to animate him in the present undertaking, by a view of the past triumphs of Barbarism over Science. W[arburton]. [The Cell of Poverty and Poetry, situated in *Dunciad A* in the neighbourhood of Rag Fair, was shifted in *1743a* to the neighbourhood of Bedlam. Warburton's reference to 'a little unendowed Hall' is obscure; but, in view of the mention of 'Professors' immediately afterwards, the Hall may perhaps be identified with Sion College, close to Bedlam. Dr. Joseph Trapp, Professor of Poetry at Oxford from 1708–18, was, at the time Warburton's note was written, President of Sion College; and on April 26, 1743 he had published a *Concio ad Clerum Londinensem.* . . . He was a frequent subject of ridicule by the wits.][105]

I find this identification quite implausible. A much more obvious explanation of Warburton's 'obscure' allusion would be to take Grub Street as the seminary in question. Since it may appear highhanded to assume airily that all previous commentators have missed such an important point, I shall set out my reasons as fully and scrupulously as possible.

(1) Negatively. Trapp is an unlikely candidate for such a key role. Only once in all his work did Pope mention him: in the 1728 version of *The Dunciad*, at A.II.381, his identity was cloaked by the word 'T——'. But this we learn from a manuscript source, since when the names were spelt out in full a year later, he had already been removed from the text. The only reference in Pope's correspondence dates back to 1710. Henry Cromwell had praised poems by Trapp included in Tonson's *Miscellany*: Pope replies less warmly, but adds that he does not have 'any sort of prejudice to him [Trapp] as a priest'.[106] Moreover, Trapp was an ardent Tory, and the butt chiefly of *Whiggish* wits – of Dunces such as Oldmixon, indeed. Swift may not have liked him very much, but Trapp certainly took the same side as he in various pamphleteering battles, notably in 1710–11.[107] It is hard to believe that so random and unformed a relationship should have been used to underpin the central attack on Dulness, when so many active enmities were available. Moreover Trapp was President only from 1742 to 1743, which would date the reference quickly.[108]

(2) Another negative point. The case is much the same with Sion College. This *was* near Bedlam, indeed Grub Street and Sion were almost equidistant from the hospital. On the other hand there are several arguments working against this identification. The College was not 'unendowed'. On the contrary, since its foundation in 1630, it had amassed amongst other things a notable library.[109] More important, it would be a most inappropriate setting for the 'scribbling' activities singled out by Warburton. Trapp was only one president amongst many, and neither starvation nor 'Journals, Medleys, Merc'ries . . .' were associated with this foundation. Sion could not properly be regarded as the 'home' of Cibber [B.I.266]; its potential resonance through the poem would be negligible, and it is certainly not mentioned by name anywhere – in text, notes, preliminaries or appendices. It never figures in the poems or correspondence of Pope, and to the best of my knowledge is not used with satiric intent by any major Augustan writer. Of course, the fact that it is not so used elsewhere does not prove that Pope could not have chosen to do so in this instance. But that, I think, is to multiply hypotheses beyond need – a fact that becomes apparent when we contrast the situation as it applies to Grub Street.

(3) As already shown, Grub Street was not merely near Moorfields and Bedlam; it was often so described. (As against Sion College 'lost' inside the City within the walls.) Grub Street might with perfect propriety be described as 'unendowed'; it was a poor region, and Pope never lets us forget that. The objection might be made that a street is not a hall. But Grub Street was constantly referred to by the satirists in such terms. Throughout his *Tale*, Swift speaks of the 'Society' of Grub Street, the 'Academy of Wits' located there, the 'College' of modern Aeolists, the 'Corporation of [hack] Authors', the 'Corporation of Poets', the 'Walks' of Wit, the 'spacious Commonwealth of Writers', 'Seminaries' planted by 'the *Grub-street* Brotherhood', and so on. As for professors, there is the familiar allusion to the '*Grubaean* Sages', with their 'Precepts and their Arts'. Again, in a work which has generally been taken as Swift's, the *Letter to a Young Poet*, the writer deplores the absence in Dublin of a Grub Street. He desiderates this institution by pointing to the existence of

parallel foundations ('a Court, a College, a Playhouse . . .'), and outlines a plan by which 'our poetical Vapours . . . might fall into one Quarter of the Town', instead of being scattered through 'every Street' at large. He proposes that 'some private Street, or blind Alley of this Town' should be set up as an 'apartment for the Muses'. This comes very close to Pope's idea of 'a bleak recess', 'conceal'd from vulgar eye'. In the case of the *Letter*, the application to Grub Street is made quite explicit. (See Ch. III.)[110]

An even more striking piece of evidence can be found in the work of another Scriblerian: the preface to *John Bull* (1712), by Dr John Arbuthnot. I have used part of the passage as an epigraph to this chapter, but certain phrases may be singled out here: 'The whole University of *Grub-street*', 'the Matriculates of that famous University', 'O *Grubstreet*! thou fruitful Nursery of tow'ring Genius's!' Arbuthnot's narrator boasts of having received his education amongst 'the Learned of that Society', and laments the 'approaching Barbarity that is likely to overspread all its Regions' (cf. Warburton's note). He uses, too, the notion of the 'Brethren' of Grub Street, common to all such passages of satire, in which the street is institutionalised.[111] It is found, for example, in the preliminary material for Fielding's *Grub Street Opera* (1731), where the introduction is written by 'Scriblerus Secundus', a pseudonym indicating the extent of Fielding's debt to Pope, Swift and their friends.[112] Once again we see how the iconography of Grub Street, as it was customarily described, is matched by the details of the cave of Poverty and Poetry. The two localities can surely be merged into one.

(4) Grub Street was traditionally the 'home' of Dunces. The 'sacred Dome' of Dulness is specifically stated by Pope to be coterminous with the cave: and Cibber 'no sooner enters, but he Reconnoitres the place of his original'.[113] Grub Street was known for poverty, scribbling, calumny, 'Scribling' was its special occupation. It can be seen, then, that both the text and Warburton's note fit Grub Street snugly: neither suits Sion College, except by an effort of wrenching. Cibber had obvious links with Grub Street, none that is recorded with the College. Grub Street was a familiar recourse in contemporary satiric economy; its identity could be spotted by an

alert reader, whereas a joke resting on an allusion to Sion would be hard to penetrate, and not very pointed when grasped.

(5) The overriding reason stems from these facts. At the cave, the goddess shows her chosen king 'all her works' (B.I.273). These are without exception literary productions. Like the 'Journals, Medleys' and the rest, the list which Pope provides would suit an enclave of bad writers: scarcely, a theological backwater. Moreover, *The Dunciad* is stuffed throughout with references to 'bards' (at least six times), poets, authors, stationers, swans, muses, wits, critics, songsters, riddlers and the like. Their productions are named as images, similes, metaphors, tragedy, comedy, farce, epic, figures, odes, plays, lays, folio commonplace books, quartos and octavos, a birthday ode, long and painful pages, points, antitheses, puns, bawdry, Billingsgate, prologues, prefaces, notes, prose, verse, sermons, characters, essays, songs, sonnets, epigrams, and so on. The journey to the shades in Book III is led by what the argument calls 'a mad Poetical Sybil',[114] described in the text as one

> In lofty madness meditating song;
> Her tresses staring from poetic dreams . . . (B.III.16)

Similarly, the central vision of this book is that of Settle: a former City poet, not a superannuated select preacher. In other words, most of this material aligns very well with Grub Street; only contingently and fortuitously with Sion College.

Most recent critics, I think, have tended to play down excessively the direct *literary* satire of the poem. There is a metaphysical aspect to Dulness: but her principal avatars are always the writing profession. Warburton explains quite adequately, in my view, the trajectory of the poem; and if this is the case, then no other symbol could have been devised which would tie together the various layers of the poem than the home of bad poetry. Since 'the Restoration of the Empire of Dulness in Britain' is the theme (note to B.I.1), it is peculiarly just that this *coup d'état* should be organised from 'The College of the Goddess in the City, with her private Academy for Poets in particular'.[115] Only one place could reasonably be thought of as the habitat of the 'hacknied Town scribler' (note to B.I.37), and this of course was Grub Street.

(6) One item of external evidence may be mentioned. Not long after the first version of *The Dunciad* appeared, that strongly pro-Pope organ the *Grub-street Journal* began its career (cf.Ch.VI). In the issue for 20 August 1730, no. 33, an article was printed in the *Journal* entitled 'Proposals for erecting a College for the habitation of Grub-street Authors, by Giles Blunderbuss, Esq; Historiographer to the Grubean Society.' This mock proposal connects with Swift's many variants on the notion of a Grub Street academy. Here it is enough to note that 'Blunderbuss' suggests a removal from Grub Street itself to more spacious quarters nearby. These are to be near Fore Street, and Moorfields is fixed on as the ideal spot. Blunderbuss notes as a recommendation the proximity of the Artillery Ground ('that great famous seat of war') and, also anonymously, 'the vicinity of that college, which already occupies the south-side of those fields'. Among other details supplied in connection with the new Grub Street there is a reference to the walls as a 'station for booksellers after the old manner'. The article as a whole provides a series of parallels with the satiric practice of *The Dunciad*; here I wish merely to bring out its relevance to the topic we have been considering. Pope, I would contend, took the hint, but not quite *au pied de la lettre*. He moves the dome of the Dunces to new quarters in his revision, to be sure, and these are located within earshot of Bedlam. But they stand not in a new Grub Street, constructed on the great fen of Moorfields. If we are as readers alive to all the hints which the poem provides, the cave can be placed at no other point than the road which entered Fore Street a matter of two hundred yards westward: the 'old' Grub Street, of course.

Turning from the object of attack to the method, we ought to note the emphasis on 'the wond'rous pow'r of Noise' (B.II.222). Literary incompetence is imaged by cacophony; the two are actually forced together syntactically in phrases like 'Noise and Norton . . . Dennis and Dissonance' (B.II.238). It is therefore of special interest to find mention of Dulness summoning 'her own Grubstreet choir' (B.II.123). Throughout the poem we have the swelling 'Chapel-royal throat' (B.I.319); the 'warble round' of the sirens (B.IV.541); and 'singing peers' (B.IV.49). There is the French horn (B.IV.278), trills and notes (B.IV.57), fiddling kings (B.IV.598), and 'loud Bow's stupendous bells resound' (B.III.278). Increasingly, these aural effects take on a sinister and less musical cast: 'warb'ling Polypheme' is taught to roar (B.III.305); screams issue forth (B.III.160, 306); 'chromatic tortures' threaten, as hums and snores break out (B.IV.55). Overtones of war are again present: the young rake, given a duncely education, 'stunn'd with his giddy Larum half the town' (B.IV.292). The Angel of Dulness, an *alter ego* of Cibber, 'wings the red lightning, and the thunder rolls' (B.III.256). If Handel is allowed his freedom to compose as he wishes, 'Jove's own Thunders follows Mars's Drums.' (B.IV.68). To counteract this threat, a last trump is blown, and all the retinue of Dulness assembled. Elsewhere, in an audacious pun, we hear 'the heavy Canon [of Christ Church] roll' (B.IV.247). The words *loud/loudly* are reiterated; terms like 'echo, hum, bray, bellow, strain, sound, bawl, peal' abound.

This richness of aural content serves two main functions. It fixes the Dunces as gibbering fools whose 'Music' never 'meanly borrows aid from Sense' (B.IV.64). The climatic moment occurs in Book II, with the shouting match and its accompaniment of grating catcalls. 'Tis yours to shake the soul' the Goddess tells her devotees:

> With Thunder rumbling from the mustard bowl,
> With horns and trumpets now to madness swell,
> Now sink in sorrows with a tolling bell;
> Such happy arts attention can command,
> When fancy flags, and sense is at a stand.
> Improve we these. Three Cat-calls be the bribe
> Of him, whose chatt'ring shames the Monkey tribe:
> And this his Drum, whose hoarse heroic base
> Drowns the loud clarion of the braying Ass. (B.II.226)

At that, a thousand tongues are heard 'in one loud din', and the famous passage of 'discordant' braying begins, with an unusual profusion for Pope of simple onomatopoeia (*chatt'ring, jabb'ring*). In the contest itself, Blackmore proves himself king brayer. Amidst all the 'moans' rending the welkin, and the 'harmonic twang' of the asses, the 'sonerous' poet carries away the prize, just as his voice carries to distant Tothill Fields, Hungerford and Westminster. The passage reminds us that a Dunce is never more at home than when acting like the donkey he is. Moore-Smythe has already been characterised (B.II.45) by reference to 'empty words . . . and sounding strain'. This is again a specifically literary emblem, though noisy inanity might possibly have been applied to men and women in any walk of life. Significantly, Bedlam was a byword for clamour: a contemporary spoke of members of Parliament making 'a hideous noise like so many Bedlamites'.[116]

Secondly, sound effects are used to drive home another prominent motif, the idea of the factious, brawling crowd:

> Dire is the conflict, dismal is the din,
> Here shouts all Drury, there all Lincoln's-inn;
> Contending Theatres our empire raise . . . (B.III.269)

It is noteworthy that Drury Lane and Lincoln's Inn Fields had a characteristic in common apart from housing a theatre. Each was frequently the scene of affrays at this time. The 'din' thus becomes representative of discord at large, as well as the quarrels between the theatres. And 'discord', in this context, means not only the cosmic breakdown, which recent critics have dwelt on so much – it points once again to the noisy street battles of eighteenth-century London. At best 'the noise of the streets was indeed deafening', what with the clatter of the carriages and the cries of vendors. Sanity, in Pope's poem, is forced to cover its ears against the hubbub, like Hogarth's Enraged Musician.

There is a subsidiary point here. *The Dunciad* is to a remarkable degree an *open-air* poem. A sense of expansiveness is apparent at all times; something the constant iteration of place-names, spread across the City, does much to promote. The text is littered with allusions to St James's, the Fleet Prison, Hockley Hole (twice), Chancery Lane, Guildhall, Ludgate, and so on. Sometimes the place is used with little more than figurative intent (Billingsgate; Drury Lane, at B.I.322). More often, however, the effect is to enhance the reader's sense of an *alfresco* scene, where turbulence is the norm. It has been wittily said, 'One of the few activities in which the upper and lower classes could find a common, happy meeting ground [in the eighteenth century] was street fighting.'[117] Here again the poem reflects the actuality of the age. A higher proportion of conspicuous life was led in the streets; historical events of consequence much more frequently took place out of doors. Public occasions, of ceremony or of function, went on in the streets. We need consider only the cases of Defoe, whose experience might be said to attain its most significant moments in the market place. His *Shortest Way* was burnt outsideWestminster Hall; he stood in the pillory in Cornhill, Cheapside and the Strand; he marched with a deputation into the Houses of Parliament. A few lines after mentioning the sight of Defoe in the pillory, indeed, Pope writes in the person of Curll:

> And oh! (he cry'd) what street, what lane but knows,
> Our purgings, pumpings, blankettings and blows? (B.II.153)

It is a rhetorical question. The cudgelling of publishers, the tossing of Curll himself in a blanket, were indeed quasi-public 'happenings', arranged for their display value. Yet they were also part of diurnal reality for the Londoner of 1740. Violence was a commonplace; perhaps Grub Street and its denizens were a little more at risk than the average.

Pope mentioned Grub Street by name only five times in the revised text. One additional reference (A.I.184) was dropped. In every case, the literal sense is present or available. (This is in contrast to his use of the term elsewhere, for example in the *Epistle to Arbuthnot*, where the figurative meaning is dominant).[118] Of these, the most valuable usage occurs in the third book, where Settle in his rapture compares Queen Dulness with Berecynthia:

> Not with less glory mighty Dulness crown'd,
> Shall take thro' Grub-street her triumphant round;
> And her Parnassus glancing o'er at once,
> Behold an hundred sons, and each a Dunce. (B.III.135)

Just as the bad poets aspiring to the art of sinking are allotted the 'Lowlands of Parnassus' as their quarters, so Dulness is assigned the lease of an actual plot of ground.[119] (Our key phrase never appears in *Peri Bathous*, though the topics and the individuals taken up are often identical. This suggests that it was the special needs of the plot, and the specially chosen setting, which dictate Pope's employment of the term in *The Dunciad*.) The simple truth is that Dulness *does* take 'her triumphant round' through Grub Street; the gallery of characters which follows (Ward, Jacob, Welsted, Dennis, Gildon, etc.) makes up a selection of first-choice Dunces. Ward is actually confronted with an ale-house (B.III.147), just like the one he had kept in Moorfields – another piece of live social history, to set against the stews, coalyards, and roundhouses mentioned elsewhere. Real poets went to Bedlam; real rioters practised cudgel-play or wrestling at Hockley Hole; real trainbands carried out their exercises on Moorfields (Cibber is ironically commended by Aristarchus for his knowledge of '*Old Battle-array*').[120] Real Dunces, like Defoe and Gildon, lived in the vicinity of Grub Street. The poem makes them re-enact these experiences at the removed (but no less painful) level of fiction. For all Pope's comic invention, the joke would have been much less good if there had been no reality on to which to base the grotesque transformation acts of his poem – no Bedlam, no city riots, no Grub Street.

*   *   *

As everyone knows, Dryden's *Mac Flecknoe* (1682) was the most important single model for the mock-heroic of *The Dunciad*. Apart from anything else, the earlier poem 'gave Pope the idea of a succession to the throne of Dulness'.[121] However, some of the implications of this carry-over have been missed, because one significant point of comparison has escaped detection. The throne of Thomas Shadwell is set up in the very same quarter of the town as the 'gorgeous seat' of Cibber (B.II.1). Cripplegate is the home of Dulness in both cases. It is no accident that Pope specifically recalls Dryden's poem at this moment: the seat 'far outshone/Henley's gilt tub, or Fleckno's Irish throne.'

At the outset there is a direct verbal recollection, not indicated in the Twickenham edition. When Pope describes the Dunces' cell, removed in the second version to the vicinity of Bedlam, he begins:

Close to those walls where Folly holds her throne . . . (B.I.29).

Compare the setting provided for Shadwell's imperial residence:

Close to the Walls which fair *Augusta* bind,
(The fair *Augusta* much to fears inclin'd)
An ancient fabrick, rais'd t' inform the sight,
There stood of yore, and *Barbican* it hight:
A watch Tower once; but now, so Fate ordains,
Of all the Pile an empty name remains.[122]

Dryden's archaising vein mirrors the dilapidated state of the place;
Dunces, like rats, infest decaying mansions. The passage continues:

From its old Ruins Brothel-houses rise,
Scenes of lewd loves, and of polluted joys.
Where their vast Courts the Mother-Strumpets keep,
And, undisturbed by Watch, in silence sleep.

In the light of Aubrey Williams's research, it is hardly necessary to
stress that Queen Dulness in Pope's poem functions as Magna Mater,
i.e., in one signification, mother-strumpet or madam. As with the
original site of the Dunces' cave, Rag Fair, a halo of brothels extends
around the sanctum of folly. That the watch turned a blind eye to
certain notorious areas of the town is well attested; some years later
party no. 7 of the Bow Street force was deputed to patrol this area,
but in 1740 the policing function was slackly performed – not to
speak of 1680.[123]

Dryden moves on to a splendid setpiece concerning the nursery
theatre briefly in occupation here during the Restoration. In this
house 'Queen's are form'd, and future Hero's bred'. Unfledged actors
are taught to rant and posture. Fletcher and Ben Jonson are banished
in favour of fairground drolleries:

. . . gentle *Simkin* just reception finds
Amid this Monument of vanisht minds:
Pure Clinches, the suburban Muse affords;
And *Panton* waging harmless War with words.

Punning, we recall from Book IV, is a major acquirement of the
Dunces. And the 'suburban Muse' is another word for the Smithfield Muses, the deities who preside over harlequinades, puppet-
shows or any other duncely spectacle.[124] In another sense, too, Pope
equally places his throne-room in a 'monument of vanisht minds' –
Bedlam.

On this spot, then, 'as a Place to Fame well known', Fleckno decides to set down Shadwell in readiness for his coronation. There is a hint that the dramatist Dekker has prophesied that 'in this Pile should Reign a mighty Prince', but as far as I can discover this is a facetious rather than a literal reference, corresponding to the vision of Settle in *The Dunciad*, Book III. At all events, the coronation is duly publicised throughout the town, and we are given one of those brief itineraries which are so characteristic of Augustan satire:

> Rows'd by report of Fame, the Nations meet,
> From near *Bun-Hill*, and distant *Watling-street*.

The City proper (Watling Street) is 'distant'; close at hand is the unmistakably suburban Bunhill Fields, where Cripplegate was in 1680 almost on the point of straggling into semi-rural scrubland. Bunhill Row had recent associations with John Milton; but equally to the purpose its southern end lay a bare hundred yards from the northern tip of Grub Street. And through that street the 'Nations' of bad authors would assuredly troop on their way to the coronation ceremony.

The remainder of *Mac Flecknoe* is familiar enough and need not concern us. The point is that Shadwell's far from peaceful province in 'Acrostick Land' turns out to lie within the limits of Cripplegate. Earlier commentators assumed that the theatre near the Barbican must have been the old Fortune playhouse, which had been situated north of the Barbican off Golden Lane. But some acute detective work by Leslie Hotson has shown that the Restoration nursery was situated elsewhere.[125] There was first of all a booth or playhouse built in Finsbury Fields, 'commonly called Bun hill', in 1671. For nine weeks that summer the nursery occupied that site until some of the young actors defected. But in October of the same year Lady Davenant's proposal to erect a playhouse in the Barbican was opposed by parishioners of St Giles'. They alleged that the foundation of the theatre would 'tend to the great evill and inconveniency' of the inhabitants, arguing that a playhouse should not be permitted 'so neere the Bowells of the City'. Nevertheless, the theatre was built and it is doubtless to this which Dryden alludes. Hotson argues with some cogency that the nursery stood south of the Barbican, in a court later named Playhouse Yard, and that the building was taken over by the Anabaptist meeting house which Rocque indicates on this site. This identification has the incidental merit of bringing the nursery closer to the city walls, and that is of some relevance in considering the thematic significance of the passage.

This section of *Mac Flecknoe* does indeed rehearse much of the satiric 'happening' which constitutes Book I of *The Dunciad*. The nursery was opposed by residents of Cripplegate on the grounds that it would lead to disorders. The theatre is itself an epitome of Duncehood in action; it rejects the honoured traditions of drama in favour of low pantomimic entertainments. Readers of Sybil Rosenfeld's enjoyable study of *The Theatre of the London Fairs in the Eighteenth Century* will know what that portends: for Dryden as for Pope, drolls were to legitimate drama as birthday odes were to Homer.

Secondly, the fact that the playhouse lay just outside the City walls is given deliberate emphasis. 'Augusta' had been 'much to fears inclin'd' around the time of the Exclusion Crisis and the Popish Plot. Yet the phrasing suggests a permanence in the situation – the absence of an auxiliary verb removes the notion as well as the grammatical fact of tense. We are led to suppose that the city is in a constant state of siege and disquiet. The agencies of this unrest are concentrated *outside* the walls of the ancient Augusta – the use of the Roman term implies the integrity of the Roman settlement, rather than the modern city whose liberties extend further out. The nursery, unlike Bunhill Fields and the northern part of Grub Street, lay just inside the liberty of the city. But the 'suburban Muse' flourished in districts like Smithfield and Farringdon Without, which strictly came under the jurisdiction of the City – as well as places like Southwark which had their own ancient municipal life, yet remained wards of London without the walls. Suburban status, as today, was not a matter of administrative history, but of social and geographical realities.[126] The growing suburbs had long been felt to constitute an obscure threat. Dryden and Pope may not have sided with the City Corporation on many political issues, but imaginatively they were at one with the ancient community here. The place of maximum squalor and lewdness, where policing is most inadequate, naturally lies away from the compact centre of organic 'London'. The same idea might be put in a slightly different way. Paradoxically the taint of urbanism, as Pope for one discerned it, lay most heavily on the fringes of the town, where haphazard development had proceeded, not unchecked but under too little restraint. The point of maximum danger, correspondingly, is the edge of the town, where callow urbanism is in process of destroying the age-old countryside. Not for nothing do Juvenal's Umbricius and Johnson's Thales deliver their philippics against the city from just outside its bounds – 'Indignant THALES eyes the *neighb'ring* town' (My italics).

The suburban muse, then, with all its baneful cultural implications, was properly set down in Cripplegate. Dryden used as its symbol a theatre in Paul's Alley. To find a more potent and expressive vehicle, Pope had only to shift the seat of Dulness two or three hundreds yard eastwards. Grub Street was half within the liberty of the city, half without: as literal a state of suburbia as one could ever imagine.

Men and Places

For the Dunces, the point of no return is the church of St Mary le Strand. Queen Dulness sets up her throne there (A.II.23):

> Amid that Area wide she took her stand,
> Where the tall May-pole once o'erlook'd the Strand;
> But now, so ANNE and Piety ordain,
> A Church collects the saints of Drury Lane.

According to Aubrey Williams, this siting of the action, just beyond the boundary of the City and Temple Bar, is 'highly significant, for at the Strand began the jurisdiction of Westminster'. He continues:

> Then, where Drury Lane enters the Strand, the dunces enact their ludicrous parody of the epic games. The exact geography of the games seems partly determined by the fact that the Strand and Drury Lane were the actual sites of many printing-houses and theatres, and so could mark the encroachment of literary dulness on Westminster.[127]

All this, so far as it goes, is excellently said. But if we are to chart 'the exact geography' of the games, then there is much more to be said. On the negative side, it is not wholly true that many printing houses were located in the Strand. Booksellers' shops were numerous in Fleet Street particularly, and such famous members of the trade as the firm of Tonson were actually in business a few yards from St Mary's, 'over against Catherine Street', as many an imprint records. The printing trade as a whole was centred much farther east.[128] But there are more positive additions to be made. Firstly, the maypole (removed as lately as 1718) carries obvious associations of bawdy fun and pagan ritual. The Dunces act with the unthinking atavism of a Hocktide reveller. They do not know what their own jollities portend, but they indulge with religious fervour. More important is the range of ideas evoked by the mention of Drury Lane. As the mention of 'saints' (prostitutes) makes plain, the district north-westwards from the games' venue had an unsalubrious reputation. In particular, it was down in this direction that the Great Plague had spread. Drury Lane connoted only secondarily theatreland. Nor was the concentration of coffee-houses, which modern descriptions of the area tend to single out, its most marked feature for men and women of the time. Sociologically this district was rather heterogeneous; it had a genuine bohemian flavour, which the other haunts of Dulness lacked. Wits and aristocrats *would* have visited this part of town, whereas they would never willingly have strayed into Moorfields or Rag Fair. Despite that, it cannot be denied that for the most part Drury Lane was linked in the contemporary mind with organised vice. An early letter from Pope to Henry Cromwell makes the point. The issue is raised in prose: 'If I may be allow'd to object against any thing you write . . . it shou'd be that Passage in yours, where you are pleas'd to call the Whores of *Drury-Lane*, the Nymphs of *Drury* . . .' And then, amusingly, in verse:

> If Wit or Critick blame the tender Swain,
> Who stil'd the gentle Damsels in his Strain
> The Nymphs of *Drury*, not of Drury-Lane;
> Be this his Answer, and most just Excuse—
> 'Far be it, Sirs, from my more civill Muse,

> Those Loving Ladies rudely to traduce.
> Alleys and Lanes are Terms to vile and base,
> And give Idea's of a narrow Pass;
> But the well-worn Paths of the Nymphs of Drury
> Are large & wide; *Tydcomb* and I assure ye.'[129]

The obscene touch here is only what contemporary readers would have expected every time the name 'Drury Lane' came up. Its squad of 'Loving Ladies' were for a long time the chief resident personnel. The topographic aspect is explicitly stressed on many occasions, so that we find references to 'a woman of great note in the hundreds of Drury' in the *Grub-street Journal*.[130]

For the severe moralist, the existence of the theatre did not improve matters, especially in the region about Russell Street. In 1730 the shopkeepers and traders appealed to the Westminster Sessions, in whose jurisdiction of course they lay:

> Several people of the most notorious characters and infamously wicked lives and conversation have of late . . . years taken up their abode in the parish. . . . There are several streets and courts such as Russell Street, Drury Lane, Crown Court and King's Court and divers places within the said parish and more particularly in the neighbourhood of Drury Lane infested with these vile people. . . . There are frequent outcries in the night, fighting, robberies and all sorts of debaucheries committed by them all night long to the great inquietude of his majesty's subjects.[131]

(Note, in passing, the word 'infested'.) Certainly this was no district in which to cultivate Thorowgood's bourgeois habits or to put the Protestant ethic into practice. Narcissus Luttrell describes a violent Jacobite riot which took place in Drury Lane itself in 1695,[132] and there were others later. Naturally the night-cellars and gaming establishments which had sprung up promoted crime, and it is interesting to note that Jack Sheppard began life as a carpenter's apprentice in Wych Street, off Drury Lane. He never moved his centre of operations very far away.[133] There was a cockpit in the street, too.[134] Whether Pope would align these features of the landscape with the theatre may be doubted. But he certainly knew the byways of the region. As we shall see, he gives as the address of one of Curll's authors Vinegar Yard, a mean court right up against the playhouse.

The whole district around Covent Garden and St Giles' requires a book to itself. Gay speaks of *'Drury's mazy courts'* and Garth of 'fam'd St *Giles*'s Pound'.[135] It was an area linked with rookeries and thieves' dens, around the crowded labyrinth of Seven Dials. Hogarth had set the first stage of cruelty in this vicinity, and the harsh image clung on. In fact St Giles' figures in the background of 'Noon', and one part of the parish forms the basis for Gin Lane.[136] The lodging-houses and gin-shops of this area were infamous even in a London less nice than our own; after the plague had gone, we find typhus setting in with peculiar virulence. Most of the houses were not especially old; it was a seventeenth-century development. But it was the worst part of the city as far as insanitary boarding went. Un-skilled Irish labourers, lascars, negroes flooded into the district. Coloured beggars even became known as 'St Giles' blackbirds'. As with the 'hundreds of Drury', adjoining the parish to the south-east, 'St Giles' in eighteenth-century art – literary or graphic – means trouble.[137] Dunces and highwaymen mingled there. The parish of St Paul's, Covent Garden, harboured at one time both the most infamous of bawds, Mother Douglas, and the most notorious of booksellers, Edmund Curll.[138] The sociological accident coincides with the literary assertion: to publish is to act as a pimp on behalf of artistic prostitution.

These associations can be traced in the work of many of Pope's contemporaries. But, to limit ourselves to his own circle of friends, Garth and John Gay had given recent expression to this view of Covent Garden and its environs. The former writes in *The Dispensary*:

> Long has this darling Quarter of the Town,
> For Lewdness, Wit, and Gallantry been known.

Whilst *Trivia* shows us a rowdy game of football, juxtaposed ironic-ally with Inigo Jones's 'famous temple'.[139] This blend of spacious amenity, as regards the actual buildings, with tumultuous and anti-social conduct furnishes just the kind of human oxymoron which the Scriblerians delighted to observe.

The St Giles' – Drury Lane – Covent Garden area, then, can be seen to contain the usual ingredients of a home of the Dull. It embraced a greater range of poverty and affluence than most districts of this kind. But the other characteristics appear as usual: connections with crime, plague black spots, organised vice, the visible squalor of Gin Lane, a high concentration of immigrant labourers, crowded housing, an abundance of night-cellars and garrets, labyrinths of impenetrable courts and alleys. The residence of particular minor writers whose genuine existence is attested seems almost an accidental addition.

Earlier we found similar circumstances in the case of other regions – Grub Street, West Smithfield and Rosemary Lane. I shall consider in Ch. II the extensive belt of poverty-line London which bordered on that notorious sink, the Fleet Ditch. Overall, we can distinguish four main centres of this kind. These regions adjoin one another and, in the case of Smithfield, they actually merge. However, they may be roughly divided as follows:

(1) ROSEMARY LANE. The parts just outside the City at the southeastern corner, near the Tower. Mainly located in the parish of St Botolph without Aldgate, and Portsoken Ward. This district includes Rag Fair itself, the headquarters of the Dunces in the first version of the poem. It also embraces Goodman's Fields, the Minories, Nightingale Lane.

(2) ST GILES' CRIPPLEGATE. More or less coterminous with both the parochial and the municipal limits designated by that name. Contains Grub Street itself, and in addition Red Cross Street, Jewin Street, Old Street – as well as Moorfields and Bedlam. Joined with area (1) by Hounsditch and Petticoat Lane.

(3) FLEET *and* FARRINGDON. This is the largest area, covering most of Farringdon Ward Without, and also certain adjacent regions, notably the parish of St Andrew, Holborn. Skirts the western edge of the old City wall, and includes Bridewell, Fleet Street, Shoe Lane, the environs of Newgate, the Fleet Prison and the lower reaches of the Fleet River. Linked with area (2) by the notorious Smithfield slum, reaching as far as the southern tip of Clerkenwell, but all draining into the Ditch.

(4) ST GILES' *and* COVENT GARDEN. Includes Drury Lane and that part of the Strand immediately contiguous. Adjoins area (3) to the east.

It would be possible to devise other zones of this kind, most obviously in the Borough of Southwark – where the Mint served as an epicentre of the disease which was Dulness, not to mention other human disabilities. But these are the sectors of London most directly relevant to the imaginative working of *The Dunciad.*

It will be immediately apparent from the map that these four areas ring the ancient walled City. The point to be made is that they do not actually *invade* the limits so defined. This is not to say that they do not fall within the jurisdiction of the municipality. Actually, a high proportion of the first three areas lies within the 'liberties' of the City, i.e. parts within the 'rules' of the Corporation and its courts, but outside the walls. This is a significant fact. In the early eighteenth century, the heart of the City itself was not subjected to special strain. The population of the City within the Walls declined steadily over the course of the century. The City without the Walls, after growing in the Restoration era, remained fairly static. It was the outlying parishes which grew most quickly. Some of these in effect were surburban, and largely escaped the problems of poverty and sanitation associated with rapid growth. It was the zone surrounding the ancient City, the inner ring of parishes in such vicinities as Holborn, Stepney and Clerkenwell which felt these problems most acutely.[140]

It was in those secondary regions, surrounding the City Walls, where the Dunces were most highly concentrated. This point has been obscured by Aubrey Williams's reading of Pope, which – acute and valuable as it is – fosters one central misconception. Williams sees the gallery of Dunces as a literary embodiment for a process visible in the world at large – 'the extension of City standards into the court'.[141] He charts with some care 'the path pursued by the dunces in their riotous peregrinations about London' and implies that we can see this itinerary as an emblem for the passage of Troy-novant from the City to Westminster.[142] However this is to reckon only with a selection of the facts. It is important to recognise that the Dunces, for the most part, did not live in the City, narrowly defined. They cannot be simply equated with the brokers and stockjobbers, the merchants and importers, the shopkeepers and moneylenders: for the good reason that they themselves had no real stake in the life of the City. It is not just that they had no seat on the aldermanic bench of the Corporation. Many of them lived in Westminster (i.e. area (4)); many others resided in, and frequented, parts of the town nearer Whitehall than the new Guildhall which went up in the 1730's. The truth is that when the Dunces reached St Mary le Strand, and set up their maypole at that spot, they had returned to their own background. When they made their next halt, at Bridewell Bridge, they were virtually home. The journey from Mansion House to Fleet Ditch was not for them (as it *was* for the Lord Mayor and his party) a voyage out. It was not even an aimless peregrination. It was a homecoming.

Just how familiar Pope was with the haunts of his victims, and how carefully he plotted their movements, we can gauge from one striking piece of his evidence. This is to be found in his 'Further Account of the Condition of Edmund Curll' (1716). My analysis of the text is based partly on comments by Elwin and Courthope, and by Ralph Straus; but substantially the passage remains unexplicated. This is a great pity, for without assistance we can hardly make anything of Pope's satire. His interest in his literary opponents, *prior to* their transmutation into literary vehicles of his own manufacture, entails several obligations on us as readers. Unique amongst satirists, the Scriblerian group kept a detailed file on their victims over a period of many years. Their final satiric references are chosen with pointed accuracy. Indeed, there is a malicious brand of specificity which marks out all Pope's practice. It follows that we have to be alive to what may look at first to be the stray particulars, if we want to grasp the general implications of his attack.

The passage is occasioned by a determination of Curll (as Pope has it in his narrative) to summon his various authors for a kind of sickbed salon. The bookseller, in 'a lucid Interval' amid the fits of madness occasioned by the poison Pope had administered, sends out a messenger to call in his flock. There follow 'Instructions to a Porter

76

how to find Mr. *Curll*'s Authors'. Delightfully circumstantial, these instructions provide us with Pope's first, and fullest, reference guide to his map of Dulness. In succession we are given the description of each needy hack and his likely whereabouts. Pope skips briskly from one address to the next; I shall follow at a more leisurely pace, proceeding not *seriatim* but taking the authors one by one. (Here we shall not be primarily concerned with the identity of these men and women, a question to be studied elsewhere.)[143]

The porter is to search first for the house historian, 'at a Tallowchandlers half way under the blind Arch'. This possibly refers to Petty France, Westminster, in view of the facts, first, that the parts of Westminster adjoining Tothill Fields were made up of mean streets at that time; and second, that Aaron Hill came to live in Petty France some years later.[144] (He had also written a history of the Ottoman Empire in 1709.) More probably, the location in mind is another Petty France, shortly to disappear, which at that time lay in Bishopsgate Ward Without, near modern Broad Street, and became 'New Broad Street'. The burial ground of St Botolph's lay here. The original Bethlehem Hospital had been sited here, though Bedlam now stood a few yards west. This is, in short, an archetypal duncely address, within easy reach of Grub Street, conveniently situated for access to Bedlam, and placed squarely within the liberties.

It is a short step to the second point of call, 'At the Bedsted and Bolster, a Musick-house in *Moorfields*, two Translators in a Bed together'. The two unfortunate hacks cannot be positively named, and I have not managed to locate the precise site of the music house. Ned Ward seems to have been connected with one such establishment.[145] Whether he can really be regarded as a translator (despite his version of *Don Quixote* 'Merrily translated into Hudibrastic Verse') is an open question. But there can be no two opinions about the character or social concomitants of the address supplied. Moorfields, as we have already seen, had a reputation for clandestine sexual assignations, orthodox or unorthodox. Again its proximity to Bedlam and to Grub Street was such that Pope and Swift appear to use the name as a mode of alternative description. Certainly a Dunce domiciled in Moorfields had done nothing, by his choice of a residence, to infringe his status.

Thirdly, the porter is sent to 'the *Hercules* and *Still* in *Vinegar-yard*', in search of 'a School-master with Carbuncles on his Nose'. Who the latter was, I am not sure. Vinegar Yard is easier to identify; this was an alley off Drury Lane, the very next along from Playhouse Yard. In 1720 Strype described the alley as 'indifferent broad, but ordinarily built and inhabited'.[146] The topographer is careful in choosing his words, and generally errs on the side of charity – somewhat by contrast with his predecessor, Stow. We may safely conclude that Vinegar Yard was a narrow court, tainted by the local associations, likely to contain a 'bagnio' (or bordello) and inferior lodging-houses. The tavern was doubtless as mixed in character and clientele as was its very title. From its convenience for the theatre, it looks as though the schoolmaster perhaps served on the dramatic side of Curll's staff. But that is mere speculation. A more confident judgement would be that such denizens of the reigon contributed to the tide of disease, immorality and dirt flowing down Drury Lane to the Dunces' rendezvous at St Mary le Strand, a matter of two to three hundred yards away.

The next two stopping-off points call for less comment. The first is 'a Blacksmith's Shop in the *Fryars*', where a pindaric writer in red stockings, almost certainly Ambrose Philips, may be found. The district of Whitefriars, or 'Alsatia', long a refuge for every kind of fugitive, is described in the next chapter. Pope suggests that the writer of Pindarics is not merely in straightened circumstances, but that he is fleeing from poetic justice: he is a fugitive from the civilised standards and propriety of art, a debtor of the literary world. Following this, the porter is enjoined to visit 'the Calendar-mill-Room at *Exeter-change*' in quest of a 'Composer of Meditations'. This again places the action in the same quarter of London. The Exeter Exchange, not to be confused with the 'New' Exchange, down towards Charing Cross, was likewise in the Strand. Until its demolition in the early nineteenth century, it stood in the vicinity of the present-day Exeter Street, the other side of Bow Street from Catherine Street and Drury Lane – but again no more than three hundred yards from St Mary's church. There is no doubt that many of Curll's authors survived, literally or imaginatively, to earn an entry for themselves in *The Dunciad*; in fact every writer unambiguously named in the 'Further Account' turns up in the later poem – Gildon, Oldmixon, Mrs Centlivre, Blackmore. With this in mind, it can fairly be said that several of the participants in the shouting-match outside St Mary's had indeed retired to their own parlour door.

The next reference is more puzzling. Curll is made to send his porter in search of his 'best Writer against *Reveal'd Religion*'. The address given is 'the three *Tobacco-pipes* in *Dog* and *Bitch* yard'. Despite extensive enquiries, I have not been able to locate this spot with any accuracy. There was an inn called the Three Tobacco Pipes, in a squalid district near Charing Cross which included part of what is now Trafalgar Square, as well as lower St Martin's Lane (where there was one of the ubiquitous, but none the less significant, streets by the name of 'Dirty Lane'.)[147] But I suspect, without having mustered clinching evidence, that Dog and Bitch Yard is more likely to have been situated in St Giles'. This is owing to a connection with Lewkners Lane, the next address to which I shall turn.

Here we have, indeed, the most interesting of all the localities, with the richest store of legendary association. It is worth quoting the entire paragraph: 'At Mr. *Summers* a Thief-catchers, in *Lewkners* Lane, the man that wrote against the impiety of Mr. *Rowe*'s Plays'. The individual concerned was almost certainly Charles Gildon, a Dunce of Dunces. More to the present purpose is the street itself. Lewkners Lane, sometimes spelt Lutenors, Leuknors, and similar variants, subsequently became known as Newtonhouse Lane and Charles Street. Ultimately, around 1878, it took its present name, Macklin Street. It was built on what had been the grounds of Sir Lewis Lewknor, who lived in Drury Lane about 1620.[148] Early in its existence the street acquired a bad reputation, which it was unable to slough off for the better part of two centuries. Even at this date, it is easy to find ample justification for this ill name, whether we consider literary or historical evidence.

Dryden was perhaps the first to use the street as a byword for loose living. In his early comedy, *The Wild Gallant*, the bawd Lady du Lake reluctantly admits, to the embarrassment of Loveby (the gallant of the title), that her lodgings are 'in St *Luknors* Lane at the Cat and Fiddle'. Two whores employed by this same procuress live respectively in Dog and Bitch Yard and in 'Sodom'. Loveby, shamed by this public avowal, exclaims 'I am ruined! . . . plague had you no other places in the Town to name but *Sodom*, and *Luknors-Lane* for Lodgings?' 'Sodom' is hard to fix exactly on the map – naturally it does not appear under that name! However, there are abundant indications that it was in the St Giles/Long Acre district: possibly eastwards towards Holborn. The latter was a centre of homosexual prostitution, and Jonathan Wild was to write of 'a noted house in Holborn' frequented by transvestites and known as 'the Sodomitish Academy'. I believe that the context suggests that Dog and Bitch Yard could also be found close at hand, and would be inclined to place it tentatively round about St Giles'. A few years after Dryden, Samuel Butler referred to Lewkners Lane in terms which leave no doubt as to its local character:

> The nymphs of chaste Diana's train,
> The same with those of Lewkner's lane.

An early commentator, cited by Zachary Grey, supplies an almost redundant gloss: 'Some years ago swarmed with notoriously lascivious and profligate strumpets.' It was certainly not an address one would be proud to blazon as a letterhead.[149]

Roger L'Estrange said much the same thing: he called Lewkners Lane 'a rendezvous and nursery for lewd women, first resorted to by the Roundheads', a political slur Pope is not likely to have taken very seriously.[150] The point is made, but more subtly, in *The Beggar's Opera*. In direct imitation of the 'summons' technique employed by Pope, Gay has Macheath send a porter for the 'Ladies' he wishes to entertain. The assembled company, when the girls arrive, is made up entirely of the likes of Suky Tawdry and Jenny Diver. Apologising for a slight delay, the drawer at the inn tells Macheath, 'You know, Sir, you sent him as far as *Hockley in the Hole*, for three of the ladies, for one in *Vinegar Yard*, and for the rest of them somewhere about *Lewkner's Lane*.'[151] Literary men, it is plain, live in identical quarters with women of the streets – in some cases, one assumes, not just under the same roof. It is a simple but effective ploy. Yet again the Dunces are pressed into the army of poverty and vice.

If that had been all, however, they would have escaped more lightly than is the case. Lewkner's Lane was a haunt of tarts, certainly, and had its share of gin shops, night-cellars and similar establishments. Its real degeneration, and its real usefulness from the point of view of Pope, began about 1713. It was then that Jonathan Wild, shaking free of the Wood Street compter, and quitting his temporary abode in Cripplegate, came to live in Lewkner's Lane with his moll, whose favourite name seems to have been Mary Milliner. This formidable couple, lacking that collective unity of purpose which distinguishes Bonnie and Clyde, split up before very long. Within a year or two Wild had left his brandy shop in St Giles', and moved to a tavern in Little Old Bailey. However, it was in Cock Alley, a stone's throw from Grub Street itself, and Lewkner's Lane that he first made headway in his dubious business. And even in 1718, according to Charles Hitchen, Wild's brother Andrew kept a 'case' (brothel) in Newtenhouse Lane. Jonathan had left the street when Pope's 'Further Account' appeared. But there is no doubt who was the most celebrated thieftaker to have resided there in recent times: his name was not Summers. As we might expect, Jack Sheppard was just as closely connected with Lewkner's Lane. On one occasion, Defoe (?) tells us, he managed to dispose of stolen property at an ale-house in the Lane, 'a rendezvous of robbers and ruffians'. Sheppard is also said to have frequented a victualling house in this street, and to have met Edgeworth Bess there. Later the couple kept a small brandy shop there. Not surprisingly, the writer of Sheppard's dying confession makes him specify 'Lewknor's Lane' as one of 'the chief scenes of [his] rambles and pleasures.'[152] What company for the unhappy dramatic critic!

It will be possible to cover the remaining localities more briefly. The next relates to *'Tooting'* (presumably Tothill) Fields, in Westminster. However, the exact location is 'the Farthing Pye House', and that stood in the Tenter Fields, past Upper Moorfields at the edge of Cripplegate parish. Following that, in a garret 'up three pair of stair' at the laundresses 'at the Hole in the Wall in *Cursitors Alley*', the porter will find two more hacks employed by Curll, sleeping in one bed. (The volley of prepositions conveys just how remote and inaccessible the garret is: the syntax amounts to a flurry of gesticulated directions.) Cursitors Alley ran eastwards off Chancery Lane, through Castle Court, and turned north towards Holborn. It occupied the site of the Cursitor's Office, mentioned by Stow. Modern Cursitor Street corresponds broadly with the first section of the Alley. It is noteworthy perhaps that another fully paid-up Dunce, John Oldmixon, later lived in Southampton Buildings, a few yards further up Chancery Lane: he may possibly qualify for the role of 'Indexmaker', named at this point.[153] Overall, this was perhaps not quite such an unsalubrious region as some of the others. But it did border on the heavily contaminated district surrounding the Fleet, i.e. area (3), and the narrow courts hereabouts must have been a suitable habitat for the hack author.

The remaining addresses are widely spread. First, the porter is to call on Mrs Centlivre in Buckingham Court, Charing Cross; her husband was a servant of the royal household at St James's. Next, he should visit Budge Row 'for the Gentleman you used to go to in the *Cockloft*. I have taken away the *Ladder*,' says Curll, 'but his Landlady has it in keeping.' Budge Row was situated just south of Poultry, running south-east towards Cannon Street out of Watling Street. Finally, a double item which is probably the best known of these directions: 'I don't much care if you ask at the *Mint* for the old beetle-brow'd Critick, and the purblind Poet at the alley over against St *Andrews Holborn*. But this as you have time.' Candidates offered here include John Dennis, Gildon again and Oldmixon. The Mint was, of course, a refuge for debtors in Southwark. A recent habitué had been Nahum Tate, Poet Laureate moreover, who had actually died there. Defoe had possibly spent at least one period in hiding there;[154] and there were doubtless others among contemporary men of letters who were acquainted with the Mint. As for the other address, it lies squarely within the confines of area (3), not far from Holborn Bridge, where the various confluent streams rolled into the Fleet – a moral, as much as a natural, phenomenon for Swift and Gay.

The complete list furnishes us with what is practically a working gazetteer of the subculture formed by professional writers at this time. It will be noted that the addresses are distributed all over the inner suburbs, except that the easternmost region (that of Rosemary Lane) is not represented. Otherwise, the locations are dotted about the infected areas which have already been described. It is apparent, too, that only one of the addresses falls inside the City walls, and yet that few of them lie very far from the boundary – several coming within the liberties of the City. Whether Pope invented these abodes with scrupulous care, or whether he simply used real addresses of real individuals, the effect is the same. His fastidiously precise directions further indicate the part played in the moral and imaginative life of his satiric drama by London topography. The distribution of Dunces is a clue to the marriage of character and setting. This chapter has, I hope, supplied evidence to support that contention. In the following chapters, I shall draw out more general implications from this state of affairs: implications bearing mainly on the way in which we should read Pope's verse.

Epigraphs (i) Taken from Stow, p. 122. The 'Birds' described are actually usurers; but since the location is Portsoken Ward, where the cave of Dulness was originally placed, I have ventured to apply the description to the Dunces. It was noteworthy that the needy hack, 'Omicron', who probably formed the basis of Hogarth's definitive portrait of 'The Distressed Poet', lived in Hounsditch. For Pope, such men undoubtedly constituted 'the black discredit of the Age'.

(ii) Arbuthnot, p. 194.

1. Bronson, 'When was Neo-classicism?' in *Studies in Criticism and Aesthetics 1660–1800*, ed. H. Anderson, J. Shea (Minneapolis, 1967), pp. 13–35 [quoted from p. 34].

2. Geoffrey Holmes, *British Politics in the Age of Anne* (London, 1967), p. 30; G. S. Holmes, W. A. Speck, *The Divided Society: Parties and Politics in England 1694–1716* (London, 1967), p. 66.

3. Ian Watt, 'Publishers and Sinners: The Augustan View', *Studies in Bibliography*, XII (1959), 17.

4. A. S. Turberville, *English Men and Manners in the Eighteenth Century* (New York, 1964), pp. 337–55. The quotations are from pp. 337 and 341; James Boswell, *The Life of Samuel Johnson* (London, 1963), II, 446.

5. Watt, p. 185.

6. R. Paulson, *Theme and Structure in Swift's Tale of a Tub* (Princeton, 1960), p. 170n.

7. E. A. Bloom, *Samuel Johnson in Grub Street* (Providence, 1957), e.g. p. 6: 'Despite the poverty which kept him [Johnson] in Grub Street, he was not a Grubean . . .'

8. See Nigel Barton, *The Lost Rivers of London* (London, 1962), p. 28; Stow, p. 475; S. E. Rasmussen, *London: The Unique City* (Harmondsworth, 1961), p. 76ff. Spate speaks of 'a mass of slums near the stagnant ditch of Moorfields' in O. H. K. Spate, 'The Growth of London, AD. 1660–1800', *A Historical Geography of England*, ed. H. C. Darby (Cambridge, 1963), p. 530.

9. Most of the facts mentioned in this paragraph are taken from Baddeley, pp. 4–5, 18–20, 203. See especially 'The Poor of the Parish', pp. 203–14.

10. T. C. Dale, *The Inhabitants of London in 1638* (London, 1931), I, 236–9, reprinting material from the Lambeth Palace Library. Grub Street itself contained only two houses of substance (one occupied by the celebrated recluse 'Mr. Welby') but even these were not exactly mansions. In Fore Street, the most considerable property, the Greyhound Tavern, was assessed equally with Welby's house, the most highly rated in Grub Street. Forty-six dwellings, of what description one can only guess, standing in Bullens Rents, off Grub Street, attained a grand total of £50 in the assessment. Very few properties in the immediate vicinity were worth a rental of £10. For the position in Pope's lifetime, see *Grub Street* (1972), pp. 412–15.

11. William Kent (ed.), *An Encyclopaedia of London* (London, 1937), p. 158; Harben, p. 416. Eilert Ekwall, *Street Names of the City of London* (Oxford, 1954), pp. 85–6, deduces from a thirteenth-century source that the 'grub' = larva may be the origin of the name.

12. See Baddeley, op. cit., p. 2.

13. Quoted by George Poulson, *Beverlac: or, the Antiquities and History of the Town of Beverley* (London, 1829), II, 775n.

14. Stow, p. 122.

15. [Edward Hatton], *A New View of London* (London, 1708), p. 257. An earlier estimate is 6445 for the London portion in 1631 (quoted by Denton, p. 142). Denton provides figures to illustrate the decline in population during the nineteenth century (p. 143).

16. See George, pp. 410–11.

17. *New Remarks*, pp. 169–70.

18. Misprinted in George, p. 407, as 'Geo. III'. George quotes an estimate of 1710–11 (42000 for the joint parishes), which is 'clearly exaggerated' (pp. 408, 412).

19. John Timbs, *Curiosities of London* (London, 1855), pp. 335–7.

20. Denton, passim. Almost all the information in the following section derives from this source: separate references are not normally supplied.

21. The indented paragraph is from Denton, p. 16. Cf. Valerie Pearl, *London at the Outbreak of the Puritan Revolution* (Oxford, 1961), p. 13, on St Bride's, St Sepulchre, St Andrew's Holborn, and St Giles' Cripplegate 'already scarred with pestilential slum dwellings' before the Grand Rebellion. The following paragraphs are based on Denton. For a later theatre, see A. E. Wilson, 'Misfortunes in Grub Street', *East End Entertainment* (London, 1954), pp. 93–102. Actors had long been associated with Cripplegate (Denton, p. 157) and they were commonly regarded as mere vagabonds. Cibber, of course, was an actor.

22. Defoe, *A Journal of the Plague Year* (Harmondsworth, 1966), p. 57.

23. Baddeley, p. 192.

24. Baddeley, p. 196; Moore, *Citizen*, p. 340. Defoe tells the story (quoted by Moore, p. 315) of a sexton of Cripplegate who wanted the plague to continue, on account of the high burial fees he was receiving. In 1729 Bunhill Fields was the largest cemetery in London; Row's burial ground and Moorfields were also substantial; see Maitland, II, 741.

25. Baddeley, pp. 37, 208; Bayne-Powell, p. 241; Dale, pp. 238–9. There was a 'cage' for vagrants at Grub Street end mentioned in 1586 – Charles Pendrill, *Old Parish Life in London* (London, 1937), p. 203.

26. Oldmixon, p. 743.

27. Baddeley mentions 'a crack-brained enthusiast' who died in the parish and was buried in [Old] Bethlehem burial ground (p. 17). Cripplegate was notorious for such fanatics, and not merely for harmless eccentrics as Henry Welby. See also Baddeley, pp. 24, 36, 154–6, 157; George, pp. 331, 100–1, 125. Typhus was particularly virulent around 1800 in Old Street and Golden Lane (George, p. 94). By order of the Lord Mayor, houses in Cripplegate were pulled down in 1666 as part of an attempt to prevent the spread of the fire: Gomme, I, 158.

28. There is some discrepancy among the authorities, but this can be explained by changes as time elapsed. Malcolm, *London Redivivum*, (London, 1805), III, 280, gives these figures for 1710: three presbyterian meeting houses, three anabaptists, three independent. *New Remarks*, p. 167: five dissenting houses, plus a tabernacle where Anglican rites are performed. Maitland, II, 1189. See also Denton, p. 74.

   Other evidence of the dissenting influence resides in Dr Williams' Library, set up in Red Cross Street in 1729 (Presbyterian); and a school in Ropemakers Alley (Denton, p. 151).

29. See *Gentleman's Magazine*, LX (1790), 293.

30. The neighbouring properties included several breweries, notably Samuel Whitbread's on the north-west corner of the street (its site still, though the Barbican project has overwhelmed Grub Street). The best account is that

of Peter Mathias, *The Brewing Industry in England 1700–1830* (Cambridge, 1959), pp. 11, 262, etc.

31. Stow, p. 317. This corner of the City within the walls was associated with the first Earl of Shaftesbury (whose house had lain just off Aldersgate), and during the time of the Popish Plot had been regarded as a hub of protestant activity.

32. E. B. Chancellor, *The Literary Ghosts of London* (London, 1933), p. 57. For other literary connections, see Appendix B.

33. Moore, *Citizen*, pp. 1–12; Baddeley, p. 136. For Milton's residence in Jewen Street and Bunhill Row see *The Life Records of John Milton* (New Brunswick, 1958), IV, 377, V, passim.

34. *DNB*, s.v. Wild; F. J. Lyons, *Jonathan Wild Prince of Robbers* (London, 1936), p. 258 and passim.

35. Hatton is less informative, whilst Maitland derives largely from Strype. It should be noted that Strype's map of Cripplegate labels 'Moore Street' the stretch westwards from 'the Postern' to St Giles' church. This is normally referred to (as in Strype's text) by the name of Fore Street.

36. Strype, III, 93.

37. Strype, III, 93; IV, 60; Stow, p. 476.

38. Maitland, II, 906–7.

39. Stow, p. 318; Bayne-Powell, p. 167.

40. E. B. Chancellor, *The Pleasure Haunts of London* (London, 1925), p. 152.

41. Maitland, II, 908.

42. Baddeley, p. 7.

43. G. H. Cunningham, *London* (London, 1927), p. 368; *HMC* (Bath MSS) 58 (London, 1908), III, 506–7; Maitland, II, 908; William M. Sale, *Samuel Richardson Master Printer* (Ithaca, 1950), pp. 8–14. For other connections with the printing and book-selling trade, see H. R. Plomer, *A Dictionary of Printers and Booksellers 1668–1725* (Oxford, 1922), p. 150; and Henry L. Snyder, 'New Bibliographical Data for the Reign of Queen Anne', *The Library*, XXII (1967), 336–7, 345. Malcolm, *London Redivivum*, III, 306, records some improvements in and around Jewen Street on the site of formerly 'very wretched' houses. Oldmixon, p. 623, mentions the arrest of a Jacobite in his 'dirty lodging' in Jewen Street.

44. Henry Campkin, *Grub Street (Now Milton Street) London* (London, priv. prin. 1868), p. 6. A playhouse called 'the City Theatre' briefly stood in Milton Street in the 1830's (Chancellor, *Pleasure Haunts*, p. 133): a fact (had it existed earlier) which would have given an added touch to Pope's satire and would have locked the symbolism of his poem even more tightly together.

45. But see H. Bolitho, D. Peel, *Without the City Wall* (London, 1952), p. 18:

and p. 76 of an interleaved copy of G. B. Rawlings, *The Streets of London* (London, n.d.) held in Cambridge Public Library.

46. See Bryan Anstey, 'A Study of certain Changes in Land Values in the London Area in the Period 1950–64', *Land Values*, ed. Peter Hall (London, 1965), pp. 241–3, esp. map on p. 25.

47. Williams, pp. 14–15, 90ff.

48. Barton, pp. 28, 106; George, p. 91ff.

49. TE, V, 59, 267.

50. TE, V, 63–5.

51. Millicent Rose, *The East End of London* (London, 1951), p. 59. William Addison (*English Fairs and Markets*, [London, 1953], p. 75), implies that the fair is still held: but this appears to be a mistake. It should also be noted that fever was regularly transmitted through the poorer quarters via the old clothes in cast-off rags shops. See George, pp. 64–5.

52. Harben, pp. 514–5.

53. Strype, II, 13, 26–8.

54. Hawkins speaks, too, of a 'halo of bagnios' surrounding the theatre. *The Life of Samuel Johnson, Ll.D.*, ed. B. H. Davis (London, 1962), pp. 41–2.

55. See George, pp. 93, 95, 101, 345: for the low quality housing in the parish of St Botolph, Aldgate, see p. 100. On the 'rickety and verminous wooden houses' in St Katherine's by the Tower, see George passim and Rose, pp. 60, 200–1. On the dangers to be encountered round Nightingale Lane, which adjoined Rosemary Lane, cf. Chancellor, *Pleasure Haunts*, p. 176.

56. Irving, p. 260. See also Durfey, as quoted by Chancellor, p. 176.

57. George, pp. 100–1. See also p. 229.

58. *Colonel Jack*, ed. S. H. Monk (London, 1965), pp. 4, 8–9, 15. Monk is, however, wrong in suggesting that Defoe 'himself' had grown up 'in and about Stepney' (p. 312). There is no evidence to this effect.

59. *Romances and Narratives*, XVI, 182, 191, 192, 218.

60. *London*, ed. P. Cunningham (London, 1927), p. 572; W. C. Sydney, *England and the English in the Eighteenth Century* (London, 1891), II, 215; A. P. Herbert, *Mr. Gay's London* (London, 1948), p. 69; Radzinowicz, II, 175; Chancellor, *Pleasure Haunts*, p. 176; Defoe, *Tour*, I, 330; Marshall, p. 34; Straus, pp. 149–50; *New Remarks*, p. 398. For the bawdy houses around Goodman's Fields, see Marshall, p. 235. The *Observator* early in the century remarked the fact that the theatre in Goodman's Fields lay in the precincts of Rosemary Lane, which was a great convenience to the 'Ladies of Rag Fair' – see Malcolm, II, 124. Riots were frequent in the vicinity partly because of the existence of that perpetual target for destructive energies, the dissenting meeting-house. See Malcolm, II, 29, and Marshall, p. 34.

George Rudé describes the attacks on Irish alehouses in the district during the 'Mother Gin' riots of 1736, instancing the damage done to the

Bull and Butcher Tavern in Rag Fair. Curiously, he identifies Rag Fair not with Rosemary Lane but with Goodman's Fields. See *Paris and London in the Eighteenth Century* (London, 1970), pp. 201–21, esp. 208–11.

61. *Miscellanies. The Third Volume. By Dr. Arbuthnot, Mr. Pope*, and *Mr. Gay* (London, 1742), p. 62. Quoted by Johnson in the entry for Grub Street in his dictionary.

62. Boswell, II, 459.

63. Although a good deal of building was going on, as evidenced by Defoe, *Tour*, I, 375 ('A new street or range of houses taken out of the south side of the Artillery Ground near Moorfields, also an enlargement of the new burying ground, as it was formerly called, on the north side of the same ground'). See also R. J. Mitchell, M. D. R. Leys, *A History of London Life* (Harmondsworth, 1964), p. 179.

64. Pope, *Correspondence*, II, 3.

65. *Tale*, p. 181; *The Poems of Henry Carey*, ed. F. T. Wood (London, 1931), p. 151.

66. Rasmussen, pp. 76–81; Stow, pp. 301–2, 475. On the site of Moorfields proper were built Finsbury Square, Finsbury Circus and Lackington Street – the last commemorating a subsequent 'Temple of the Muses', the bookselling establishment of James Lackington which went by that name.

67. Quoted by Lyons, pp. 262–3.

68. See Patrick Pringle, *Stand and Deliver* (London, 1951), pp. 168–70; Mitchell, Leys, p. 179; Gomme, I, 161.

69. Sutherland, p. 4.

70. Defoe, *Colonel Jack*, pp. 43, 56.

71. Denton, pp. 103–4; Christopher Hibbert, *The Road to Tyburn* (London, 1957), p. 48; Jack Lindsay, *1764* (London, 1959), p. 259.

72. Denton, pp. 104, 114 (misnumbered 119). See also Max Beloff, *Public Order and Popular Disturbances 1660–1714* (Oxford, 1938), p. 82.

73. J. L. Hammond and Barbara Hammond, *The Skilled Craftsman 1760–1832* (London, 1927), pp. 206, 209.

74. Denton, p. 115.

75. Denton, pp. 104–6. A heap of charnel had been dumped on Moorfields in 1548 – perhaps as many as four or five hundred corpses. The mound lay just behind what was to become Whitefield's rostrum – Pendrill, pp. 141–2.

76. Cf. the comments of Emrys Jones on 'the gross materiality' of Grub Street poems, quoted in *Grub Street*, p. 309.

77. Thornbury, II, 197; Sydney, I, 65.

78. *The Diary of Samuel Pepys*, ed. H. B. Wheatley, (London, ed. 1952), I, 174, 250. (28 June 1661: 26 May 1662). Wrestling matches traditionally took place in Moorfields on the first three days of Bartholomew Fair – a further link with the Smithfield Muse. See Denton, p. 94.

79. Thornbury, II, 196; Malcolm, I, 91, 287.
80. *A Trip through London* (1728), pp. 52–3.
81. Sybil Rosenfeld, *The Theatre of the London Fairs in the Eighteenth Century* (Cambridge, 1960), p. 133.
82. Marjorie Plant, *The English Book Trade* (London, ed. 1965), p. 254; Plomer, p. 150. See also F. B. Tolles, *Meeting House and Counting House* (New York, 1963), p. 157.
83. *The Obituary of Richard Smyth*, ed. H. Ellis ([London], 1849), passim.
84. Denton, p. 115; Thornbury, II, 198. For Moorfields brothels, see Ned Ward's *Step to the Bath* quoted by Philip Pinkus, *Grub Street Laid Bare* (London, 1968), p. 203.
85. Sir John Hawkins, *The Life of Samuel Johnson, Ll.D.* (London, 2nd ed. 1787), p. 49.
86. Pepys, I, 214 (26 December 1661). For alehouses round Moorfields, see Besant, p. 640; and for music, Gomme, II, 137–8 and George, p. 306.
87. Denton, pp. 107–8. See also *Tricks of the Town: Eighteenth Century Diversions*, ed. R. Straus (London, 1927), pp. 74, 75. Tom Brown (quoted by Pinkus, pp. 162, 174) refers to 'Moorfields sharpers'.
88. Radzinowicz, I, 188; *Calendar*, I, 37–9; Horace Bleakley, *The Hangmen of England* (London, 1929), pp. 12–19. The execution followed a procession past the Artillery Ground. Radzinowicz also tells (I, 196) of a bookseller who had committed murder and then suicide in prison (1755). He was buried at a crossway in Moorfields with a stake through his heart. For the Artillery Company's annual march through London from Moorfields, see Read's *Weekly Journal*, 24 May 1718.
89. See H. W. Troyer, *Ned Ward of Grub Street* (Cambridge, Mass., 1946), p. 159.
90. See Holmes, Speck, p. 41; *Catalogue of Prints and Drawings in the British Museum* (London, 1873), II, 303.
91. Stow, p. 175; cf. p. 172, on Petty France; Strype, I, 192.
92. Ralph, *A Critical Review of the Publick Buildings . . . in . . . London and Westminster* (London, 1734), pp. 7–8. Defoe admired Moorgate, once it had been rebuilt and enlarged 'to give room for the city Train'd Bands to go through to the Artillery Ground, where they muster, and that they might march with their Pikes advanc'd . . .' (*Tour*, I, 354). This confessed aim allows Pope to drive a satiric coach and horses through the gateway to Bedlam.
93. By R. R. Reed (Cambridge, Mass., 1952); see esp. Ch. I, pp. 1–39.
94. Strype, I, 195.
95. See *DNB*, s.v. Lee.
96. Butt, pp. 616, 630.
97. Faber, p. 87. See also *Tatler* no. 174, and E. G. O'Donoghue, *The Story of*

Bethlehem Hospital (London, 1914), p. 252. O'Donoghue (pp. 240–2) comments on the literary associations of Bedlam, notably those with Ned Ward and Tom Brown. *Journal* (probably in the person of Defoe) satirised a Curll author who was to be given 'a safe conduct to the structure in Moorfields':– Lee, II, 48, quoting *Journal* of 28 June 1718.

98. Butt, p. 649.
99. Butt, p. 615.
100. O'Donoghue, pp. 249–51; *Journal*, I, 122n.
101. Swift, *Correspondence*, IV, 65–70.
102. *Tale*, pp. 175–6.
103. Swift, *Poems*, p. 512.
104. Plumb, *The First Four Georges* (London, 1967), p. 16. For Johnson's visit to Bedlam in May 1775, see Boswell, I, 565. Curiously Boswell does not mention this visit in his journal, as published from the Boswell papers at Yale.
105. TE, V, 271–2n.
106. TE, V, 147n, 457; Pope, *Correspondence*, I, 106.
107. See for example Oldmixon's *Critical History of England* (1724–26), I, 270; II, 270; *History* (1735), p. [633]: and *Essay on Criticism* (1728), pp. 49, 56, among many similar references.
108. E. H. Pearce, *Sion College and Library* (Cambridge, 1913), pp. 347–8, lists the names of the Presidents at this period.
109. Stow specifically observes, 'To this Library there have been already [1633] divers bountifull and well disposed benefactors, who have given large sums of money towards the furnishing it with books . . . [seven named] besides divers others; whose names, legacies, gifts, and bookes bought therewith: are (by way of a gratefull memoriall) registred in a fair Booke kept in the Library' (pp. 304–5).
110. See Swift, *Prose Works*, I, 341–2.
111. *Miscellanies*, pp. iv–vi.
112. Fielding, IX, 209–10.
113. Note at B.I. 265. The 'fogs' of Dulness (B.I. 262) would be appropriate to the traditionally marshy area of Grub Street. Incidentally, the original word for the fen ('More') happens to be the name Pope gives to the first individualised Dunce (other than Cibber) whose actions are described – James Moore Smythe (B.II. 35). The first 'Poet's form' set before us is his – 'A Wit it was, and called the phantom More.' (B.II. 50). Again bad poetry is identified with the bogs of Moorfields, the most un-bracing and soporific climate in all London.
114. TE, V, 319.
115. 'Argument to Book the First', TE, V, 266.
116. Holmes, p. 304.

117. L. C. Jones, *The Clubs of the Georgian Rakes* (New York, 1942), p. 27. On the noise of the streets, see M. Dorothy George, 'London and the Life of the Towns', in Turberville, II, 171–2.

118. Butt, pp. 601, 610.

119. Steeves, p. 5ff.

120. TE, V, 263.

121. TE, V, xxxviii–xxxix. Cf. Ian Jack, *Augustan Satire* (Oxford, 1952), pp. 116–18.

122. *The Poems of John Dryden*, ed. J. Kinsley (Oxford, 1958), IV, 1917.

123. Radzinowicz, II, 257.

124. For Simkin and Panton, cf. *Poems*, ed. Kinsley, IV, 1918 and *English Satiric Poetry*, ed. J. Kinsley, J. T. Boulton (London, 1966), 27.

125. See Leslie Hotson, *The Commonwealth and Restoration Stage* (Cambridge, Mass., 1928), pp. 176–94. This treatment supplants that of W. J. Lawrence, *The Elizabethan Playhouse and other Studies/Second Series* (Stratford, 1915) – see pp. 237–9 for an account of the Fortune theatre – and 'A Forgotten Restoration Playhouse', *Englische Studien*, XXXV (1904).

126. It is arguable for instance that present-day Watford is at least as much a suburb of London (demographically or economically considered) as is Feltham. Yet the latter lies within the GLC administrative area, the former some way outside. For the general character of the suburbs and parishes in Stuart London, and a discussion of their particular social problems, see Valerie Pearl, pp. 23–37.

127. Williams, p. 36.

128. Macky's *Journey through England* (1714–22) tells us that the main centre of the book trade had shifted from Little Britain to Paternoster Row. Certain sections of the trade were conducted chiefly in the vicinity of Temple Bar. See F. A. Mumby, *Publishing and Bookselling* (London, 1949), p. 141. However, a quick census of the printers listed by Plomer and by William Sale suggests that the actual printing shops were chiefly located nearer the heart of the City.

129. Letter of 25 April 1708: Pope, *Correspondence*, I, 47.

130. Quoted by Paulson, I, 147, from the issue of the *Journal* for 24 September 1730.

131. Quoted in George, pp. 92–3.

132. Entry in Luttrell's *Relation* for 11 June 1695, quoted by Holmes, Speck, pp. 78–9.

133. *Romances and Narratives*, XVI, 173, 214.

134. Bayne-Powell, p. 169.

135. Faber, p. 84, and see the reference to 'the rounds of *Drury-lane*' in the following section on 'how to know a Whore'; *The Dispensary* (8th edn., 1718), p. 29.

136. See Paulson, I, 168, 210–1; Wheatley, pp. 138, 155. The badges which the charity boys wear in Hogarth's prints, as in the case of Tom Nero, mark them as educated in the rough school of life, after the manner of St Giles in the Fields.

137. For other information see Paulson, I, 179; Wheatley, pp. 132–7, 285; E. B. Chancellor, *The Eighteenth Century in London* (London, n.d.), p. 134.

138. Chancellor, *The Annals of Covent Garden* (London, n.d.), pp. 61–2, 106, 198, 240–1. It is fair to record that there was at least one association of a happier kind: Robert Harley, later first Earl of Oxford, was born in Bow Street. Some other indications: a pillory was set up at the heart of St Giles', that is Seven Dials, in 1733. It was an unfortunate place for any man who happened to have incurred unpopularity, rather than glamour, by his crimes. Wild would not have survived long there. John Thrift, a mid-century hangman, was accused of murdering a Jacobite in Short's Gardens, Drury Lane, in 1750; not surprisingly, he got off when the affair reached the Old Bailey. Two years later, Thrift died at his home in Coal Yard, also off Drury Lane. The parishioners of St Paul's, Covent Garden, were strongly opposed to his burial in their consecrated ground; hangmen, like Dunces, were rudely bundled from one parish to the next. See Bleakley, pp. 62, 85–9. For other crimes and disorders of St Giles', extracted from the proceedings of the Commissions of the Peace, and Oyer and Terminer for the City of London and County of Middlesex, see Herbert, pp. 14, 31, 100, etc. For references to the whores of the 'hundreds of Old Drury', see the *Weekly Journal* for 28 May 1721; cf. Virginia Cowles, *The Great Swindle* (London, 1960), pp. 120, 174. According to Miss Cowles (p. 147), after the South Sea Bubble crash there were rich liveries on sale in the old clothes markets of Long Lane, Monmouth Street and 'Regent Fair'. The last seems to be an error for Rag Fair.

139. Garth, *The Dispensary*, p. 40; Faber, p. 73. It should be noted that the one place Gay hits on, to localise prostitution in a city teeming with prostitution, was the *exact* site of the Dunces' games – 'Where *Katherine-street* descends into the *Strand*' (Faber, p. 84).

140. George, p. 17. The same writer states (p. 78): 'The poorest parts of eighteenth-century London – the dilapidated courts and alleys, the crumbling tenements and the dangerous districts – were chiefly in the belt which had grown up round the City between the reign of Elizabeth and the end of the seventeenth century.'

141. Williams, p. 38.

142. Williams, p. 30ff. The author asserts that 'in Book II . . . contemporary London topography is an essential, meaningful part of the poem.' It is my view that this significance prevails from the very first line of *The Dunciad*, from the moment Smithfields, Rag Fair, Bedlam, and so on, are introduced.

143. Pope, *Prose Works*, I, 278–9. I am preparing a separate account of the passage, with a view to identifying the various writers.
144. Cf. Pope, *Correspondence*, III, 371.
145. H. W. Troyer, *Ned Ward of Grub Street* (Cambridge, Mass., 1946), p. 159.
146. Strype, VI, 75.
147. LCC *Survey*, XVIII (London, 1937), p. 129.
148. LCC *Survey*, V: ii, p. 30; Cunningham, p. 433.
149. *The Works of John Dryden*, ed. J. H. Smith, D. MacMillan (Berkeley/Los Angeles, 1962), VIII, 59–60; Lyons, pp. 279–81; *Hudibras*, ed. Z. Grey (London, 1799), II, 176 [Part III, Canto I, 11.865–6]).
150. Quoted by Chancellor, *Pleasure Haunts*, p. 175.
151. Faber, p. 504. Similarly Macaulay speaks of 'painted women, the refuse of Lewknor Lane and Whetstone Park': *History of England* (London, 1906), I, 286.
152. Lyons, pp. 70, 244; *DNB*. s.v. Wild; *Romances and Narratives*, XVI, 180, 194, 198, 230. There *was* a real 'Somers a Thief-taker in Newtner's Lane', mentioned in Applebee's *Weekly Journal*, 8 September 1716 – Wild figures in the same story. But Wild was already the bigger fish.
153. See *Weekly Miscellany*, 20 June 1733, quoted in *Gentleman's Magazine* (July 1733), III, 336.
154. Sutherland, p. 43.

II

The Plagues of Dulness

All, that they boast of Styx, of Acheron,
Cocytus, Phlegeton, our have prov'd in one;
The filth, stench, noyse: save only what was there
Subtley distinguish'd, was confused here.

Ben Jonson, 'On the famous Voyage'

Besides those overt-acts of treason now recounted, the most of all of which the insurgents were guilty of, they were guilty of several acts of felony, such as burning private property, and demolishing private houses, and committing several acts of robbery and open violence. . . . The crime, as applied to the fact, is palpable and direct; pulling down all inclosures, demolishing all brothels or bawdy-houses, or chapels, making insurrections, in order to redress grievances, real or pretended, is levying war within the realm, and against the King, though they have no design against his person. . . . The rabble had augmented their numbers by setting the felons at liberty. If the military had not been called in, none of your lordships can hesitate to agree with me, that within a very few hours the capital would have been in flames, and shortly reduced to an heap of rubbish.

Lord Mansfield, speech in the House of Lords, 1780

The birth of the eighteenth century was attended with four searing memories, which can fairly be called traumatic. Within the lifetime of men and women who were still active, four great events had impinged deeply on the national consciousness. I mean the Civil War, the Great Plague, the Fire of London and the Glorious Revolution. These happenings had personal and imaginative repercussions which were to last for generations; and not even the Restoration or the Dutch wars, the Popish plot or the Monmouth rebellion, made quite the same durable impact. The importance of the constitutional up-

94

heavals from the point of view of literature has often been emphasised. I do not think, however, that the impress on writers of the other two events has ever been satisfactorily described. My aim here is to sketch out some of the ways in which these occurrences prolonged their resonance within a single major form, satire, with special reference to Pope, Swift and Gay. This is a study (in A. C. Charity's expressive phrase) of events and their afterlife.

The Plague and the Fire had several conspicuous features in common.[1] Apart from their propinquity in time – they were separated by a bare twelve months, if we regard the epicentre of the plague as the end of August 1665 – they both came to be regarded as a divine visitation. Each was interpreted as a prophecy, as a warning, as a blight ordained by the Almighty; each was surrounded by numerological speculation and gnostic prediction. Equally, the spread of both events was seen as an act of sabotage by Papists, Dissenters, freethinkers, the French, the Italians and whomever one chanced to dislike. Both brought sudden destruction to the capital in the autumn of the year. Both involved evacuation on a massive scale. Both centred closely on the City of London and its immediate environs. Both spread at an accelerating tempo and smouldered for some time before gradually dying out.

The two main verbs in that last sentence are worth picking up, although I did not choose them with any extraordinary care. They lead towards a less literal-minded basis of comparison, which is itself the guiding idea of this chapter. Both plague and fire, then, are phenomena which can be described in terms of raging, consuming, seething, blazing, inflaming, and so on. Both can be called virulent or, by extension, voracious. Amongst their shared connotations, three ideas seem to be overlaid. The first is that of spreading; the second is that of destruction; and the third is that of corrosion or some form of impairment by heat. Semantically, words associated with disease have, for obvious historical reasons, come to overlap with those suggesting burning. This is an ineluctable fact of language. Its convenience for the Augustan satirists, as regards their wider rhetorical ends, will be illustrated shortly. For the moment, I want to insist on the historical and literal applicability of such notions at the end of the seventeenth century. Images of disease and of fire required only a very short fuse to activate them into poetic life. They carried with them a potent imaginative charge, derived from the recent memory of the twin cataclysms of 1665–6. If, as I shall contend, these images became the climactic symbols of Augustan satire, then they would gain additional force from their links with two climactic events of the age immediately preceding.

It is now widely agreed that Augustan rhetoric employs a defensive idiom. Jeffrey Hart, for example, has pointed out in an illuminating essay that whereas Donne, Marvell and Milton seek to create coherence through their imagery, their successors attempt rather to assert and defend an existing order. The pattern is already established, the harmony is already a going concern. Dryden's characteristic operation, says Hart, is 'to exclude, rather than to assimilate, whatever would disturb the balance of mind or state . . .' In a similar way, tone in Augustan poetry 'hold[s] in balance those disparities in experience which the metaphysical conceit would have attempted to depict as analogical identities.'[2] In other words (to extrapolate from what Hart says), Augustan idiom does not fuse but holds in equilibrium; does not create new identities but safeguards old identities. The integrity to be preserved is the one that was already observable and observed before the artistic construct was fashioned, or indeed contemplated.

Seen in this light, it is easy to deduce how the phraseology of satire in this period should revert so often to terms implying contagion, destruction, morbidity, virus and the like. Relatively little comment appears to have been made on this obsession with disease, apart from the hostile remarks of those deploring Swift's coprophilia and Pope's nastiness. The defence of these writers has, in recent years, been mainly conducted on other grounds. Yet if one wanted a quick run-down of the governing metaphors to be found in their work, one could scarcely do better than turn to Roget's *Thesaurus*, and consider the entry for 'Disease'; I append a selection from this sub-heading.

> Disease; illness, sickness . . . morbidity; infirmity, ailment . . . disorder, malady; distemper. Visitation, attack, seizure, stroke, fit, epi-

lepsy, apoplexy . . . atrophy; indigestion . . . decay . . . decline, consumption . . . paralysis . . . taint, pollution, infection, contagion . . . epi-, endemic; murrain, plague, pestilence, virus, pox. Sore, ulcer, abcess, fester, boil . . . imposthume, issue; rot, canker, cancer, carcinoma, caries, mortification, corruption, gangrene, leprosy, eruption, rash, breaking out, venereal disease. Fever, calenture; inflammation . . . galloping consumption, churchyard cough . . . neurasthenia; idiocy, insanity . . . cripple, invalid, sickroom, hospital.[3]

The relevance of these words (and others I have omitted) to such works as *The Dunciad*, *A Tale of a Tub* and many more, is surely very obvious. Here I wish to draw attention chiefly to the term 'calenture', as holding within itself the basic coupling of heat and pestilence. Other items such as 'morbidity', 'epilepsy', 'taint', are equally significant. Pope and Swift, as we know, tended to image religious fanaticism as a febrile kind of disorder, rising and subsiding spasmodically with the lunes. It is interesting to note, therefore, that Wyld's *Universal English Dictionary* glosses 'contagions' with a secondary, figurative meaning, 'catching, liable to spread from one person to another', and gives as instances 'enthusiasm, laughter, gloom, mirth, religious fervour &c.' Either the modern or the ancient sense of 'enthusiasm' will do. The point is that moral and social decay was, for the Scriblerian group, *catching*; and the enthusiast was only a particularly striking case of the way in which folly was transmitted by contact with the foolish. His fits might be especially noteworthy for their epidemic character – but then all Dulness was epidemic, because all Dulness was pestilential. The metaphor of plague explains the phenomenon; at the same time, it acts as an icon for the condition. I do not go so far as to say that Pope and Swift chose the image because of the dominance of the Great Plague, and its forerunners, in the national imagination; and that their idiom therefore predetermined their human outlook at large. That is the *reductio ad absurdum* of rhetorical criticism. Professor Wimsatt once referred scathingly to 'the confident school of ritual origins (where the myth of American Independence might be derived from firecrackers on the Fourth of July) . . .'[4] And there is, quite seriously, some danger that our present approach to satire, with all its virtues, may produce a situation where attitudes to folly in the post-Renaissance phase of humanism are seen to derive from the availability of the *Encomium Moriae* framework. But, having said this, I do believe that the eighteenth-century satirists were, at some level, impelled to dramatise their moral dialectic along the lines they did because of the potency of certain images at that precise moment in history. An obvious example is the pox. Swift's ready recourse to this idea, culminating in his mock-panegyric, 'Pethox the Great', can easily be misinterpreted if we forget the virulence of the disease at this time – the facility with which it could be picked up, the difficulty with which it could be cured, the frequency of hereditary conditions, the savage side-effects it carried with it, and so on.

I am arguing three things. Firstly, that the recollection of the disasters oᶠ a generation before still operated powerfully in people's minds at the opening of the eighteenth century. Secondly, that the characteristic idiom of Augustan satire (whether the actual vocabulary, at a local level, or the wider rhetorical and fictional resources used) makes use of this residual memory, though often at a subliminal level. And thirdly, that the images centrally derived from the historical events (plague/epidemic/burning etc.) were peculiarly suited to the things these satirists actually wanted to say – peculiarly effective weapons for exposing the kind of danger they saw in the contemporary world.

But it is possible to go farther than this. I want now to suggest that the conditions of life in London at this period were such as to reinforce this choice of idiom. I wish to propound, by means of concrete illustrations studied in some detail, the view that the Scriblerian party – though they may have borrowed their controlling metaphors from the events of Restoration London – developed their central dialectic with close reference to the London of fifty years later. Of course, one specialised instance is provided by Grub Street, a district with its own peculiar human ecology and satiric economy.

The great satirists were born in the century of revolution. Within their lifetime they experienced every kind of disturbance which a nation can undergo. There was international conflict, with the struggles between states exemplified by the War of Spanish Succession and that of Jenkins' Ear. Far from achieving peace in their time (the plan for perpetual peace which the Abbé de Saint-Pierre drew up in 1715 was a symptom of the general bellicosity of the age), men saw Europe constantly riven by turmoil. Swift was conceived whilst the Dutch wars smouldered: he lived on to see the relatively marginal Jenkins' Ear affair escalate into the War of Austrian Succession.[5] But it was internal dissent which most characterised the period. Pope was born in London almost with the Revolution. As a man of twenty-seven he was an interested bystander as the first considerable Jacobite rebellion was put down.[6] He died at fifty-six, a single year too early to witness the second. These rebellions were not, to contemporaries, the pitiful sallies of a hopelessly lost cause which they have become in modern eyes. Both the Fifteen and the Forty-five were less romantic, less operatic, less chivalric than legend instructs us. For the men and women of Pope's generation they represented a genuine threat to the stability of the Hanoverian regime.[7]

But it is not only the major flashpoints which make an age or a society insecure. As well as the big constitutional upheavals, there was a steady undertow of popular disturbance. Seditious movements ranged from the alleged plots to assassinate William III in the 1690's to a series of minor affrays set off, for instance, by the Gin Act (1736). I shall argue that *The Dunciad* offers us, on one level, an imaginative reconstruction of an eighteenth century riot. In the following sections I shall develop this point with reference to two particular outbursts of violence, which illustrate the passion and enthusiasm with which people took sides in a century once regarded as the epitome of torpor. First the premonition, then the enactment.

The Crowd in Action

I have borrowed this heading from George Rudé's suggestive book, *The Crowd in History*.[8] Its appropriateness stems from the fact that *The Dunciad* is, apart from anything else, a poem about civil commotion. Not only the riotous gathering in the streets which occupies much of Books I and II, but also the later parade of '*Farces, Operas, and Shows*', and the complex action of Book IV, are relevant to this theme. There can be few poems which are richer in crowd scenes. A number of scattered instances may be named at random:

> And now had Fame's posterior Trumpet blown,
> And all Nations summon'd to the Throne.
> The young, the old, who feel her [Dulness's] inward sway,
> One instinct seizes, and transports away.
> None need a guide, by sure Attraction led,
> And strong impulsive gravity of Head:
> None want a place, for all their Centre found,
> Hung to the Goddess, and coher'd around.
> Not closer, orb in orb, are seen
> The buzzing Bees about their dusky Queen.
> The gath'ring number, as it moves along,
> Involves a vast involuntary throng,
> Who gently drawn, and struggling less and less,
> Roll in her Vortex, and her pow'r confess. (B.IV.71)

> Dire is the conflict, dismal is the din,
> Here shouts all Drury, there all Lincoln's-inn;
> Contending Theatres our empire raise,
> Alike their labours, and alike their praise. (B.III.269)

> Thro' Lud's fam'd gates, along the well-known Fleet
> Rolls the black troop, and overshades the street,
> 'Till show'rs of Sermons, Characters, Essays,
> In circling fleeces whiten all the ways:
> So clouds replenish'd from some bog below,
> Mount in dark volumes, and descend in snow. (B.II.359)

> And thou! his Aid de camp, lead on my sons,
> Light-arm'd with Points, Antitheses, and Puns.
> Let Bawdry, Billingsgate, my daughters dear,
> Support his front, and Oaths bring up the rear:
> And under his, and under Archer's wing,
> Gaming and Grub-street skulk behind the King. (B.I.305)

The work is filled with references to the 'crowd', or similar terms. Confining ourselves to the revised version of the poem, we find mention of 'the vulgar herd' (B.IV.535); the 'sable shoal' and 'black

blockade' formed by 'a hundred head of Aristotle's friends' (B.IV.
190), described by Aristarchus as 'that rabble' (B.IV.209); the 'hundred sons' of Dulness, mentioned with careful emphasis twice in five
lines (B.III.134); the 'sea of heads' belonging to the sleeping Dunces
(B.II.410); the 'black troop' with their 'show'rs' of sermons and
essays (B.II.360); the 'desp'rate pack' of mud-divers (B.II.305); the
'guild' awoken by the shouting-match (B.II.250); the 'industrious
Tribe' of authors (B.II.33); the 'mass of Nonsense' (B.I.241); the
'progeny' of the Dunce, Cibber (B.I.228); the 'Mob of Metaphors'
(B.I.67); whilst the word 'crowd' actually occurs seven times. Every
manifestation of Dulness indeed – whether pedantry or venal bookselling or the promotion of opera – is characterised by a tropism
towards such aggregative units. Dunces find safety in numbers.

Nor are these collectivities either neutral or inert. Their 'union' is
illusory: it promotes anarchic disorder. To quote the 'harlot form' of
opera:

> O *Cara! Cara!* silence all that train:
> Joy to great Chaos! let Division reign . . . (B.IV.53)

There is something oppressive about all these assemblies ('Now
crowds on crowds around the Goddess press . . . Dunce scorning
Dunce beholds the next advance . . .') (B.IV.135). They are not
merely 'clam'rous' (B.II.385); they are bent on displacing others:

> In flow'd at once a gay embroider'd race,
> And titt'ring push'd the Pedants off the place . . . (B.IV.275)

At times the imagery takes on even more sinister overtones:

> Then thick as Locusts black'ning all the ground,
> A tribe, with weeds and shells fantastic crown'd . . . (B.IV.397)

The bellicose nature of the Dunces is suggested by Pope's phrasing:

> Around him wide a sable Army stand,
> A low-born, cell-bred, selfish, servile band,
> Prompt or to guard or stab, to saint or damn,
> Heav'n's Swiss, who fight for any God, or Man. (B.II.355)

Elsewhere the language resounds with contempt:

> Millions and millions on these banks he views,
> Thick as the stars of night, or morning dews,

> As thick as bees o'er vernal blossoms fly,
> As thick as eggs at Ward in Pillory. (B.III.31)

Once again the last line brings back the poetic context from apparently free-ranging metaphor to closely specified contemporary actuality: the actuality of crime and punishment which lies so close to the duncely milieu. Finally, the fullest description of the crowd's composition, which comes after Queen Dulness has proclaimed her games:

> They summon all her Race: An endless band
> Pours forth, and leaves unpeopled half the land.
> A motley mixture! in long wigs, in bags,
> In silks, in crapes, in Garters, and in rags.
> From drawing rooms, from colleges, from garrets,
> On horse, on foot, in hacks, and gilded chariots:
> All who true Dunces in her cause appear'd,
> And all who knew those Dunces to reward. (B.II.19)

One could scarcely have a more explicit statement in poetic terms of the sociology of Duncehood.

It is interesting to compare the picture thus built up with Rudé's analysis of the pre-industrial crowd. He begins, it is true, by excluding from consideration

> crowds that are casually drawn together like sight-seers; crowds assembled on purely ceremonial occasions or crowds taking part in religious or academic processions; or 'audience' crowds . . . who gather in theatres or lecture halls, at baseball matches or bullfights, or who used to witness hangings at Tyburn Fair . . . Equally, we should generally exclude those more active, or 'expressive' crowds that come together for Mardi Gras, participate in dancing orgies or student 'rags', or attend revivalist meetings to hear Billy Graham or Father Divine, as they listened two hundred years ago to George Whitefield and the Wesleys.

Now all of these (except perhaps the first) are categories into which one *could* fit the crowd movements of *The Dunciad*. There is a strong processional flavour to the Dunces' own itinerary, as was appropriate to a parodic Lord Mayor's Show; and in so far as Dulness partakes of both academic and religious vices, Rudé's phrasing meets the case. Again, the crowd in the poem does spend a good deal of its time

listening to their Queen or to other spellbinders. The element of a
sporting contest is unmistakable; and the road to Tyburn is a very
short one indeed. Orgiastic symptoms are just as unmistakable, and
not only in the second book. Lastly, what Rudé says about revivalist
meetings comes especially close because such events did indeed take
place in the neighbourhood of Moorfields. In the British Museum
Print Room there is an engraving of 1739 called, appositely enough,
'Enthusiasm Displayed: or the Moorfields Congregation'. This is an
attack on Whitefield. But in another sense the scribblers of Grub
Street formed a standing Moorfields congregation.

Despite these considerations, I think it is plain that the goings-on
in *The Dunciad* fall into the residual categories, as well, found in
Rudé's analysis. The historian states that 'main attention will be
given to political demonstrations and to what sociologists have termed
the "aggressive mob" or the "hostile outburst" – to such activities
as strikes, riots, rebellions, insurrections, and revolutions'.[9] The
activities Pope recounts are not in any obvious sense political. That
they are often aggressive or hostile has already been indicated. That
they have the character of an outburst, a riot or an insurrection may
be less easily granted. Again, a somewhat exhaustive tabulation of
particular references is the best way of carrying forward the argument.

Apart from the allusion to the 'sable Army', we find many other
points at which Pope emphasises the quasi-military aspect of the
events. Thus the contentiousness which is endemic to folly is satirised
by means of the ancient disputes concerning the date of Easter:

> . . . Happy! had she seen
> No fiercer sons, had Easter never been.
> In peace, great Goddess, ever be ador'd;
> How keen the war, if Dulness draw the sword!
> Thus visit not thy own! on this blest age
> Oh spread thy Influence, but restrain thy Rage. (B.III.117)

Pope's note runs, 'Wars in *England* anciently, about the right time of
celebrating *Easter*'. War and ceremonial are thus connected; the plea
made by Settle's ghost in this passage is to be in vain, for Dulness
has already drawn her sword in effect. Her final triumph, moreover,
is one based on superior numbers, like any ordinary military success.

Later on in the same book, Settle refers to the aldermen of the City in significant terms, speaking of

> Their full-fed Heroes, their pacific May'rs,
> Their annual trophies, and their monthly wars . . . (B.III.281)

'Peaceful' is little more than a sneer, harking back to the 'bloodless swords and maces' of B.I.87. 'Monthly wars', as Pope's note tells us, refers to the periodic exercises of the City trainband 'in the *Artillery Ground*'. This was located – where else but in Moorfields? The cockpit of civic fribbles is near the arena of literary foolery: appropriately, since the 'monthly wars' could just as well mean the periodical infights of Grub Street, too.

Settle constantly recurs to the theme of dissension among the retinue of Dulness. On the surface he deplores it: but that is only Pope's way of making him testify to its existence:

> Ah Dennis! Gildon ah! what ill-starr'd rage
> Divides a friendship long confirm'd by age?
> Blockheads with reason wicked wits abhor,
> But fool with fool is barb'rous civil war.
> Embrace, embrace my sons! be free no more!
> Nor glad vile Poets with true Critic's gore. (B.III.173)

As a matter of fact the only embracing going on (as the next line reveals) is a homosexual coupling. But Dunces are inalienably at war: if not amongst themselves, with 'wicked wits', that is genuine literary talent or true social propriety. The atavistic return of 'barb'rous civil war' in the mentality of these satirists is something I shall turn to presently. Likewise the dominating imaginative role played by the notion of consumption by fire:

> All sudden, Gorgons hiss, and Dragons glare,
> And ten-horn'd fiends and Giants rush to war.
> Hell rises, Heav'n descends, and dance on Earth:
> Gods, imps, and monsters, music, rage, and mirth,
> A fire, a jigg, a battle, and a ball,
> 'Till one wide conflagration swallows all. (B.III.235)

No giants, outside Settle's crazed prophecy, but only pigmy battalions of Dunces 'rush to war' in the event. At the end the fires are all dimmed. '*Art* after *Art* goes out' (B.IV.640), the precise result of war, according to many versions of cultural history available to Pope. Similarly we find Settle speaking of the lawless insurgence of the bad poets, 'Each Songster, Riddler':

> Some free from rhyme or reason, rule or check,
> Break Priscian's head, and Pegasus's neck;
> Down, down they larum, with impetuous whirl,
> The Pinders, and the Miltons of a Curl. (B.III.161)

If that is not a riot, it is uncomfortably like one. Not even the eighteenth century accepted headbreaking in the streets as a part of ordinary civilised behaviour, lax as they were in these matters. One is less sure in the case of the fierce logicians (that epithet occurs frequently) who 'Came whip and spur, and dash'd thro' thin and thick' (B.IV.197), something the young blood might have attempted without the militia's being called out.[10]

Pope puts into a more express form his sense of the Dunces as taking part in a revolution against good sense. The main evidence comes in Book IV. Here we have a portrait of the crowd in action which approaches the analysis of Gustave Le Bon. As Rudé puts it, not unfairly, Le Bon

> was inclined to treat the crowd . . . as irrational, fickle, and destructive; as intellectually inferior to its components; as primitive or tending to revert to an animal condition. His prejudices led him to equate the 'mob' with the lower classes in society; and . . . [he] claimed [the French revolutionary crowd] tended to be composed of criminal elements, degenerates, and persons with destructive instincts, who blindly respond to the siren voices of 'leaders' or 'demagogues'.[11]

So, long before Taine or Le Bon, contemporaries saw it, much as it depresses the modern liberal historian. Large sections of *The Dunciad* are applicable, as I read the poem: the destructive element is most apparent at the end of the poem, the irrationality perhaps most in Book III. But to see how Pope shows us a crowd 'intellectually inferior to its components', easily hoodwinked by a leader, and bent obscurely on rebellion against it knows not what, we must look at one particular episode in the last book. There is indeed so much evidence that my quotation must be highly selective:

> The young, the old, who feel her inward sway,
> One instinct seizes, and transports away.
> None need a guide, by sure Attraction led,
> And strong impulsive gravity of Head:
> None want a place, for all their Centre found,
> Hung to the Goddess, and coher'd around.
> Not closer, orb in orb, conglob'd are seen
> The buzzing Bees about their dusky Queen.
>   The gath'ring number, as it moves along,
> Involves a vast involuntary throng,
> Who gently drawn, and struggling less and less,
> Roll in her Vortex, and her pow'r confess.
> Not those alone who passive own her laws,
> But who, weak revels, more advance her cause.
> Whate'er of dunce in College or in Town
> Sneers at another, in toupee or gown;
> Whate'er of mungril no one class admits,
> A wit with dunces, and a dunce with wits. ·
>   Nor absent they, no members of her state,
> Who pay her homage in her sons, the Great;
> Who false to Phoebus, bow the knee to Baal;
> Or impious, preach his Word without a call . . .
> . . . There march'd the bard and blockhead, side by side,
> Who rhym'd for hire, and patroniz'd for pride . . .
> . . . When Dulness, smiling – 'Thus revive the Wits!
> But murder first, and mince them all to bits . . .
> Let standard-Authors, thus, like trophies born,
> Appear more glorious as more hack'd and torn . . .
>   Leave not a foot or verse, a foot of stone,
> A Page, a Grave, that they can call their own . . .
> And while on Fame's triumphal Car they ride,
> Some Slave of mine be pinion'd to their side.' (B.IV.73–134)

With proleptic accuracy, this horrifying picture serves as a kind of warning against the Gordon riots.[12] The sluggish but unstoppable impetus of the crowd;[13] their social heterogeneity; their complement of 'mongrel' outcasts; their delight in rapine and destruction; their pathetic search for trophies and effigies; their careful choice of victim and rancorous envy – all this and more corresponds with what we know of the eighteenth-century city riot. When there is added the sustaining parallel between Cibber and the arch-rebel Satan (so brilliantly elucidated by Aubrey Williams), the importance of the 'riot' theme begins to show up.[14] Palpably, the civil broil has become an image of the breakdown in intellectual order which the poem takes as its subject.

There are further similarities. The Dunces obscurely imagine themselves to be oppressed (by merit), which Rudé – following Lord Granville in 1737 – sees as a characteristic of the rebellious crowd. Again, Rudé writes that the people may rise, amongst other reasons, 'because it has some deep social grievance, because it seeks an immediate reform or the millenium, or because it wants to destroy an enemy or acclaim a "hero"; but it is seldom for any single one of these reasons alone.' The social grievance of the Dunces is the strong antipathy of bad for good. The milleniary and destructive ambitions of the crowd, and their desire to do honour to their leader, are apparent on the most cursory reading of the last two books. The chiliastic fervour of Cibber is matched by the hero-worshipping zeal of the mass of Dunces:

> . . . All eyes direct their rays
> On him, and crowds turn Coxcombs as they gaze.
> His Peers shine round him with reflected grace,
> New edge their dulness, and new bronze their face. (B.II.7)

Again, the charismatic presence of Dulness herself is everywhere apparent. She glories in the absolute tyranny of King Mob:

> For sure, if Dulness sees a grateful Day,
> 'Tis in the shade of Arbitrary Sway. ·
> O! if my sons may learn one earthly thing . . .
> 'The RIGHT DIVINE of Kings to govern wrong.' (B.IV.181)

There is a parallel, too, with a series of riots led by 'Rebecca' and her daughters in the next century. Here we have a (spuriously) female leader, whose name has biblical overtones: a Magna Mater claiming allegiance from her 'children'. The religious connection is interesting, in view of the sacerdotal implications which have been discovered in *The Dunciad* by Williams and others. According to Rudé, the French

weavers of Moorfields as especially persistent and violent protesters on labour matters. Equally to point, he notes the 'surprising fact that the most riotous parts of London . . . were not the crowded quarters of St Giles-in-the-Fields or the shadier alleys of Holborn but the more solid and respectable popular districts of the City, the Strand, Southwark, Shoreditch, and Spitalfields.' The Dunces often lived in St Giles' or Holborn, but their riots take place in the City and around the Strand.[16]

Three final points. As to the composition of the crowd, Rudé sets out to refute the assumption of historians such as Dorothy George and Dorothy Marshall that the mob 'was in large measure composed of social dregs, pimps, prostitutes, thieves, and receivers.' Throughout this book I have attempted to show that Pope does indeed seek to associate his Dunces with such people, mainly by use of the actual physical environment. But, as the quotations must have made clear, he is far from asserting that all Dunces were 'social dregs' by origin. Secondly, it is notable how many eighteenth-century London riots were anti-Catholic in inspiration. The best-known instances postdate *The Dunciad*, but not by any means all. This was a fact of which Pope, even though he left Lombard Street in infancy, cannot have failed to be aware. Thirdly, it is fascinating to observe how closely 'the common pattern of the eighteenth-century city riot', as Rudé describes it, conforms to that of the poem. In the cases Rudé studied, the rioters 'operated in itinerant bands, marching (or running) through Shoreditch, the City of London, Westminster or Southwark, gathering fresh forces on the way.' So do the Dunces 'march' (B.II.423; IV.101) through the City to the boundary of Westminster, as a 'gath'ring number' (B.IV.81). The running seems to be confined to the foot races of Book II.[17]

I do not claim, of course, that Pope was so prescient that he foresaw all the historical parallels which can now, with hindsight, be drawn. I do believe that he instinctively turned to a conspicuous breach of public order when he wished to project imaginatively his sense of a breakdown in social values. As I shall argue presently, rebellion meant to the Augustans something more than the cultural lesion which it connotes for writers of this century (and indeed, to some extent for Arnold too, protected from the more violent continental *coups* of the nineteenth century). In 1740 rebellion still sparked off in men's minds the idea of desperate constitutional collision – a fissure, not in social consensus but in the rule of law itself: brother killing brother. If this is so, then it is fair to see in *The Dunciad* the image of a febrile state, on the verge of a reign of terror:

> Beneath her foot-stool, *Science* groans in Chains,
> And *Wit* dreads Exile, Penalties and Pains.
> There foam'd rebellious *Logic*, gagged and bound,
> There, stript, fair *Rhet'ric* languish'd on the ground. (B.IV.21)

Dulness, the great insurrectionist, is also the great tyrant, commissar of the secret police. So it will always be, Pope implies. This is not by way of literal prediction, of course. The poetry is simply that much more effective because of the immediacy with which civil war then seemed to threaten, and because of the way contemporaries thought about such turmoil.

There is a danger that we shall exaggerate the importance of this element in the total workings of the poem, once we have discovered it: as with the topographic background. This is a risk which attends most attempts to explicate poetry written in such different conditions from our own. By isolating the submerged religious allusions in Pope, we are liable to falsify his intent: not because they are not there, but just because they *are*, so self-evidently to a reader of Pope's day. As soon as we pick out a strand in his thought or imagery, which has passed from automatic reception to recondite 'demonstration', we tend to give that strand more significance than it should really possess. But this is one of the penalties of exposition.

Nor do I wish to suggest that the reading of the poem I have offered, with its emphasis on the seething crowd, furnishes what critics of the age called 'a complete key' to *The Dunciad*. The view of Pope's work which is made possible by reference to documentation and analysis of the eighteenth-century urban riot is only a partial vision. But I would contend that it does harmonise with the insights we already bring to that work, based on more familiar responses and bodies of information.

The events of *The Dunciad* call to mind another form of urban protest or demonstration. As well as the riot, they suggest the political procession or symbolic carnival which was the Augustan equivalent of a modern sit-in. The processional element in the poem has not been very fully explored; it can, I think, be illuminated by considering two external factors.

The first concerns a reference in a letter by Alderman John Barber. Surprisingly, this immensely helpful clue seems to have been disregarded by all previous commentators, yet it has been in print more than a century and a half. Neither the Twickenham editor nor Aubrey Williams mention this letter, even though it would strengthen much of what they say. Barber was printer of the *London Gazette*, a leading figure in the Stationers' Company, and Lord Mayor of London in 1732–3. Writing to Swift on 24 August 1732, he alludes to the coming Lord Mayor's Day (30 October) and continues:

> It would add very much to my felicity, if your health would permit you to come over in the spring, and see a pageant of your own making. Had you been here now, I am persuaded you would have put me to an additional expense, by having a raree-show (or pageant) as of old, on the lord mayor's day. Mr. Pope and I were thinking of having a large machine carried through the city, with a printing-press, author, publishers, hawkers, devils, etc., and a satirical poem printed and thrown from the press to the mob, in public view, but not to give offence; but your absence spoils that design.[18]

Or did it? These words were written five years after Pope had been in the throes of composition; but its suggestion of medieval guilds, Terrae Filius and public display may well have been in Pope's mind much earlier. The difference was that in 1732 there was a Lord Mayor, who was a Tory and a friend of the Scriblerians. Barber was a friend of Swift of very long standing – he had suffered for his part in putting out *The Public Spirit of the Whigs* in 1714 – and he was no bumbling alderman to be taken in by a passing joke. The poem to be thrown to the mob may not have been *The Dunciad* – something more within the compass of a broadside sheet would be required – but it would be a work of the same order. In the event, Pope's satirical offering to the mob, guying the literary profession in a 'public' mode, was circulated in a more conventional fashion. The procession of hawkers was simply built into the internal structure of the poem (A.II.13ff.).

Second, there is the annual procession to commemorate the Popish Plot. This was instituted in 1679, possibly with the knowledge of Shaftesbury, and every November right into Hanoverian times it was re-enacted to the accompaniment of bonfires, huzzas and side-skirmishes. The torchlit caravan began, appropriately, at Moorfields, and moved via Bishopsgate, Hounsditch, Aldgate, Leadenhall Street and Cornhill through Cheapside down to Temple Bar. There the waxwork figure of the Pope which had been carried along would be burnt, his richly dressed body having been lifted down from its chariot. On the bar itself, as reconstructed by Wren, one of the embossed figures was that of Queen Elizabeth; and on to this statue a shield would be placed, bearing the legend 'The Protestant Religion, Magna Charta.'[19] No one born a Londoner, least of all a Papist, could fail to be aware of this yearly ritual.[20] I do not suggest that Pope was necessarily conscious of the custom when he devised his supreme poetic fiction; though there is nothing in psychological or aesthetic theory which would rule that out. It does seem possible, to put it no higher, that subconsciously he had the memory of this gruesome procession activating his imagination when he sent his own troop of Dunces marching through the City. Two mental tricks, by no means uncommon, could have aided this process. To start with, it would not be fanciful to suppose that Pope at some level may have identified his own persecuted church with his own name (his opponents could never resist such an easy pun). An army of zealots bearing a stuffed Pope to ceremonial carnage at Temple Bar would therefore easily serve as a surrogate for an army of Dunces bent on the ritual destruction of Alexander Pope. Secondly, we might recall a familiar fact which has been given prominence by recent experiments. This is the tendency of the mind, when abstracted by sleep or some other preoccupation, to confuse words which sound nearly alike. Thus the subjects of psychological research have been found to dream of door-keys when the name 'Torquay' is repeated quietly to them as they sleep. Could it be that the vowel-quantities in another pair of words were close enough for Pope to make an imaginative transference – Magna Charta : Magna Mater ? The shibboleth of the anti-Papists, and the talisman of the anti-Popists, mentioned in the very first line of the revised poem. It is a remote possibility, but instructive to contemplate.

To see this potential symbolism realised in literature, we have only to turn to the *Tatler*. A fairly early number by Steele is No. 41, which appeared on 14 July 1709.[21] The paper describes an exercise of arms by the Artillery Company a fortnight previously. Steele re-counts the march of a body down Moorgate from the Artillery Ground, through the City, and then their return via Aldersgate Street, the Barbican and Red Cross Street. Here the force drew up, and subsequently moved up Beech Lane (then a twisting alley, later improved as Beech Street) before taking up position in White Cross Street. Here a sort of tactical exercise was conducted, with the Lieutenant-General's contingent retreating into Chiswell Street. The action of this curious wide-game was concentrated in a zone centring on Grub Street, the radius being about two hundred yards. Forays are made through Red Lion Court, over by the Artillery Ground itself; ambushes are laid in Black Raven Court, off Golden Lane; Bunhill Row is fiercely contested. Two divisions are deployed in Grub Street, and the entire affair takes place within shouting range of that unruly citadel. Steele ends with the level-toned irony he commanded so well: 'Happy was it, that the greatest part of the achievements of this day was to be performed near Grub Street, that there might not be wanting a sufficient number of faithful historians.'

Here was one lead for Pope: it was a paper he almost certainly read. The divisions of Grub Street are the forbears of the war-like Dunces, parading through London. The conducted tour of Cripple-gate is, at the close, related directly to the other forms of aggressive life which flourished in the parish. In other words, Steele emphasises the happy accident by which military pageantry and pompous train-band zeal had its expression in the Quartier Scriblerian, where instant history was made by the hack chroniclers. It is a key instance of a literary joke which depends on (and is accompanied by) a close itiner-ary of this single, unsubstitutable area. From the start, Grub Street was a better joke because its geographical setting was so familiar, so available and so endlessly appropriate. Pope, of course, improves on the joke; but he does so by developing, not muting, its existing implications.

The Rage and the Rabble

The vocabulary of Augustan satire, then, carries within itself a buried layer of allusion to civil unrest. The 'premonition' is imagistic and rhetorical, rather than literal; but it is still true that this body of writing prefigures an important development in populist activity, indeed in social history at large. The Scriblerian lexicon anticipated events.

The clue to this state of affairs is to be found in the terror and revulsion with which Pope and Swift looked on faction. This is now a grey little word with little power to alarm us. But at a historical moment when schism appeared the great threat to progress in political, economic and cultural life, the term had a sharper ring. Not for nothing does Ricardus Aristarchus, in introducing the later *Dunciad*, refer to 'the party of Dulness'.[22] The poem itself incorporates a visionary account of a malicious faction destroying itself, and others, in pursuit of private goals. The chiliastic fervour of the Dunces leads them to parrot mindless slogans; their fierce conviction induces them to swamp London with their noxious and debilitating exhalations. They are a party.

The phrase 'cultural life' was perhaps ill-considered. It is doubtful whether the eighteenth-century mind truly recognised such a category at large. And assuredly the thinkers of the age did not regard crime or public affray as social lesions, as many people would today. They had not read their Matthew Arnold, and for them a riot in Hyde Park was only secondarily – if at all – to be deplored because it showed a lack of personal cultivation on the rioters' part. It was to be reviled as threatening an actual breakdown in the rule of law. The Augustans, we should recall, read Cicero not merely as a graceful moralist; they still combed his works for lessons in political prudence.

The tendency to read *The Dunciad* as an exploration of a gap in 'communication' betrays a similar distortion of the period. The first thing to say about the eighteenth-century notion of communication is that, broadly speaking, no such theory existed. By importing our modern categories, we give a spurious lucidity to some aspects of the age. But we blur its outlines, too, and soften its asperities. On the whole the Augustan mind was not well attuned to 'cultural' considerations. Both Pope and Swift, I believe, harboured deeper fears than the mere loss of cultivation in personal living. It is a pardonable exaggeration to say that their literary forebodings project a state of affairs almost exactly equivalent with that of the actual French Revolution, as it impressed itself on the mind of their successor Burke. They feared the storming of the English Bastille.

More significant, then, than any 'cultural' development is the growing importance of the popular affray as a *political* instrument in the eighteenth century. Historians disagree as to the precise nature of this change, and it would be rash to place too much weight on the 'partisan' basis of riots at large. But in using the term I do not mean that all disturbances were motivated by a straight Whig/Tory clash, though some were: the Mug-House riot of 1716 would seem to be one. Nor do I postulate any definite ideological alignment in such persistent troublemakers as the Spitalfields weavers. The point is not that these varied groups all had a common 'radical' banner – clearly they did not. But behind the different religious, economic, racial or social issues which stimulated disorder, there is one shared characteristic. All the rioters believe that by carrying out a public demonstration, as a group, they will be able to further their ends. Almost invariably, their demonstration ran into pillage, arson or both. Pope implies that the Dunces are experts in '*Battle-array*', like their leader, Cibber (who actually 'met the *Revolution* at Nottingham face to face', as Pope jibingly puts it).[23] The phrase is hardly metaphoric at all; and as usual the biographic hint is to the purpose. Dunces are heirs of the armies of the seventeenth century, which had laid waste so much of the country. They are destroyers by profession.

Symptomatically, the age which was so fertile in riots gave us the Riot Act. This was indeed among the very first measures of the first

Hanoverian king. It is 1 George I, stat. 2, c. 5 (1714), and survived in England and Wales right up to the Criminal Law Act of 1967. Eighteenth-century jurists were much concerned to provide a workable definition of the various modes of unlawful assembly. A rout, for instance, has been held to mean an affray caused by an assembly on the move – like, let us say, the Gordon rioters or the Dunces. Riot itself has been interpreted to refer to a 'tumultuous disturbance of the peace by three or more with an intent mutually to assist one another against any who oppose them, in the execution of some enterprise of a private nature.' (The last phrase is designed to exclude the notion of insurrection, where some public cause is at issue.) But all modes of affray must be shown to induce 'the terror and affright of the people' for a prosecution to lie.[24] It is hardly necessary to remind ourselves of the nature of the duncely 'enterprise', or the horrific quality of the 'dread Empire' of Chaos (B.IV.653) with its promise of unending night.

Among popular disturbances of the age, two are of special interest. Both link Grub Street even more firmly with tumult. The Wilkite affrays of 1768, which have been so thoroughly explored by George Rudé, confirm Pope's imaginative thesis in a variety of ways. We find Wilkes greeted by huzzas at the junction of Chancery Lane and the Strand; by St Clement's church, his supporters actually went so far as to take over as carriage-horses in their delight. The resemblance to the cries of 'God save King Cibber!' (B.I.320), or the brays which roll down Chancery Lane (B.II.263) are too obvious to need emphasis. The hacks' quarter of St Giles' and Drury Lane was, inevitably, convulsed during the riots. St Bride's, in the vicinity of the Fleet Ditch, was a parish which resounded again and again to the cry of 'Wilkes and Liberty'. Wilkes indeed was elected as alderman for the ward of Farringdon Without (the corresponding civic division) in January 1769. It is interesting to note that the popular hero had been born in St John's Square, Clerkenwell, in 1725: little more than a decade later, Samuel Johnson was to be in occupation of the nearby St John's Gate – profession, hack writer. It is not a very long step to Grub Street proper: a bare quarter of a mile from Wilkes's birthplace to the parish of Cripplegate.[25]

No less interesting, though more indirect, are two other features of Professor Rudé's research. He quotes Alexander Wedderburn, writing to George Grenville on 3 April 1768:

[the south of England has become] a great Bedlam under the dominion of a beggarly, idle and intoxicated mob without keepers, actuated solely by the word *Wilkes*, which they use as better savages do a walrus to incite them in their attempts to insult Government and trample upon law.

The phraseology here is a standing testimony to the imaginative accuracy of the poem Pope had written over a quarter of a century earlier. The noisy and inebriated Wilkites mouthing their shibboleths are at one with the devotees of Colley Cibber. Secondly, it is intriguing to note that many of the citizens arrested in 1768 for riotous assembly, or similar offences, prove to have been parishioners of St Giles', Cripplegate or St Luke's, Old Street. Perhaps they did not have so far to march as others – but that in itself made the inner suburbs a home of the riotous. Among those listed by Rudé, we find a lighterman of Old Street, convicted of breaking windows at the Mansion House riots, and given one of the stiffest sentences. Another given to protest by defenestration was a watch-finisher of Jewin Street. A weaver of Golden Lane is also named. Moving slightly further afield, we encounter a porter of John Street, Clerkenwell, and the wife of a clothes-dealer in Nightingale Lane – a street abutting on Rosemary Lane, where old clothes and Dulness alike proliferated.[26] It would appear that whenever serious disturbance broke out in London, Cripplegate could be relied on to supply its quota of hooligans and hoodlums.

It is the Gordon Riots, however, twelve years later, which supply the most striking authentication of Pope's charge. In a number of ways the events of June 1780 sum up the history of popular insurrection in the eighteenth century. It cannot fail to impress us, then, that they prove equally to enact many of the implied predictions of *The Dunciad*. Of course, I do not mean that Pope literally divined the shape of things to come, as Burke perhaps did in the case of French history. I am suggesting rather that the poet's creative mind shaped events along lines that were, so to speak, already immanent in history. His poem acts out fictively a myth of social disorder, which the anti-popery riots chance to follow with curious mimicry. But this is a contingent fact: *The Dunciad* would still be an impressive vision of the anarchic city even if the Protestant Association had never existed. We are being neither perverse nor anachronistic, then, if we congratulate Pope on writing better than he knew. Events come to his support so often because he went so often (and at such an early imaginative stage) *to* events in the devising of his myth.

A single piece of evidence gives eloquent proof of the relevance of the happenings of 1780. It was only at this juncture that Samuel Johnson for the very first time planned to visit Grub Street. He was over seventy years old; he had been living in London continuously for more than half that span; and he was in no doubt that he ought to have paid his respects before this time. Fanny Burney tells the story to Mrs Thrale:

> Since that time, I have had the pleasure to meet him [Johnson] again at Mrs. Reynolds's, when he offered to take me with him to Grub Street, to see the ruins of the house demolished there in the late riots, by a mob that, as he observed, could be no friend to the Muses! He inquired if I had ever yet visited Grub Street? but was obliged to restrain his anger when I answered 'No', because he acknowledged that he had never paid his respects to it himself. 'However,' says he, 'you and I, Burney will go together; we have a very good right to go, so we'll visit the mansions of our progenitors, and take up our own freedom together.'[27]

Typically, the comic byplay illustrates a larger truth. The septuagenarian writer, once a hack domiciled over the way from Cripplegate, invites the young author of *Evelina* to inspect 'the mansions of [their] progenitors' – the only bit of London literary men could call their own. And when, we may ask, does he feel impelled to do so? Why, when the street is recovering from the after-effects of a riot. Grub Street was in a proper state to receive its own at such a moment: conflict and destruction were its lifeblood.

Johnson had taken a close interest in the progress of the riots. He noted in a letter to Mrs Thrale on 9 June 1780 that a masshouse in

Moorfields had been burnt down (conceivably the same 'house' he was to visit with Fanny Burney). Three days later he inquired with an air of some desperation, 'Who can guess the caprice of the rabble?'[28] It is a refrain taken up by others. Horace Walpole, an equally interested spectator, had been using similar phrasing for some time. During the Wilkite troubles, he had written to Mann, 'Since our riots and tumults, I conclude you are glad when you do *not* hear from me; it is a symptom that we are tolerably quiet; for you can have no fear of me, who live out of the storm. It is true, our mobs are subsided . . .'[29] The word 'mob' is ubiquitous. A concordance of Walpole's work – which would be a most valuable operation if enough computer-programmers could be recruited at Yale – would show how often he falls back on the word around this period. Johnson did not live 'out of the storm', and his fears were almost as marked. Even men of great physical courage found themselves beset by apprehension. For a time it must have seemed as if the empire of Chaos had indeed come: the destruction of Lord Mansfield's famous library must have appeared as a ghastly fulfilment of Settle's demented prophecy:

> Heav'ns! what a pile! whole ages perish there,
> And one bright blaze turns Learning into air. (B.III.77)

By one of those strange connections which begin to look less and less like pure coincidence, William Cowper chose to single out Pope and Swift amongst the many valuable books destroyed. His poem was enclosed in a letter dated 22 June 1780:

On the Burning of Lord Mansfield's Library : Together with his MSS. By the Mob, in the Month of June 1780.

> So then – the Vandals of our isle,
>   Sworn foes to sense and law,
> Have burnt to dust a nobler pile
>   Than ever Roman saw!

> And MURRAY sighs o'er Pope and Swift,
>   And many a treasure more,
> The well-judged purchase and the gift
>   That grac'd his letter'd store.

Their pages mangled, burnt, and torn,
The loss was *his alone ;*
But ages yet to come shall mourn
The burning of *his own.*[30]

Cowper here associates vandalism, burning, mangling, as common foes of the tradition represented by Swift, Pope and Mansfield himself. The 'mob' are by implication *un*lettered, incapable of the 'storing' function which humanist lore revered (as with Swift's bee). The Gordon riots, in other words, operated as an agency of Dulness. The populace, volatile and doomed to the temporary, takes its revenge on the stable and the permanent. It has but one weapon: indiscriminate carnage. That a mob bent on throwing Pope, along with other Catholics, to the flames should concentrate many of its activities in Cripplegate is almost too apt to be credible.

A lively, though not meticulously accurate, account of the disturbances has been given by Christopher Hibbert in *King Mob.* To set his narrative alongside *The Dunciad* is to become aware of an uncanny prescience on the part of Pope. The most striking way of making the point, indeed, will be simply to juxtapose quotations, with brief reference to other surveys of the riot.

The trouble first reached serious proportions on Friday, 2 June, with the meeting at St George's Fields. This was a large open space in Southwark, and as Hibbert says,

> By night it was a dangerous place and only the most foolhardy citizens took a short cut across it unarmed. In daylight gangs of streetboys chased each other around the wooden shacks of beggars and the bushes near stagnant ponds, while apprentices from the workshops at Newington Butts and from the maze of streets between Bandly Leg Walk and Angel Street ['angel' doubtless connoting prostitutes], came out to play football or to make love in the long grass. For many years it had been a favourite place for open air meetings, demonstrations and religious meetings . . .

It was, in other words, exactly like Moorfields on the other side of the river. The riots started in a natural habitat of Dulness. Similarly the gangs of Dunces chase one another round London, after emerging from their shacks in the 'maze of streets' in St Giles', and recreate themselves with boisterous athletics round the stagnant pool that was the Fleet Ditch. They demonstrate with religious fervour and quasi-erotic immodesty. After this assembly, the rioters marched (as do the Dunces) to the West End. They moved down Fleet Street to the Strand, towards Charing Cross. Whenever they passed a church they would give three cheers (exactly so, the acclamations and bawlings of Pope's poem take place outside St Mary le Strand). The rioters progressed a little farther, since Westminster was their destination; the Dunces are content to petition Parliament with noise:

> Thames wafts it thence to Rufus' roaring hall,
> And Hungerford re-echoes bawl for bawl. (B.II.265)

Whilst the rioters were hanging about outside the House of Lords, awaiting news of how their petition had been received, they began to 'jeer or laugh' at the Foot Guards, who retorted with a somewhat impotent charge.

> This treatment [writes Hibbert] while enraging many of the demonstrators made others laugh so much that they could not get up from the ground, where they rolling about in paroxysms of infectious laughter.

It seems hardly necessary to remind ourselves that an identical blend of rage, laughter, reeling and paralysis runs through *The Dunciad*:

> Heav'n rings with laughter: Of the laughter vain,
> Dulness, good Queen, repeats the jest again. (B.II.121)

Many of the rioters were drunk, of course. Many lay down at Westminster, as do the drugged circle of Dunces at the end of their games. Samuel Romilly, on his way to listen to the debate in the Lords, encountered a group of people

> assembled round a female preacher who by her gestures and actions seemed to be well persuaded, or desirous of persuading others that she was animated by some supernatural spirit.

At one point Dulness does actually change from a false deity into a priestess:

> The Goddess then, o'er his anointed head,
> With mystic words, the sacred Opium shed. (B. I.287)

Like all proselytisers, Dulness has her 'Chosen' (B.I.273); she pours her 'Spirit' over the land (B.I.8).

Again, the link with Bedlam is explicit. Horace Walpole had written of Lord George Gordon as the 'lunatic apostle', and added:

> It is to be hoped this man is so mad that it will soon come to perfection unless my plan is adopted of shutting up in Bedlam the few persons in this country that remain in their senses. It would be easier and much cheaper to confine all the delirious.

When the Protestant Petition was presented at the House of Commons, a certain Colonel Holroyd told Gordon that initially he had regarded the leader of the rioters as mad 'and was going to move that you might be sent to Bedlam'. But now, he went on, he saw that there was method as well as madness, and if Gordon went once more to the mob, he would move that the Tower, instead, should receive him. If Gordon was not completely dissociated at this stage (Dickens perhaps exaggerates the wildness of his fanaticism), he was certainly a man of marked neurotic tendency; in later years he was simply mad. But this is not all. During the riots themselves, there had at first been a plan to release the lunatics along with the convicts. This was abandoned; but witnesses testify to the reactions of the inmates of the hospital. The Bedlamites, excited by the glare and the noise, shrieked deliriously; many danced with glee. There is a deep poetic accuracy in Dickens' choice of a hero for *Barnaby Rudge*.[31]

It was on the following day – Saturday, 3 June – that Grub Street itself became involved. About nine o'clock in the evening violence flared up near Finsbury Yard, in Moorfields. Hibbert comments:

> Moorfields was one of the poorest districts, just to the east ['some way to the north-east'?] of the ragged tumbling slum quarter of St Giles', portrayed in Hogarth's 'Gin Lane', and north of Bedlam. It was a part of London where many Irish labourers had lodgings and where the doss-houses were frequently full of Irish vagrants who paid a penny a night to sleep on the lousy, rat-ridden straw.

A merchant 'of Irish extraction' called Malo was the target for the mob. He seems to have been singled out not principally because he was a Catholic (some of the victims of the depredations were in fact themselves of the Protestant faith), but because he was believed to favour the employment of Catholics, generally Irishmen. The rioters, not altogether without justification, saw this as a threat to their own livelihood. As we saw earlier, there had always been a high proportion of unskilled Irish labourers in Cripplegate Ward. In 1740 this had been one more way in which the rich connotations of the opprobious term 'Grub Street' could be filled out. In 1780 the circumstances came home to roost: the first serious damage done by the Gordon rioters was that wreaked on Grub Street and its immediate environs.

Thanks more to the irresolution of the crowd than to any preventive measures (though seventy-three militia-men were belatedly called in from the Tower), comparatively little physical harm was done on the first night. But on the Sunday, things changed – as Hibbert explains.

It was a hot dry day with not a breath of wind in the air, and the people seemed content to sit idly around on doorsteps and in the streets and to lie on the hot dry ground in Middle Moor Fields and the Tenter Grounds. They seemed unwilling, a Guards Officer noted, to wander far away from the district and the Artillery Ground usually crowded on a Sunday afternoon was strangely quiet.

As the evening cooled the excitement mounted. At about eight o'clock the crowds converged, as if instructed during the day to do so, on a Catholic chapel in Ropemakers Alley. Some women who lived next door to the chapel leaned out of a first floor window and begged the people below to be careful. Their entreaties were greeted with a hail of stones and brickbats, which had been collected to smash the windows of the chapel, and the women hastily withdrew and fled in terror from the back door of their house.

The intoxicating sound of smashing glass was the awaited signal. Hundreds of street-boys and girl prostitutes ran excitedly up and down Ropemakers Alley and the courts adjoining, shouting that the fun had started.

It continued unabated in Moorfields for two horrifying and long-remembered days and nights. Every Catholic chapel in the district was burned to the ground; Irishmen were attacked with sticks and knives whenever they were recognised; quiet and inoffensive Catholics were insulted, spat upon and their clothes torn off their backs; their houses were broken open and their furniture and books and pictures and carpets were tossed on to raging bonfires in the middle of the streets.

Cellars were invaded and food and wine were brought up to be consumed in Bacchanalian parties around the fires; while the Pope and St Patrick were burned in effigy on the sites of burned-out chapels and Irish taverns.

This was indeed the party of Dulness let loose. A riot of destruction and gluttony, sustained by perverted religious principles.

> How keen the war, if Dulness draw the sword! (B.III.120)

It was this scene, in and around Grub Street, which suggested to Dr Johnson that he might go and acknowledge his descent from the hacks of yesteryear. It was this scene, too, which Dickens described in a paragraph of impassioned energy in *Barnaby Rudge* (Ch. III), and which Hablot K. Browne illustrated with a kind of maniacal comedy. This is the hellish city of the eighteenth century satirists come to life.

According to J. P. de Castro, a Catholic pawnbroker in Golden Lane was amongst the worst sufferers. His house was pulled down and, not content with that, the mob burnt all his goods in their store at Old Street. Catholic property in Bunhill Fields was also gutted. Thus two streets associated with the most resolute Protestants among major English authors, Milton and Defoe, were ravaged in the cause of anti-popery. It is a matter for gratitude that Bunyan's grave in Tindall's burial ground, just next to Bunhill, was not desecrated by some meandering rioter. The Catholic chapel seems to have been situated in White Street, off Little Moorfields, parallel with Ropemakers Alley. It was in this street, curiously, that the leader of the Cato Street conspirators was found and arrested in 1820. Forty years earlier a bonfire was set up in White Street. In Moorfields itself four young men were strung up after conviction for taking part in the riots. Grub Street continued its unhappy alliance with jailbirds, rakehells and small-time anarchists. The prophecy uttered by Settle in which Dulness is apotheosised contains only the prediction that Rome will be brought low; the rioters attempted to bring down her church too. The minister of the Catholic church died two months later; his death, the *Annual Register* thought, had been hastened by the events in June. He had begun his career as minister when the chapel stood in Butler's Alley, directly off Grub Street itself. When Pope wrote his poem, that is, the main target of the rioters would have lain in the very precincts of Grub Street. Their centre of operations was deflected a couple of hundred yards when the chapel moved, possibly to the site of the former Anabaptist conventicle in White Street, at some date subsequent to 1765.[32]

The bonfires in Moorfields having lit the way, the riot now spread to other parts of the City. For the remainder of that ugly week, we hear little of the region. On the Wednesday night we catch a glimpse of Gordon himself 'haranguing the multitude' there, in a vain attempt to stem the tide and to get them to disperse. On the same evening, according to one story, the party who assailed the Bank dragged off one man to Moorfields in order to ensure his secrecy on an embarrassing discovery he had made. But there is little firm evidence.

However, this is not all that can be said on the subject of the Gordon riots. Again and again in descriptions of the events we come on phrases which instantly call up the world of *The Dunciad*. To take a few examples more or less at random – there is the poet Crabbe observing of the rioters, 'They boldly paraded the streets with colours and music.' Compare the triumphal progress of Cibber to St James's:

> Lift up your gates, ye Princes, see him come!
> Sound, sound ye Viols, be the Cat-call dumb!
> Bring, bring the madding Bay, the drunken Vine . . . (B.I.301)

Cibber's minions 'shine' with reflected grace and bronzed face (B.II.9); their 'motley' troop pours forth in garish abundance, with 'silks, crapes, Garters' as well as rags (B.II.21). Crabbe saw the parade on the morning of Tuesday, 6 June; later that day the rioters carried off Lord Gordon in his chariot (the Dunces had their quota of those: B.II.24). The route taken was up Whitehall, along the Strand and Fleet Street, down Cheapside and Poultry to Mansion House. Not even Pope, with his inventive mock-heroic mind, dreamt up so total an invasion of the Lord Mayor's procession. Here fact does more than underline Pope's joke: it gives it another, uncovenanted, level of meaning.

We may pass over such obvious items of information as the fact that prostitutes were amongst the earliest recruits to the army of destruction. Or that the prisons, bordering the Fleet for the most part, were the major focus of attention for much of the time. Or that the garrets of Smithfield were searched, not for hacks (who could certainly have been found there on occasion) but for fugitives. Or that one of the largest vigilante corps, said to be two thousand strong, had to be set up in Cripplegate. Or that dead bodies were dumped into that universal receptacle, the Fleet Ditch. It is more interesting to note, first that the riots were said to provoke the 'largest exodus since the plague', and second that the riots, like the Fire, were initially blamed on foreign *provocateurs*. Historical evidence is only documenting a connection which poetic imagery had long before asserted.[33]

Fire and Fever

Bonfires raged through the Gordon riots – and other eighteenth-century insurrections – as they blaze through Augustan literature. Combustion was at once the symbol and the agency of anti-popery. The zeal of the anti-Pope faction, that is the Dunces, was likewise attended with conflagration. That crowds and fires went together had been noted by Samuel Johnson as early as 1738: at a time when Grub Street was in a sense his spiritual home, five years before the revised *Dunciad* appeared. His Juvenalian picture of the capital, *London*, contains the thought:

> Here malice, rapine, accident, conspire,
> And now a rabble rages, now a fire . . .[34]

The very grammar links *rabble* with *fire*, whether or not the second is actually caused by the first. As a student of Jacobean city comedy has written, London backgrounds reflect 'the intricacies and unpredictable though constant hazards of the city, which is at once familiar yet hostile and impersonal.'[35] A major hazard of the time was the loss of property by fire, either by accident or malicious arson. Physical fire protection was only just growing up, and insurance was still in its infancy. The mob accordingly had a strong weapon in their hands when they resorted to fire-raising, as the Sacheverell riots in 1710 conspicuously illustrated. A natural visitation could also become a convenient means of offence for the disaffected. An act of God might be taken over to further the actions of the godless.

Naturally a good deal of contemporary concern with the matter can be traced back to the Great Fire. The fear of a recurrence of that disaster shaped the attitude of all Londoners. So we find reprints of a book like *An Account of the burning of the city of London, as it was published in . . . 1666*, which was issued in its third edition (1721) with the 'opinion of Dr. [White] Kennet . . . and Dr [Laurence] Eachard', expert witnesses in theological rather than pyrotechnical matters. Defoe characteristically has a good deal to say on the matter. One of the most obvious examples occurs in his section on the city of London in his *Tour*. He devotes a number of paragraphs specifically to the new buildings erected after the Fire, and discusses the changes in the urban landscape which have resulted. Then, a few pages later, he reverts to the theme:

> And as I am speaking of Fire and burning of Houses, it cannot be omitted, That no where in the World is so good Care taken to quench Fires as in *London*; I will not say the like Care is taken to prevent them; for I must say, That I think the Servants, nay, and Masters too in *London*, are the most careless People in the World about Fire, and this, no doubt, is the Reason why there are frequently more Fires in *London* and in the Out-parts, than there are in all the Cities of *Europe* put them together; nor are they the more careful, as I can learn, either from observation or report, I say, they are not made more cautious by the inumerable fires which continually happen among them.

Defoe goes on to list the factors which make London particularly 'well furnished for the extinguishing fires when they happen.' These include the number of water-courses and piped water supplies; the great number of 'admirable engines' owned by the parishes; and the care of well-equipped fire insurance offices. Defoe had earlier listed the four principal societies, and estimated that more than seventy thousand separate properties in the metropolis were now covered against fire risk.[36]

I have not been able to ascertain whether Defoe's claim regarding the high rate of fire-damage, relative to other European cities, is as much of an exaggeration as it looks. Early actuarial figures are not complete enough to make such comparisons reliable. But it does appear that, on a subjective plane, the inhabitants of London *thought* they were uniquely exposed to loss and danger from this source – an understandable legacy in their minds from the calamity of 1666.

Pope was never one to waste such a psychological circumstance. His poem reverberates with the words *fire, flames, flamy, burns, smokes, blaze conflagration* and so on. One trivial instance will exemplify the way in which he utilised topical facts to his own artistic purposes. I quote from the earlier version, although both text and note survive intact in 1743.

> Grubstreet! thy fall should men and Gods conspire,
> Thy stage shall stand, ensure it but from Fire. (A.III.309)

Pope's note at this point may be supplemented by the Twickenham editor's helpful gloss:

> In *Tibbald's* Farce of *Proserpine* a Corn-field was set on fire; whereupon the other Playhouse had a Barn burnt down for the recreation of the spectators. They also rival'd each other in showing the Burnings of Hell-fire, in Dr. *Faustus*. [Twick.ed: On Oct. 26, 1727 – just about the time that these words were written – a riot occurred at the opening performance of Cibber's *Henry VIII* at Drury Lane, owing to a cry of 'Fire!' raised among the audience. Several people were injured, and one woman crushed to death . . . Pope may have had the circumstance in mind.]

It is worth stressing that the two playwrights involved here, Theobald and Cibber, were the two successive King Dunces. Pope's point is clear. Grub Street in its theatrical aspect – Drury Lane, say – deals in the perishable, like its literary organ; even though here there are no physical copies, but merely plays, to undergo the process of destruction. As everyone knows, eighteenth-century theatres were notoriously likely to go up in flames. Pope therefore gets further satiric purchase by associating theatres and fire. It is a reminder that the actual buildings in which the harlequinade and operas of the Dull were performed were as short-lived as their repertoire. Slightly earlier, in 1721, there had been fears that Drury Lane was in danger of falling down; whilst in 1722 one of the common playhouse 'riots' (the normal word used) erupted against Cibber himself.[37]

Much the same innuendo is found in Book I. There, the chosen bard (let us take Cibber) retires to his library and runs his eyes over his unique collection of trash and showily-bound lightweight authors. To this 'Gothic Library' his fellow-hacks are admitted:

> Here all his suff'ring brotherhood retire,
> And 'scape the martyrdom of jakes and fire. (B.I.143)

Their wretched productions, if not granted the sanctity of their King's library (there is possibly a joke on Bentley here, who had come to prominence while keeper of the royal collection), will suffer one of two fates. Either they will be reduced to the arse-wiping function or else they will be used to light fires. I do not think there is any strong sense here that the books will burn on account of heretical content, i.e. will be placed on the index.

It is this very same library, of course, which provides the kindling for the great ritual bonfire in this book. The pyre is carefully built up, in a manner the Smithfield Muses who are invoked at the start might well approve; for was not Smithfield the place above all in England to carry out a ritual cremation?

> Of these twelve volumes, twelve of amplest size,
> Redeem'd from tapers and defrauded pies,
> Inspir'd he seizes: These an altar raise:
> An hecatomb of pure, unsully'd lays
> That altar crowns: A folio Common-place
> Founds the whole pile, of all his works the base:
> Quartos, octavos, shape the less'ning pyre;
> A twisted Birth-day Ode completes the spire. (B.I.155)

Cibber goes on to address these volumes:

> 'O born in sin, and fourth in folly brought!
> Works damn'd, or to be damn'd (your father's fault)
> Go, purify'd by flames ascend the sky,
> My better and more christian progeny!
> Unstain'd, untouch'd, and yet in maiden sheets;
> While all your smutty sisters walk the streets.' (B.I.225)

As often, there are important biographic allusions here, which have been well explained by the Twickenham editor.[38] But the wider effect of this 'tender and passionate Apostrophe', as Pope calls it, is to link Dulness even more closely with the life of the streets. At the moment in which purification should be taking place, by ceremonial sacrifice, we are forcibly reminded of the filth that surrounds folly. Fire and dirt go together, as they are generally made to do.

Shortly afterwards, the ceremony proper:

> And thrice he lifted high the Birth-day brand,
> And thrice he dropt it from his quiv'ring hand;
> Then lights the structure, with averted eyes:
> The rowling smokes involve the sacrifice.
> The op'ning clouds disclose each work by turns,
> Now flames the Cid, and now Perolla burns;
> Great Caesar roars, and hisses in the fires;
> King John in silence modestly expires;
> No merit now the dear Nonjuror claims,
> Moliere's old stubble in a moment flames.
> Tears gush'd again, as from pale Priam's eyes
> When the last blaze sent Ilion to the skies. (B.I.245)

I ronically only Dulness herself can douse the flames. It would take a whole campaign of extended forays in practical criticism to tease out all the meanings here, quite apart from the Ovidian and Virgilian recollections. Pope himself supplies further jokes in his annotation, bringing in asbestos amongst other things. It is enough, perhaps, to mention the brilliant metaphysical wit enshrined in the phrase, 'Moliere's old stubble' to which the note adds, 'A Comedy thrashed out of Moliere's Tartuffe.' Pope's imagination dances from one variety of fire to the next: at one moment we have a smouldering cornfield after the harvest, at another a Guy Fawkes celebration, at another possibly a royal fireworks display ('the Birthday brand') – or might this indeed suggest a child lighting candles on a cake?[39]

By this means the poet has linked the Dunces with a rather grisly rite. But he has also shown us their works as ripe for incineration; and he has prepared us for the rumbustious crowd scenes of the following book. Cibber's face, at the start of Book II, is itself a sort of burning-glass; and throughout the section we are given constant reminders of this trope. Of Curll's urine, for example, we are told,

> His rapid waters in their passage burn. (B.II.184).

It is Settle's prophecy in Book III, however, which takes up the notion most centrally. The apotheosis of Dulness involves an extension of territorial rights, to regions

> Where spices smoak beneath the burning Line (B.III.70)

and reaches even Tartary:

> Heav'ns! what a pile! whole ages perish there,
> And one bright blaze turns Learning into air. (B.III.77)

There is a paradox here. Queen Dulness, herself, a heavy cloud-compelling monarch, tedious and cold, can yet 'burn' up learning and civility, as a very cold object burns by the transference of heat.

At the climax of Settle's vision, we see the progress of barbarism as Gothic ignorance settles over Rome and even the Popes themselves become instruments of destroying ancient civilisation.

> Padua, with sighs, beholds her Livy burn,
> And ev'n th' Antipodes Vigilius mourn.
> See, the Cirque falls, th' unpillar'd Temple nods,
> Streets pav'd with Heroes, Tyber choak'd with Gods:
> 'Till Peter's keys some christ'ned Jove adorn,
> And Pan to Moses lends his pagan horn;
> See graceless Venus to a Virgin turn'd,
> Or Phidias broken, and Apelles burn'd. (B.III.105)

It is unlike Pope, who has justifiably been termed the most consistently varied of our poets, to repeat a key rhyme-word at so close an interval. Here the idea of 'burning' seems to have taken so compulsive a hold on his imagination that no alteration, no elegant variation, no more or less accurate synonym would do. The simple monosyllabic word comes back with heavy insistence to clinch this horrific description of the self-induced ruins of Rome.[40]

At the very end of the poem, with the triumph of Dulness, eternal night comes to quench the fires of learning with its own black combustion. To a Hanoverian, this must have suggested the trampling down of civic and political morality by the jobbing administration

(as Pope thought of it) of Robert Walpole, and later Henry Pelham.
The passage is so well known that selective quotation should be
enough:

> Before her, *Fancy*'s gilded clouds decay,
> And all its varying Rain-bows die away.
> *Wit* shoots in vain its momentary fires,
> The meteor drops, and in a flash expires.
> As one by one, at dread Medea's strain,
> The sick'ning stars fade off th'ethereal plain . . .
> Thus at her felt approach, and secret might,
> *Art* after *Art* goes out, and all is Night . . .
> *Religion* blushing veils her sacred fires,
> And unawares *Morality* expires.
> Nor *public* Flame, nor *private*, dares to shine;
> Nor *human* Spark is left, nor Glimpse *divine*! (B.IV.631–52)

Wit has become a frenzied, irregular kind of flame; its luminosity is
no longer steady or controlled. The Queen of Ignorance has assumed
absolute power, and with that London becomes a city very like Hell –
a point that emerges most plainly from Aubrey Williams's reading.
The city of endless night is, in fact, dark as Milton's Hades is dark:
the flames are sensible ('felt') but not visible.

This emphasis on the destructive power of fire could be further
explored along two different lines, one broadly 'rhetorical' in character, the other historical or documentary. Under the first aspect, we
might recall the statement by Jeffrey Hart which I quoted earlier
(p. 96). Fire is a powerful emblem of a process which serves to 'disturb the balance of mind or state' (thus one speaks of a rebellion
breaking out, catching alight, spreading like wildfire, razing institutions to the ground, and so on). More specifically, fire came to be
associated with religious zeal, that is enthusiasm. And possibly because of the Gunpowder Plot, the notion seems often to have been
associated in the seventeenth and eighteenth centuries with constitutional upheaval:

> True Zeal is an *Ignis lambens*, a soft and gentle Flame, that will not
> Scorch one's hand; it is no predatory or voracious thing: but *Carnall
> and fleshly Zeal*, is like the Spirit of Gunpowder set on fire, that tears
> and blows up all that stands before us.[41]

This is Ralph Cudworth, preaching to the House of Commons as early as 1647. But eighty years later, it is still apt to think of the zeal of the Dunces as being 'like the Spirit of Gunpowder set on fire'. The 'bright blaze' which destroyed Rome, which 'turns Learning into air' (B.III.78) and which reduced Lord Mansfield's library to ashes are one and the same. All can be seen as ceremonial fireworks lit as part of the triumph of Dulness.

This leads us to the historical aspect. The only preservative against Popery which the Gordon rioters could think of was to demolish Catholic churches. Equally, in 1710, the pro-Sacheverell mob had gutted meeting-houses and conventicles to proclaim its horror of dissent. Even the Spitalfields weavers, those ubiquitous protesters (often, significantly enough, choosing Moorfields as their venue),[42] engaged in fire-raising. Their normal method of destroying Irish properties, for instance in the riots of 1736, was to break down the house with crowbars and other non-inflammatory tools. But they did burn an effigy of an unpopular master on other occasions;[43] and if the damage was less, the symbolism is hardly impaired. That the demolition of chapels was an invariable accompaniment of any sizeable riot in the eighteenth century is illustrated by the very terms of the Riot Act itself. Section IV proclaims:

> And be it further enacted by the authority aforesaid, That if any persons unlawfully, riotously, tumultuously assembled together, to the disturbance of the publick peace, shall unlawfully, and with force demolish or pull down any church or chapel, or any building for religious worship certified or registred according to the (Toleration Act) . . . or any dwelling-house, barn, stable or other out-house, that then such demolishing, or pulling down, or beginning to demolish, or pull down, shall be judged felony without benefit of clergy, and the offenders therein shall be judged felons, and shall suffer death as in the case of felony, without benefit of clergy.[44]

This was the act which was read (or more strictly its critical passage read) before the Spitalfields rioters in 1736,[45] and on subsequent occasions through the century. Looting, as with the Dunces, was secondary. The rioter engaged in destruction principally with regard to public or official residences (as with that of the Lord Chief Justice in 1780), and this indicates that he was dealing out a symbolic blow rather than seeking personal gain. Very rarely did the mob attack a bank, possibly because this institution had not yet become in the mind of the underprivileged an agency of repression. Religious buildings were the most regular target, and it is in connection with religion that Pope mentions duncely conflagrations (not without a private joke). Settle is made to boast:

> '. . . long my Party built on me their hopes,
> For writing pamphlets, and for burning Popes . . .'
> (A.III.282)

The note explains this juxtaposition of hack literature and ritual cremation:

> He (Settle) had managed the Ceremony of a famous Pope-burning on *Nov.* 17, 1680 . . .

This whole note, retained in the later version of the poem, is worthy of attention. Its astonishingly minute information should flatten at one blow the view that knowledge of the life-histories of the Dunces is extraneous to any literary assessment of the work.

Two final points may be mentioned. First, it is interesting that the fire insurance companies, so highly extolled by Defoe, were concerned over the prevalence of arson at this period. In 1716, for instance, two offices jointly announced a reward for information leading to the discovery of certain active fire-raisers.[46] This makes it all the more suitable that the King Dunce should be presented as a pyromaniac by inclination as much as by profession. Second, fire had long been linked imaginatively with portents and monstrous prodigies – as in, say, *Julius Caesar*. It is Settle, once more, who makes clear that the literary or theatrical aberrations of Grub Street are infractions of the natural order: breaches of cosmic order heralded by roaring flames, as breaches of civil order were announced by bonfires in the streets.

> Another Aeschylus appears! prepare
> For new abortions, all ye pregnant fair!
> In flames, like Semele's, be brought to bed,
> While op'ning Hell spouts wild-fire at your head. (B.III.313)

At the very jaws of the underworld, Dulness like a savage dances round the flames she has conjured up.

The threat of fire was insistent, and the memory of the events of 1666 recent enough to cut deeply into men's minds. But on the whole it was a threat either to property or to the peace;[47] law-abiding people could generally think that it wouldn't happen to them, and except in a very extreme case, such as the Gordon riots, the person of a private individual was unlikely to be in jeopardy. But not so with the other great nightmare – the plague. This could strike at anyone, however he or she might attempt to stay out of trouble. Appropriately, the Great Fire had stopped short at the very edge of Grub Street: Cripplegate church had had its windows scorched, but the structure had stood.[48] On the other hand, the Great Plague had raged through the parish for weeks on end.[49] As we have seen, disease had always been hard to combat in the fenny ground by Moorfields. If a writer wished (as many did) to present London as a breeding-ground for pestilence of every kind, Fleet Ditch was his most obvious symbolic recourse. But as far as actual mortality figures go, Cripplegate was as bad as Farringdon Ward Without.[50]

In 1728 there appeared under the imprint of James Roberts – sometime associate of Curll, publisher of Dunces but also of their chief enemies – a pamphlet called *A Trip through London*. This is an orthodox exercise in a genre owing something to the Roman satirists, something to Ned Ward and something to serious topography. Its opening words are representative:

> *London*, like the Ocean, that receives the muddy and dirty Brooks, as well as the clear and rapid Rivers, swallows up all the Scum and Filth, not only of our own, but of other Countries . . . continually emptying and discharging themselves into this grand Reservoir, or common Sewer of the World.

The writer's progress takes him from near Charing Cross, where a shower typically takes place, down the Strand and Fleet Street, through Little Britain into Cripplegate. Now we begin to realise the nature of the 'Scum and Filth' on the surface of London society. '*Hackney-Coachmen, Porters*, and all sorts of *Handicrafts* abound in *Cripplegate* Parish.' We are told that 'Mechanicks of both Sexes'

are rife in its population. Its low literary productions are mentioned
and its resident collection of quacks and frauds too. A whole paragraph is devoted to 'the Beggars of this Parish'. All round we are left
in no doubt as to the social character of the region.[51]

This emphasis on low surroundings is important. It was a commonplace of the literary imagination. Writers constantly saw disease
as coming to silent life in unobserved crannies, the hidden ulcers of
the city. The trope could be applied to the spread of both the Plague
and the Fire. For the latter, we need only recall Dryden's *Annus
Mirabilis*:

> Such was the Rise of this prodigious fire,
> Which in mean Buildings first obscurely bred,
> From thence did soon to open Streets aspire
> And straight to Palaces and Temples spread.[52]

The bacillus of Dulness, 'bred' in the nooks and alleys of Cripplegate, 'conceal'd from vulgar eye' (B.I.33), aspires to the open street –
the broad Strand for instance – and finally reaches St. James's, the
Chapel Royal, seething Westminster. The 'reservoir' of filth is likewise described as a receptacle for thieves and prostitutes. A City
Marshal who certainly knew the underworld well was Charles Hitchen, the homosexual and corrupt officer familiar to students of the
career of Jonathan Wild. In his attack on Wild, *The Regulator* (1718),
Hitchen apostrophises the city whose good order he was supposed to
maintain:

> *O London! London!* so much fam'd for thy good Order, by what Means
> is it now come to pass, that thou art become a Receptacle for a Den of
> Thieves and Robber, and all sorts of villainous Persons and Practices.[53]

Admittedly, this is hollow rhetoric, cheap and insincere into the bargain. But it shows precisely exactly the kind of moral topos available
to Pope when *The Dunciad* was taking shape; and it is this which lies
behind the calculated obscenities of the poem, as of those of *Peri
Bathous*.

A more substantial debt is to a work once greatly admired – perhaps excessively so – and now, as is the way, unduly deprecated.
Samuel Garth's *Dispensary* deserves more than its routine textbook

mention, if only because its satiric plant was so valuable when Pope retooled, as it were, for *The Dunciad*. Well, no: not only because of that, for it is a spirited and well sustained piece of mock-heroic poetry in its own right. But it *is* a fact that Pope continued to respect Garth long after the first burst of esteem for *The Dispensary* had been forgotten. Not the least pertinent factor here, I would suggest, is the manner in which Garth invokes Disease, 'most propitious Pow'r', and relates this to the social geography of London. He writes of the bills of mortality for St Giles' parish, the 'dreadful Shambles' round about the Fleet Ditch, and the 'Lewdness' of Covent Garden. In other words, he showed how health as a moral concept might be shadowed forth through the facts of what would later have been called public health. Thus to relate ethics and ecology is the special achievement of *The Dunciad* – but Garth had given the clue. Sometimes the allusiveness comes close to Pope's own, though the cadence is still that of Dryden:

> So thus at *Bothos*, when the *Gyants* strove
> T'invade the Skies, and wage a War with *Jove*;
> Soon as the *Ass* of old *Silenus* bray'd,
> The trembling Rebels in confusion fled.

But it is above all for his evocation of 'that devouring Harpy call'd *Disease*' that Garth was useful to the later poet.[54]

It would be possible to go through many minor productions of the Augustan era with the aim of illustrating the tenacity of the 'disease' image. But such tabulation is of limited utility, unless we can show that currency implies imaginative charge, as well as mere voltage in the circuit waiting to be switched on. One or two striking examples should suffice. There is, for example, a glaring fact on which I have never seen a comment. The historic Jonathan Wild was born in Wolverhampton about April 1683. This fact was well enough known to contemporaries: Defoe (if it is he who wrote the life mentioned earlier) gets the place and year both right. Captain Alexander Smith, who it is pretty safe to say was not Defoe (though one can never be sure) says 1684. Occasionally 1682 is found. Fielding, however, in his very free biography, substitutes a more evocative date:

> To omit other stories, some of which may be perhaps the growth of superstition, we proceed to the birth of our hero, who made his first appearance on this great theatre the very day when the plague first broke out in 1665. Some say his mother was delivered of him in an house of an orbicular or round form in Covent Garden, but of this we are not certain. He was some years afterwards baptized by the famous Mr. Titus Oates.[55]

Now it is conceivable that the text signifies 'on the anniversary of the outbreak of the plague'. But note first, that Fielding explicitly removes his account from the realms of legend (he means to be believed, he implies): second, that a fictitious London address is given for the accouchement, which any reader of the Defoe life – or its numerous rivals – would *know* to be fictitious. The joke about the roundhouse, or parish gaol, suggests that truth is being handled with some discretion. And then it would be unlike such a careful ironist as Fielding to leave an ambiguity like this if he didn't want it there. We are surely justified in concluding that this is one of the signs of a notable birth, to which Fielding has just been alluding, and that he intends the sentence to convey the meaning 'in the year 1665, around the end of April' (when the Plague did set in with increased virulence). If that is so, then the further deductions need little comment. Fielding is associating the reign of the Great (Bad) Man, the archcriminal, the commandant of the underworld, with the phenomenon of bubonic plague. Wild hits London in its seamiest quarters, just as the plague did: both began on the same day.

Jonathan Wild came out, in the *Miscellanies*, too late to be useful to Pope. Its hero had been named once or twice by Pope, in the conventional equation with Walpole:

> Down, down, proud Satire! tho' a Realm be spoil'd,
> Arraign no mightier Thief than wretched *Wild*,
> Or if a Court or Country's made a Job,
> Go drench a Pick-pocket, and join the Mob.[56]

Other references to disease in the writer's works are comparatively muted. 'Plague' and 'sore' are used in close proximity to 'Fool' in the fourth satire of Donne imitated: more neutrally, in the same poem, we have 'The whole Artill'ry of the Terms of War,/And (all those Plagues in one) the bawling Bar . . .' In the second Donne satire, poetry is said to be 'Catch'd like the plague, or love, the Lord knows how . . .', where the subliminal notion is that of venereal disease. Similarly in the *Epistle to Arbuthnot*, the 'Plague' is that incident to poets, i.e. the constant desire of his inferior brethren to badger him with their own lines. In the *Epistle to Bathurst* there is a bare reference to 'Some War, some Plague, or Famine they foresee.' Fever and pox appear together in the imitation of Swift.[57] But over all it is an unimpressive list, nothing beside Swift's catalogue of physical ailments and debilities. The truth is that Pope evolved a more indirect way of dealing with the 'unhealthy' implications of Dulness.

The language of *The Dunciad* is deeply infested: there are poetic 'Maggots', crawling about the crannies of the Cave, along with 'spawn' waiting to be hatched by 'a warm Third day'. There are showers of sermons, replenished like clouds 'from some bog below' (B.II.363). There is mention of ordure, evil vapours, a strange mutant 'vast egg': it is like a biological catastrophe brought about by the on-set of Dulness. One has the sense as one reads of observing weird medical research through a microscope:

> None want a place, for all their Centre found,
> Hung to the Goddess, and coher'd around.
> Not closer, orb in orb, conglob'd are seen
> The buzzing Bees about their dusky Queen. (B.IV.77)

This buglike quality of the Dunces is dramatically effective for more than one reason; but I draw attention to it here as it contributes to the disease motif – the festering, germ-ridden insect-world of the scribblers.

But the main hint was given by Gay, with the episode of Cloacina in *Trivia*. There is a particular link here, with the localisation of the episode in the vicinity of the Fleet Ditch (see the next section); but the device of projecting squalid, anarchically sexual, morbid Dulness through a mud-besmirched underworld landscape is of general in-terest. The joke exploits a psychological, if not then a verbal pun. At that date the predominant meaning of 'underworld' was the nether regions, Hades. An older usage, that of the lower world, i.e. this earth, survived as late as Rowe. But primarily the term connoted hell. Only in the nineteenth century did the modern sense of 'the lowest stratum of society' develop, according to *OED*. Nevertheless, it is not too hazardous to suggest that the 'nether world' of Hades and the nether world of criminal society had some imaginative fusion in Pope's mind. In *The Rape of the Lock*, canto IV, the 'dusky' spright Umbriel visits his home in the infernal regions, and

> Down to the Central Earth, his proper Scene,
> Repair'd to search the gloomy Cave of Spleen.
>   Swift on his sooty Pinions flits the *Gnome*,
> And in a Vapour reach'd the dismal Dome.
> No cheerful Breeze this sullen Region knows,
> The dreaded *East* is all the wind that blows.
> Here, in a Grotto, sheltred close from Air,
> And screen'd in Shades from Day's detested Glare,
> She sighs forever on her pensive Bed,
> *Pain* at her Side, and *Megrim* at her Head.
>   Two Handmaids wait the Throne: Alike in Place,
> But diff'ring far in Figure and in Face.[58]

The resemblance of this passage to the description of the cave of Dulness (that is, I have argued, Grub Street) is very marked. That description has already been quoted (p. 57), and here I shall merely pick out a few of the more striking parallels. The home of Dulness, like that of Spleen, is called a 'Dome' (B.I.265). Both cells are 'conceal'd from vulgar eye' (B.I.33), or screened from the light. Each is racked by 'keen, hollow winds' (B.I.35); one is a 'sullen Region', the other a 'bleak recess'. One is termed a 'Grotto', the other – with little more than elegant variation – as 'Cave' (B.I.34). Queen Dulness is attended by four guardian virtues; her rival Spleen has two handmaidens. In the earlier poem one of the attendants, Ill-nature, has her bosom filled with lampoons: in the later, there are allusions to Curll's chaste press, 'sepulchral Lyes' and 'all the Grub-street race'. With the Cave of Spleen 'A constant Vapour o'er the Palace flies'; with the Cave of Poverty, we are told, 'In clouded Majesty here Dulness shone'. Spleen changes bodies 'to various Forms', and

> Strange Phantoms rising as the Mists arise;
> Dreadful, as Hermit's Dreams in haunted Shades,
> Or bright as Visions of expiring Maids.[59]

'Fiends' and 'Spectres' throng the cave. Compare *The Dunciad*:

> All these, and more, the cloud-compelling Queen,
> Beholds thro' fogs that magnify the scene.
> She, tinsel'd o'er in robes of varying hues,
> With self-applause her wild creation views;
> Sees momentary monsters rise and fall,
> And with her own fools-colours gilds them all. (B.I.79)

With the exception of a few details of special significance (the 'momentary' monsters of Grub Street, say), these descriptions are interchangeable. That could be put another way: Pope bridges the gap between the eighteenth century and the modern senses of the word 'underworld'. He asserts, poetically, that the Hades of his time is the squalid 'Chaos dark and deep' infected by rogues, vagabonds, pimps, prostitutes – and hack writers. Hell, indeed, has its urban ghetto very much like Grub Street. The voyage from this world to the next in *The Dunciad*, significantly, takes the form of a descent into the filthy depths of the Fleet Ditch; the voyager is Jonathan Smedley. I shall return to this passage in the next section. At this point I stress only the explicit way in which the inferno is identified with the dirt of contemporary London. Pope's season in hell is spent on the shores of the Thames, shared by 'all from Paul's to Aldgate' (B.II.346).

It is tempting to recross some familiar ground, and illustrate the appositeness of the satire from eighteenth-century conditions. But this would be otiose. *The Dunciad* is not a report of the sanitary commissioners, and a detailed account of London squalor would not add very much to our appreciation of the poem. It is enough to accept the broad outline, as many authorities have handed it down to us. The streets were noisome in every respect; stench, ordure, germs, decomposing bodies of animals, malarial pests, slime and vomit – with such candidates as these, it is impossible to draw up an order of offensive magnitude. If things were bad in the daytime, they were worse at night. It did not need the Scourers or the Mohocks to make going abroad a perilsome affair. There were virtually no street lights; an attempt had been made to provide these in 1684 but 'the experiment was not a success . . . the fat used was derived from animals' intestines.' In 1734 a new scheme was introduced which 'dispelled some of the nocturnal gloom.' But in general London streets in Pope's day were dark as well as 'squalid and pestiferous'.[60]

Some parts of this general picture are relevant to the theme of this chapter, and these may be examined a little more closely. For example there is the condemnation which had been issued in 1636 by the College of Physicians (an institution bordering almost on the Fleet Ditch), regarding the spread of the plague by 'the neglect in cleansing sewers and town ditches, the presence of standing pools of foetid water, uncleanliness of the streets, the toleration of laystalls so near the living quarters, especially on the City's northern side . . .'[61] As we have seen (pp. 46–7 above), Moorfields was especially noted for this latter inconvenience. It is well known that foul ditches and sewers did much to encourage the plague in Shakespeare's London, but it may be forgotten that the notorious outbreaks of the infection in Jacobean and then in Restoration London were only the most serious among many. Somewhere on the continent, the plague was always raging fiercely; and epidemics, major or minor, persisted in England throughout the seventeenth century. In 1720 the plague flared up in the South of France. A national hubbub ensued, with a hotly contested Quarantine Bill and a series of warnings from Defoe among the consequences. Pope's great friend, Dr Arbuthnot, was called in by the Government to give advice. Later typhus, or 'gaol fever' as it was popularly named, became a greater scourge. This was a libel, inasmuch as the prisons were not the only insalubrious parts of the city. Contagious disease might just as aptly have been called 'suburban fever'. It was the malarial marshes on the outskirts of the ancient settlement – the ring of liberties between the walled city and the outparishes – which recorded the heaviest casualty figures every time the plague struck. And it struck often. Smallpox, too, had a high incidence rate in these districts. Several times I have referred to drains and ditches. The 'kennel' down the middle of the street was the most obvious form these took; but there were other conduits of one kind or another, filled with stagnant water and disagreeable jetsam. They ranged from the mighty Fleet Ditch, the great sink of London, to small culverts winding through the backways of the poorer dis-

tricts. Many were, of course, literally sewers: all fulfilled this function to some degree. Two important riders follow from the point
of view of the satirist. Firstly, there was a built-in joke in the name
'Grub Street', whether the writers knew it or not. The place incorporated in its very title (grub=ditch) an allusion to the major
single blot on the London landscape, and one of the main agencies of
disease.[62] Secondly, the presence of so many drains supplied the basis
for a striking satiric *motif* – the cloacal trope so widely encountered
in Augustan contexts.

Ian Watt has written that 'the whole subject of the cloacal image
in Augustan polemic cries out for the attention of some curious and
intrepid scholar.'[63] This is not the place for a full enquiry into the
subject, even supposing my qualifications matched, as they do not,
Watt's desiderata. Nonetheless, it is possible to suggest lines for research, and to list in a tentative way some of the rhetorical needs
which the figure met, in its graceless but effective fashion. Consider
this brief outline:

(1) The image served once again to link moral 'health' and sanitary welfare. It utilised the readily available facts of contemporary
existence, known to all readers, in order to enforce a wider social,
ethical or artistic judgement. A sewer, to put it crudely, would be a
much less potent image today because we rarely if ever see such a
thing; it has become another mode of the 'underworld', as distant
from most people's experience as Styx or as hell. (2) There was a
long tradition of idiomatic usage. The Cloaca Maxima had been as
notorious in its way as the Fleet Ditch, and Roman authors had developed its figurative applications – thus Plautus uses 'cloaca' of the
stomach of a drunken woman. (But the serious anatomical sense
appears to have grown up only in English.) Moreover, there was at
least one famous aphorism – 'A woman is a temple built on a sewer'
– which carried the right overtones of slightly comic disgust. Swift,
as we shall see, was to develop this idea with telling particularity.
The basis for the notion is very obvious: the orifice which both receives one kind of effluvium and disgorges its own. The drain collected its filth 'down below', as, according to this view, the female
pudenda did. A ditch could run beneath imposing buildings, as a

fair countenance concealed the nastiness below. (3) A sewer was a kind of public receptacle, into which any man could drop his own personal excretions; it was known to spread illness; if often flooded right over, and forced a channel into previously pure streams; and it was a tunnel between the upper and the lower world, between the city and the great river. Open sewers indeed were among the few direct communicating links from one part of London to another, in some areas of the town where the streets were little better than a maze. For all these reasons the 'cloaca' could easily be used to symbolise the way of life of the dregs of society, either morally or sociologically. In particular, it connoted, almost without the author's consciously desiring it, a measure of *sexual* corruption.

It was the Fleet Ditch above all which contained in itself these various implications. Or, to put the matter another way, it was the Ditch that dramatised in real life the imagistic possibilities of the term. On a third level, the mythological aspect was represented by the tutelary goddess of all sewers, Cloacina. John Gay had annotated *Trivia* thus: 'Cloacina was a Goddess whose image Tatius (a King of the Sabines) found in the common-shore, and not knowing what Goddess it was, he called it Cloacina from the place in which it was found, and paid it divine honours.'[64] Pope writes more curtly, 'The *Roman* Goddess of the Common-shores'.[65] Initially, however, she had been Cluaca Venus, the purifier. The satirists treat her as a kind of befouled Venus; the writers who are her devotees (living, as it were, on the edge of her mansion) likewise besmirch a noble name – that of literature.

In the ditches of London we find the Dunces plunging and wallowing and floundering. Like the strange water-beasts of *Peri Bathous*, they pride themselves on their capacity to sink ever more deeply into the mire. There are, to be sure, moral implications here – to dive headfirst, with one's backside uppermost, was to assume the very posture of folly – but mainly the value of this picture is a *comic* one. The Dunces are forced to suffer the indignities meted out by farce in every age. Instead of custard-pies in the face, Curll receives 'brown dishonours', having just slipped on a pool of urine made by his mistress. With such a passage, though it would technically be possible to relate the phraseology to the commonplaces of Augustan thought, it seems more tactful simply to leave unqualified the sheer bawdy exuberance:

> A place there is, betwixt earth, air, and seas,
> Where, from Ambrosia, Jove retires for ease.
> There in his seat two spacious vents appear,
> On this he sits, to that he leans his ear,
> And hears the various vows of fond mankind . . .
> In office here fair Cloacina stands,
> And ministers to Jove with purest hands.
> Forth from the heap she pick'd her Vot'ry's pray'r,
> And plac'd it next him, a distinction rare!
> Oft had the Goddess heard her servant's call,
> From her black grottos near the Temple-wall,
> List'ning delighted to the jest unclean
> Of link-boys vile, and watermen obscene;
> Where as he fish'd her nether realms for Wit,
> She oft had favour'd him, and favours yet.
> Renew'd by ordure's sympathetic force,
> As oil'd with magic juices for the course,
> Vig'rous he rises; from the effluvia strong
> Imbibes new life, and scours and stinks along;
> Re-passes Lintot, vindicates the race,
> Nor heeds the brown dishonours of his face. (B.II.83–108)

Here Pope makes an equivalence between Curll's fishing the 'nether realms' of Whitefriars for wit and sexual intercourse with Cloacina; such congress drugs him for the race ahead, as with a Tour de France cyclist. Characteristically Pope introduced into the later version the allusion to the 'Temple-wall'. This localises the event in the vicinity of Fleet Street, an area to which we can now turn more directly.

Artery of Dulness

If there had been no Fleet Ditch, the satirists would have had to invent one. The existence of such a notorious sore on the surface of London life proved to be an immense, though uncovenanted, gain to the Scriblerian party. The Ditch served their rhetorical needs perfectly. It symbolised, with an extraordinary fineness of imaginative 'tolerance', the squalid nature of Dulness. There are two main reasons for this special aptness.

(A) In the first place, the Ditch simply *was* all the things which Pope wishes to imply the home of the Dull should be. It was the literal embodiment of a cloacal metaphor. It did run beneath the street in places and so did constitute a link with the 'underworld'. It was a carrier of disease, smelly, unsightly, opaque with dirt, infested not only with bacteria but with hogs and human carcasses. The great Lord Clarendon seems to have been among the first writers (in that *History* which Tories of Pope's generation so venerated) to spell out the associations of the City of London into a moral formula: 'The Sink of the ill-humour of this Kingdom'.[66] A succession of later authors developed this hint with special reference to the Ditch until its name became a synonym for social, as well as physical, malady. Pope, Swift and Gay are notable for the literary effectiveness of their use of the idea, and not because they devised it.

It is important to remember just what purposes a ditch, any ditch, then served. The 'grubbe' of Grub Street would be first of all a water supply, for all its impurity. But in addition it might be used for a variety of functions, ranging from the burial of suicides to the demarcation of parish boundaries.[67] The Fleet itself was commandeered for every undignified need urban man can mentally compass. It was a latrine, a pigsty (or residential trough, one might say), a criminal escape-route, a primitive fire-precaution, and several other things as well. Of the portion of the ditch which ran through the Smithfield region, Mrs George observes:

> The Field Lane district was intersected by the filthy channel of the Fleet ditch (called in 1722 'a nauceious and abominable sink of nastiness'), into which the tripe dressers, sausage makers and catgut spinners, who shared the Lane with professional thieves, flung their offal.[68]

For centuries rubbish had been thrown into the Ditch, an existing right which men and women of the eighteenth century jealously preserved. It is natural that the Plague was particularly destructive along this appalling watercourse.[69]

For generations, there had been a vague resolve to do something about it. Stow records an effort to cleanse the 'dike' in 1502 and 1589, and efforts to remove the mills which had operated along the upper stretches, contributing further to the contamination of the stream.[70] The later developments have been summarised by T. F. Reddaway, and his account may be given verbatim:

> In former times the Fleet river had been navigable up to Holborn Bridge, but as the years passed it had gradually deteriorated into a shallow and evil-smelling sewer. Navigation had ceased and, in the middle of the seventeenth century, a not overparticular age, its condition had been described as 'very stinking and noisome'. Silt from the upper reaches, and mud and refuse from the growing streets in its valley had gradually choked it, with the result that, despite occasional cleansings, its condition more or less regularly troubled the minds of those in authority. During the reign of James I various projects had been put forward for clearing out accumulations down to the true floor of the channel, embanking its sides with brick, stone or timber, and then flushing it out at intervals from a reservoir constructed above Clerkenwell. The most detailed had envisaged grates on the upper waters to intercept debris and silt, a warden to remove carrion and bulky matter when the tide was out, and a vast grate at Bridewell to stop the Thames bringing up filth on the rising tide. Little seems to have come of them, and as the years passed an expanding population had added to the difficulties. The Commissioners of Sewers (in 1653) . . . clearly set out the evils which had arisen from this last cause. The river, they declared, from Hockley in the Hole to the Thames, was 'by many encroachments thereupon made by keeping of Hogs and Swine therein and elsewhere neer to it, the throwing in of Offals and Garbage . . . and by reason of many houses of office erected built and standing upon and over [it] and otherwise not only stopped . . . and become unpassable with boats . . . but also become [a] very . . . great prejudice . . . not only to the neighbourhood . . . but to the City of *London* and County of Middlesex.'[71]

Pope, we may interpose, did not invent the link between excretion and the Ditch which his poem joyfully celebrates.

As Reddaway continues, this valley 'where the crowded poor bred plagues, and divided authority clogged the wheels of reform, was something that the planners of 1666 could not possibly overlook.' Accordingly they drew up plans in due course for a canalised river, forty feet wide, navigable up to Holborn Bridge. There would be wharves on each bank and severe building restrictions in the environs. Compensation for lands adjoining the Fleet which had, in effect, to be compulsorily purchased caused some difficulty and delay; but ultimately work was started on the new scheme with plans drawn up by Robert Hooke, under the oversight of Wren. Even now there were a number of practical problems which impeded the project. This was despite the unusual lack of corruption displayed by the main contractor, Thomas Fitch. As Reddaway observes,

> throughout [the contract] he was hampered by the mud and refuse coming down from Turnmill Brook [that is, precisely the outflow from Smithfield which Swift describes in his 'City Shower'] and the streets round the channel. Piles of rubbish, wood and building materials, illicitly left on the wharves he was levelling were almost as great a hindrance . . . Warfare and weather both affected progress. Heavy storm caused floods in Turnmill Brook, and war with the Dutch brought the ravages of press-gangs.[72]

Thus once again we find the connection between the seamier parts of London with the depredations of war, coupled here with a reference to the city shower which Swift was to convert into a Virgilian image of Grub Street.

Nevertheless, Fitch went about his duties in a conscientious way, and by 1674 the work was completed. Unfortunately, the costly and imaginative enterprise of building the canal was not a success. The district soon reverted to its character; in Reddaway's words,

> In an area with all too few open spaces the broad stretch on each side of the channel was a temptation too great to be resisted. They were used as standing-grounds for carts, as storage places for timber, and as dumps for rubbish . . . Carts and coaches alike passed so often . . . that the pavements were broken and the roofing of the vaults threatened.

There were many critics of the scheme, Ned Ward among them, who gave as his view the statement that the cellar warehouses were so damp as to be useless 'except to Frogs, toads, and other vermin.' Thus did a duncely haunt revert to type, with an ecological shift not unlike the 'entropy' which Edwards sees as the process of Dulness in its metaphysical aspect. It quickly emerged that there was much more need for a north-west thoroughfare at this point than for a canal, which benefited only a limited number of coal merchants. Shoe Lane, of which more presently, was the main road then in existence, and it was not much of a street. Ultimately the authorities bowed to the inevitable, and just after the first version of *The Dunciad*, in 1733, the canal was arched over from Holborn Bridge down to Fleet Bridge. The central strip became a covered market. Then in 1766 the remainder of the canal, down to the Thames, was covered in, shortly before that hotly debated architectural feature, Blackfriars Bridge, went up. The Fleet Market survived till 1829 (the year before Grub Street, as such, disappeared), when Farringdon Street was built. The Canal, then, must be accounted a failure. Reddaway believes that 'an evil slum had been made attractive', and that the balance is in favour of the scheme.[73] But there is plenty of contemporary evidence that the region of the Fleet Ditch was still regarded as a fetid, rank and disagreeable place after the construction of the Canal. Certainly Pope and his friends found it no less available for their satiric purposes.

(B) This circumstance can only be understood in the context of another factor which gave the Ditch its peculiar applicability. The fortunes of the Fleet River have been encapsulated in a neat formula, that is decline from a river to a brook, from a brook to a ditch, and from a ditch to a drain. But this drop in the world was not entirely a function of what went on in, or on, the channel itself. A good deal of the disrepute into which it sank can only be explained by reference to the places it ran through or near or alongside. The Fleet, in a word, was a conduit which linked virtually all the most wretched corners of the city.

A few examples should suffice. The Ditch did not actually drain Grub Street, since it was the Walbrook which arose in the Moorfield swamp and flowed sluggishly down to the Thames near London Bridge, some half a mile to the east of the Fleet's own 'estuary'. But there was scarcely any other haunt of the Dunces which was not transversed by the Fleet or its tributary streams, as it meandered down from Hampstead through King's Cross, Clerkenwell, Holborn and Blackfriars. For example:

(a) Prisons. A representative list is Defoe's survey of 'Public Gaols' in his *Tour*. Four important prisons named in the first six – Newgate, Ludgate, the Fleet, and Bridewell – were all immediately contiguous to the Ditch. The 'New-Prison' and 'New-Bridewell' were both in Clerkenwell, near to the stinking middle stretches of the Fleet. There were roundhouses in Farringdon Ward Without.[74]

(b) Smithfield, with all its unpleasant associations (see pp. 37–38) was drained by Turnmill Brook, which fed the Ditch. Because of the lie of the land, a great deal of refuse was shipped out of this region (notably the offal of slaughter-houses) along the same undesirable waterway.[75]

(c) To the north lay Clerkenwell, with an almost equally repugnant set of associations, ranging from bear-baiting and cudgel-play to organised crime. Here too many writers found their home (see below pp. 159–60).[76]

(d) The whole of the ward of Farringdon Without was an epitome of the worst sides of eighteenth-century London life. Holborn with its notoriety for sexual irregularities of every kind; the area round Lincoln's Inn Fields, where riot and violence were daily phenomena; and the region round Fleet Street itself, where the less reputable side of the publishing trade was established and every kind of crime flourished: these and districts like them made up the ward.[77]

There were other, special, reasons for the bad character of the region. Whitefriars, for instance, had for centuries been a licensed refuge of the dissolute. There was Bridewell, too, which as a house of correction combined some of the sadder features of Bedlam with those of the ordinary gaol. In short, had the Ditch been as limpid and sparkling as Helicon, it would have had a bad name. The guilt it bore by association was that attaching to places such as Newgate, Saffron Hill, Smithfield, Whitefriars and Holborn. The Newgate Calendar recorded the daily experience of men and women who lived by the Fleet. In turn, the humours of the Fleet cling round many a Newgate pastoral, for it was across the Ditch that the road to Tyburn ran; just as these same humours eddy thickly round the Goddess Dulness herself. Rising fogs prevail in every quarter which the Fleet reached; its moist influence, 'cloud-compelling' like that of the Queen, 'spawns' pests and 'maggots' such as nonsense took to itself. To beat the bounds of the parish of St Bride's or St Dunstan's,[78] to make a perambulation of the Fleet Rules, was to take a walk on the wild side. We need look in detail at only a limited number of the named localities to see the distressing reality which lay behind the vibrant metaphor Pope made out of the Ditch.

If we begin at the mouth of the Fleet river, near to the point where the Dunces gathered for their games, there was on the right (western) bank the precint of Whitefriars.[79] On this region Macaulay has written a superb passage, blending as usual massive and calculated overstatement with delicate precision of detail:

> We may easily imagine what, in such times, must have been the state of the quarters of London which were peopled by the outcasts of society. Among those quarters one had attained a scandalous preeminence. On the confines of the City and the Temple had been founded, in the thirteenth century, a House of Carmelite Friars, distinguished by their white hoods. The precinct of this house had, before the Reformation, been a sanctuary for criminals, and still retained the privilege of protecting debtors from arrest. Insolvents consequently were to be found in every dwelling, from cellar to garret. Of these a large proportion were knaves and libertines, and were followed to their asylum by women more abandoned than themselves. The civil power was unable to keep order in a district swarming with such inhabitants; and thus Whitefriars became the favourite resort of all who wished to become emancipated from the restraints of the law. Though the immunities legally belonging to the place extended only to cases of debt, cheats, false witnesses, forgers, and highwaymen found refuge there. For amidst a rabble so desperate no peace officer's life was in safety. At the cry of 'Rescue' bullies with swords and cudgels, and termagant hags with swords and broomsticks, poured forth by hundreds; and the intruder was fortunate if he escaped back into Fleet Street, hustled, stripped and pumped upon.[80]

In placing the pindaric writer (Ambrose Philips) at an unseemly address in Whitefriars (see p. 78), Pope was suggesting that the hack

151

writer wished 'to become emancipated from the restraints' of poetic law. It is notable that Cripplegate was likewise renowned for its population of forgers and highwaymen. 'Alsatia', as the district was also known, was long celebrated for street brawls; Shadwell's fine comedy *The Squire of Alsatia* (1688) fills out some of these associations. In Hogarth's *Industry and Idleness*, Plate 9, Tom Idle is shown betrayed by a prostitute in an infamous house of Blood Bowl Alley (later Hanging Sword Alley), in the heart of Alsatia.[81]

More directly relevant are the literary associations. In earlier years a good deal of the book trade had been centred in Whitefriars, and it is still common to find printers settled in this area at the time of *The Dunciad*. Stanley Morison records several cases where the imprint of a newspaper indicates Whitefriars as its provenance. John Ogilby was in business here; John Purser, another printer of the period, had establishments successively in Shoe Lane, just across Fleet Street, and in Salisbury Court. From 1724 onwards this latter square had a more distinguished member of the trade as an occupant, namely Samuel Richardson. At first the famous printer-novelist took a house 'in the centre' of the Court; but by 1755 this structure was unsafe, at any rate for the purpose of carrying on the printing trade, and Richardson did not renew the lease. Instead he built a new printing plant, with an adjoining residence, on the north of Salisbury Court, reached from Fleet Street via Whitefriars Street. Among writers, both Shadwell and Dryden lived in this district; whilst there is a persistent, if unconfirmed, story that Defoe fled to the sanctuary of Alsatia to escape his creditors. Amongst Pope's acquaintances the printer William Bowyer, jr., was living in Whitefriars around 1740, as an extant letter from the poet makes clear.[82]

Here we have the classic set of duncely circumstances – crime, debtors, prostitutes, street-affrays, the book trade, minor authors and the rest. It is almost as if the baneful influence of the Fleet had predetermined the character of the region. Much the same applies to Bridewell. The infamous House of Correction is mainly of interest with regard to Swift. But it figures too in Defoe, in Hogarth's *Harlot's Progress*, in Ned Ward's *London Spy* and elsewhere. It was closely associated with Bedlam on the one hand and with the other gaols of the Fleet on the other: indeed, as the Webbs showed many years ago, the distinction between the prison proper, intended for the reception of felons, and the house of correction, intended for vagabonds and the incorrigibly idle, gradually vanished over this period.[83] The hospital was largely destroyed in the Great Fire, but was speedily rebuilt. Among the new developments was a new stone bridge, erected to replace the former wooden Bridewell Bridge. This was apparently designed by Wren himself, possibly on the model of the Rialto at Venice. It was this graceful footbridge which can be seen in Hayman's illustration of the mud-diving episode of *The Dunciad*; the artist has even perched the Goddess herself on the parapet of the bridge.[84] It is a succint comment on the connotations of Bridewell. Pope selected the venue with several obvious considerations in mind. There was the 'flagellation' of naked men and women (mentioned at B.II.270); the links with the Fire, with Bedlam, with vagrancy and idleness (Pope and Swift are generally ironical when they imply that they wish to find a good 'hospital' where superannuated Dunces may rest their bones); and above all the proximity of the Ditch (Stow in fact calls it Bridewell Ditch). A sizeable portion of the land belonging to Bridewell had to be taken to enlarge the quay when the Fleet Canal improvements were under way. This cannot have improved the vicinity to any marked degree: Bridewell Lane was generally clogged with debris and rubbish. Finally, had Pope known about it, he would undoubtedly have found applicable the events of 1780, when the Gordon rioters opened up Bridewell and the militia were forced to maintain a presence there for some two months. There were many felons active in this district during the riot, possibly because it was the custom to dispatch transported convicts from Blackfriars Stairs. With his customary propriety Pope has his Dunces gather at a place of assignation otherwise reserved for jailbirds.[85]

Moving up the Fleet we encounter a succession of such milieux. Fleet Street itself carried over many of the darker doings of Whitefriars. Beggars or vagrants were strongly in evidence, streetfights were commonplace, printers and journalists were already concentrated here. Curll had several places of business in and around the street; Lintot, Gilliver, and Jacob Robinson all set up shop there; Pope, indeed, used Robinson's shop as a sort of poste-restante for Warburton's correspondence in 1740.[86] At least one celebrated woman criminal, Sarah Malcolm, familiar through Hogarth's graphic study, was executed in Fleet Street;[87] a few years before Moll Frith had operated her thief-taking business from the same address.[88] The district from Temple Bar to the Ditch was notorious for alehouses and brandy shops, as Jonathan Wild's reply to Hitchen indicates;[89] drunks regularly fell right into the Ditch, and came up probably little less besmeared than Pope's divers. In 1756 it was stated that 'the most flagitious of the poor' lived in this locality.[90] Inevitably, the Plague was especially virulent 'in dirty alleys and festering courts about the Fleet River and the debtors' prison, horrible for their mixed poverty and dissoluteness'.[91] The prison itself stood a little way off, to the north-east of the modern Ludgate Circus. It was destroyed in the Fire, and again during the Gordon Riots. Supplies for the Prison were brought up the Ditch,[92] and the stench of the place must have penetrated into the heart of the gaol.

The Fleet was, of course, the debtor's prison first and foremost. The common side was especially notorious on account of the wretched conditions in which its inhabitants lived. It was here that Pickwick found Alfred Jingle, reduced to a shadow of his previous plausible substance. The existence of great cruelties in the fearsome dungeons of the Fleet was brought to light just as *The Dunciad* came to birth. A commission of enquiry headed by the philanthropist Oglethorpe was appointed in 1727, and in due course they produced a horrifying indictment of the way in which debtors' prisons – notably the Fleet – were managed. Much of the blame fell on the Warden of the Prison, Bambridge, whose name has gone down to history with no happy associations thanks to Hogarth's painting which depicts Bambridge's appearance before the Committee in 1729.[93] However, the severities of the gaol were by no means confined to the extortions of a single warden of sadistic character. Within a few years, well before the appearance of the revised *Dunciad*, Hogarth had added further dimensions to the iconography of the Prison. Tom Rakewell is seen in Plate VII of the *Rake's Progress* confined to a stone cell and attended by three gruesome personages.[94] His debts had been contracted in another duncely environment, St Giles': his only remaining port of call was to be Bedlam. The Fleet was the road to Bedlam, as it was to every place of ultimate humiliation in eighteenth-century London. In Defoe's *Complete English Tradesman* (1725), we are told of the wit turned tradesman whose saga ends in bankruptcy, with 'the Epilogue in the *Fleet Prison* or the *Mint*'.[95] The social prejudices of Defoe and of Pope were not, of course, identical. None the less this decline in fortune resembles that suffered by many a Dunce; as we have seen, hack writers did find themselves in the debtors' sanctuary at the Mint, and several, including Defoe, Settle and Theophilus Cibber, underwent confinement in the Fleet Prison.

Other gaols within close proximity of the Ditch were Ludgate, Newgate (where Tom Idle lay in fiction, Jack Sheppard in reality, and Defoe found himself on two occasions at least),[96] the House of Correction in Cold Bath Fields, west of the Ditch, and the two Clerkenwell prisons. There was, too, the Old Bailey, which owned a variety of associations with the most desperate malefactors of the age. Modern Fleet Lane, in the shadow of Holborn Viaduct station, lies at the very centre of this region.[97]

No contemporary could fail to be aware of the pageantry of Newgate. The 'Memoirs of Malefactors', published by successive Ordinaries of Newgate Prison (among whom was Thomas Purney, listed by Pope as one of Curll's authors), constituted one branch of literary Dulness in action. We recall, too, the dying confessions of men like Sheppard and Wild which are numbered amongst Defoe's contributions to the literature of roguery. Pope specifically mentions this practice in a note to the 'Epilogue to the Satires', Dialogue II:

> *Fr.* Yet none but you by Name the Guilty lash;
> Ev'n *Guthry* saves half *Newgate* by a Dash.
> Spare then the Person, and expose the Vice.[98]

'Lash' is a graphically appropriate verb, since it calls up so many of the brutal connotations of the gaol. It is striking that Pope adumbrates such a topic – central to any assessment of the artistic ends of *The Dunciad* – with reference to the habits of the underworld, social and literary. The fact is that Pope regularly frames a response to his most basic dilemmas as an author in terms of concrete allusion to the actuality of his times. We recall, too, that Newgate was the place of confinement for the most desperate and dangerous criminals; and that gaol fever raged there on many occasions.[99]

One custom overshadowed all others, as regards the criminal ecology of this part of London. This was the almost royal progress of a condemned criminal from the prison to the scaffold at Tyburn. The ostensible business was simply to convey the convict from Newgate gatehouse, at the edge of the ancient city, to the junction of Tyburn Lane and the Oxford road – that is to say, to present-day Marble Arch. In reality the procession was ritualised into a kind of black mass version of the journey to Calvary.[100] The extent of the parody may be gauged from the fact that, amongst the stations of this particular journey, there was a halt at the Bowl on the corner of St Giles' High Street and Hog Lane. Here the convicted man would be offered a drink, almost as Christ was given wine mixed with gall prior to His crucifixion. (A popular highwayman could also count on a following of 'a great multitude of people, and of women who bewailed and lamented him,' as St Luke has it.) The other circumstances of this journey will be taken up in relation to Swift's 'City Shower'. Here it is sufficient to remark that the major ceremonial acts were performed around Holborn Bridge, on Snow Hill or outside St Sepulchre's church. Old Bailey, where Jonathan Wild set up his thieftaking business, ran south from this point, parallel to the Ditch on the other side of the Fleet Prison. From 1752 the body of the criminal was brought back for dissection to Surgeon's Hall in Old Bailey. Prior to that, as in the case of Tom Nero, the anatomy was conducted in Monkwell Street, over towards Cripplegate.[101]

There were plenty of other reasons why a well-bred young person would not have been conducted to this district. The reputation it bore is well caught in a passing remark by Boswell when he first came up to the capital: 'I then thought of having obscure lodgings, and actually looked up and down the bottom of Holborn and towards Fleet Ditch for an out-of-the-way place. How very absurd are such conceits! . . . When a man is out of humour, he thinks he will vex the world by keeping away from it . . .'[102] Of course, many Dunces

likewise looked up and down the Ditch for a lodging; the difference
was that they were seeking not isolation from their 'world' – duncely
society flourished in this very quarter – but a cheap place to rest their
head. As we have seen, one of Curll's authors, very likely John Oldmixon, is located by Pope 'at the alley over against St *Andrews
Holborn*'. Professional writers slightly higher in the social scale, such
as John Hughes, might take up residence in the better addresses over
Holborn, in this case Red Lion Street.[103] Most inhabitants of Farringdon Ward Without, nevertheless, occupied less auspicious quarters. Hogarth places his second stage of cruelty outside Thavies
Inn; whilst the area round about Lincoln's Inn was infamous for
many generations as a scene of riot, dissolute behaviour and robbery.[104] As to Holborn itself, it had acquired a special name for the
practice of unnatural vice. When Thomas Amory, in *John Buncle*,
said of Curll that his translators 'lay three in a bed at the Pewter
Platter Inn in Holborn', one suspects that there may be more behind
the joke than innocent rumour.[105] Curiously enough, one writer I
have definitely located as a native of Farringdon Ward was the ally
of Pope, and principal informant on the doings of the hacks; namely
Richard Savage, who was born in Fox Court, Holborn, and baptised
at St Andrew's.[106] His birth, however, was somewhat exceptional in
its circumstances. Certainly it was a common exercise for respectable
people to find the quickest way out of Farringdon. Miss Sterling,
in *The Clandestine Marriage*, would list it among the dull districts she
wanted to quit for the dear regions of Grosvenor Square; whilst the
author of *A Trip through London* (1728) makes his representative
parvenu a citizen of the ward. Since it also included such blackspots as Shoe Lane, with its sponging-houses, its cockpit, its prostitutes and its nooks and alleys; as well as Stonecutter Street, where
dark deeds were accepted as part of life – in this light, it is obvious
why the effective parish of the Fleet was shunned by the better
classes.[107] To do them justice, the Dunces would possibly have
shunned it too, if they could have afforded to.

To the north of the ward lay Smithfield. The numerous unhappy
associations of this district have been noted. The name had indeed
become a sort of semantic coral reef, in which there were encrusted

myriads of fossilised allusions, practically all of them pejorative in character. When Pope used this proper noun in the first couplet of his great poem, he was gaining the effect otherwise attainable only by a string of opprobious epithets. It is true that these submerged meanings were quite outside the control of the satirist to make or unmake. The point is that he did nothing to neutralise them or to silence them. Primarily we are to think of the low farces of Bartholomew Fair, to which Pope directs our attention in his note. At the same time, the attentive reader is perfectly free to summon in his mind any number of notions connected with Smithfield – the thieves' kitchen, the legacy of Jonathan Wild, the crowd of aliens among the inhabitants, the filth and garbage of the market, the wretched living conditions. It should not occasion surprise by now that after the Gordon riots the officers charged to seek out the main culprits reported back dolefully from Smithfield: Chick Lane and its environs made up 'almost a town in itself' where a republic of thieves lived securely isolated.[108] Pope, of course, rams home the message. He remarks in a note (A.III.281) that Elkanah Settle 'kept a Booth at *Bartlemew-fair* . . .', and at length was charitably received into the nearby Charterhouse. When we add that Turnmill Lane became known as 'Sodom', the picture is nearly complete.[109] It seems almost inevitable that a writer of the time (actually in the *British Journal* of 24 April 1728) should compare 'the Droves that are carried to Tyburn with those sent to Smithfield for the same purpose.'[110] The Fleet Ditch bore along with its sluggish flow a perpetual slaughter-house, both animal and human.

Such then was the ward of Farringdon Without. Its main constituent parishes all had the Ditch as an eastern boundary at some point although St Bride's straddled the Fleet. St Dunstan's ran as far west as Temple Bar, which might indifferently be caparisoned with the head of a highwayman or a Jacobite.[111] St Andrew's, Holborn, stretched from Holborn Bridge to Chancery Lane; it included part of Smithfield, as did St Sepulchre's. By a species of urban blight, familiar to modern sociologists, the baneful influence of the Ditch seeped damply over the most remote parts of each parish.[112] It could be felt almost as far as it could be smelt.

Technically, the Fleet Rules stretched rather less than a mile,[113] though it is doubtful whether unfrocked clergymen performing unlicensed marriages in the Prison worried about the matter. As a result, the upper reaches of the River, above Holborn Bridge, were less immediately thought of in connection with the squalor that the name portended. All the same, Clerkenwell was traversed by the same fearful sewer as Blackfriars and Holborn. In some ways, this part of London serves as a link between·the Fleet and Cripplegate. Its overall character was perhaps a little less unsavoury than that of its southern neighbourhood. But it was nothing to boast of; and a minor writer like Henry Carey who came to settle there,[114] or a hack like John Duick who eked out a precarious livelihood in the district, would be unlikely to advertise the fact.[115] The most celebrated literary connection of Clerkenwell was St John's Gate, the home of the *Gentleman's Magazine* from 1731. Here Johnson worked for some time; in nearby St John's Street Dr Thomas Birch kept his no doubt disorderly household. Charles Ackers, a printer of more than one duncely production, operated from St John's Close.[116] The man whom Johnson has immortalised, out of the Dunces' rank where he perhaps belongs, Richard Savage, frequented the Cross Keys Inn opposite St John's Gate.[117] James Bailey, a leading member of the Stationers' Company, lived in St John's Square.[118] To shift personalities a little, it is intriguing to recall that Moll Flanders, on the run from a husband for once, took lodgings in St John's Street, or 'as it is vulgarly called, St Jones', The two prisons of this quarter also figure in Defoe's narrative of Jack Sheppard; who made his escape from the New Prison via the yard of the adjacent Bridewell.[119]

Above all, there was Edward Cave, who set up the *Gentleman's Magazine* from the old gatehouse of the Knights of St John of Jerusalem. In this incongruous setting Samuel Johnson, as his best modern biographer has it, 'found out what it was like to be a hack writer'. Such an initiation naturally took place a matter of yards from the Ditch. Cave's connection with that ever-present symbol is even more direct, however. In 1740 he dammed up a part of the Fleet near his establishment, on the northern edge of Smithfield, and built a mill to drive a newfangled spinning machine. Many people including at least one Dunce (James Ralph) thought it would have been a good thing if the whole Ditch were filled in for good. But that event had to wait till 1766; a blessing for the satirists, if for nobody else.[120]

The first writer of distinction to accept the gift offered up by the local *cloaca maxima* was Ben Jonson. His poem, 'On the famous Voyage', appeared in his *Epigrammes* of 1616. Not exactly satiric, this is rather a species of whimsical mock-heroic: daringly contrived, but not altogether successful. Two revellers, having dined well in the City, 'propos'd to goe to Hol'borne in a wherry' from Blackfriars, or more strictly from a 'Docke'

> . . . that called is Avernus,
> Of some Bride-well . . .

This is the precise site of the goings-on in *The Dunciad*; and Pope, too, could have spoken of 'The many perills of this Port'. The intrepid voyagers encounter stench, mud, oozing gases. Jonson's description isolates many of the features which the Augustan authors were to attribute to every Grubean environment:

> . . . an ayre, as hot, as at a muster
> Of all your night-tubs, when the carts doe cluster,
> Who shall discharge first his merd-urinous load:
> Through her wombe they make their famous road,
> Between two walls; where, on one side, to sacramen,
> Were seene your ugly Centaures, yee call Car-men,
> Gorgonian scolds, and Harpyes: on the other
> Hung stench, diseases, and old filth, their mother,
> With famine, wants, and sorrows many a dosen.
> The least of which was to the plague a cosen.

Though the poetic manner is consciously archaic, the range of implications achieved by Jonson points forward and not back. This is a journey from this world to the next, a visit to the shades; but it is at the same time a conducted tour of the parishes round the Fleet. There is a Virgilian downpour, whereby the travellers are 'shitten'; as with Swift's *Tale*, the great natural phenomena are reduced to a fart. Besides the open coprophilia, there are several hints of a sexual meaning; indeed, it is a cause for wonder that the Freudians have never got to work on this poem. Throughout, classical mythology is used to underpin the fiction; inevitably, the gods are a little soiled in the process, but such deflation does not seem to be Jonson's main purpose.

At length the voyagers reach 'the Stygian poole', where 'thicke frequente mists' such as envelop Dulness prevail. They pass on from Styx to Acheron, 'the ever-boyling floud'. Here 'your Fleet-lane Furies' dwell; the image changes from that of a sewer to that of a kitchen, where offal is put into a 'pastie' and the scalding steams 'make the place hell'. This is a region where (remembering that latrines were generally built over a watercourse)

> . . . each privies seate,
> Is fill'd with buttock [.] And the walls doe sweate
> Urine and plaisters [.] when the noise doth beate
> Upon your eares, of discords so un-sweet?
> And out-cryes of the damned in the Fleet?
> Cannot the Plague-bill keepe you backe? nor bells
> Of loud Sepulchres with their hourely knells,
> But you will visit grisly Pluto's hall?
> Behold where Cerberus, rear'd on the wall
> Of Hol'borne (three sergeants heads) lookes ore,
> And stayes but till you come unto the dore!

Privies, discord, noise, the Fleet Prison, plague, the bells of Old Bailey tolling for the condemned man – it is more or less an induction to Popian comedy. In the last few lines of his poem Jonson introduces an ale-house keeper, a role fit for Dunces such as Ned Ward. The very last line ends with the crude dismissive pun, '[the Muse] that sung A-JAX.' It is not the *Iliad* but a later heroic poem which Jonson brings to our mind in the event.[121]

The leap forward to Pope's lifetime involves no great feat of imaginative yoking. At the turn of the seventeenth century, Samuel Garth was to write in *The Dispensary* of 'those dreadful Shambles' round about the Ditch. Apothecaries' Hall he locates in the familiar mythological terms:

> Nigh where *Fleet Ditch* descends in Sable Streams
> To wash his Sooty *Naiads* in the *Thames*;
> There stands a Structure on a Rising Hill,
> Where *Tyro*'s take their Freedom out to Kill.

The Hall stood in Water Lane, Blackfriars. After this a whole series of poems were devoted to the humours of the Fleet. As W. G. Bell has said, 'A collection of Fleet Ditch odes would not be edifying.'[122] Even after the first portion of the Ditch had been filled in, we find references to 'that drain'd barren Sluice'.[123] The best of these poems is perhaps Arthur Murphy's 'Ode to the Naiads of the Fleet Ditch' (1761), a reply to Churchill: but this does little more than fill out Garth's conceit.

In fact Pope had only one important source among contemporaries; and that was his friend Gay. In 1720 Gay added to the second book of *Trivia* an episode of some one hundred and twenty lines concerning the goddess Cloacina. In fact, he devised a fable which serves to distance the narrative and to put the poem into a timeless continuum. Both the tone and content of *Trivia* have misled readers into imagining that its leading strategies are journalistic. Yet, as perceptive critics have recently drawn to our attention, it is a complex feat of rhetorical engineering. In one way the poem plays the usual mock-heroic game according to the standard rules (that is, a squalid and debased present is belittled by implied comparison with an heroic past). But *Trivia* is no more a straightforward mock-heroic than it is straight reportage. As with Pope, Gay takes the actual and topical as a limiting case: the poetry employs social observation to make permanent moral comment; it employs moral emblems, such as the Fleet, to state a sociological truth. In variety of resource and panache of detail, *Trivia* is great poetry; and it is time we acknowledged it as such.

Gay starts with a misleadingly conventional bit of mythologising. Just as Jove had been wont to range 'this nether world' (i.e. the earth, but a possible ambiguity is already created), so the fashion spread to 'vulgar Deitys'. Amongst them, Cloacina '(Goddess of the tide/Whose sable streams beneath the city glide)'. She falls in love with a 'mortal scavenger'. On hearing his 'cart' she approaches him, adopting the airs of a 'night-wandring harlot' and the disguise of 'the black form of a cinder-wench'. The assignation is conducted in a dark alley. Its predictable outcome, after nine months have elapsed, is the birth of a boy, 'dropt' beneath a bulk. Bulks figure largely in the legend of Grub Street, since many hacks, from Savage on, were alleged to spend their nights sleeping on them. At all events, the 'beggar's brat' thus sired grows up in the streets of London. He becomes a shoe-shine boy in a stall in the vicinity of the Fleet. Idle through lack of business, standing above 'the black canal of mud,/ Where common-shores a lulling murmur keep,/Whose torrents rush from Holborn's fatal steep,' he bemoans his sad condition. This is extremely dense poetry. The first joke, of course, is to refer to the stagnant Ditch in terms appropriate to a clear mountain stream in Arcady; 'fatal' because of the link with the procession to Tyburn. The common-shores are initially 'the land on both sides of the Fleet-ditch, where refuse gathered or was dumped until the tide came up and washed it away.' But by this time the moral overtones of the phrase were strongly evident. The open channels of refuse became a shorthand term for filth of every kind, as in Air XXI, 'Oh Mr. Constable', of Fielding's *Author's Farce* (1730).

Cloacina feels pity for her deserted child, and obtains help from the other deities in preparing a new japanning oil which will easily bring a fine polish to the most heavily besmeared shoes. She descends to the earth, and 'shoots beneath the tides' of the Ditch to await the morning, when she can make her epiphonal entrance.

> The Goddess rose amid the inmost round,
> With wither'd turnip tops her temple crown'd;
> Low reach'd her dripping tresses, lank, and black
> As the smooth jet, or glossy raven's back;
> Around her waste a circling eel was twin'd,
> Which bound her robe that hung in rags behind . . .
> The Goddess plunges swift beneath the flood,
> And dashes all around her show'rs of mud:
> The youth strait chose his post; the labour play'd
> Where branching streets from Charing-cross divide;
> His treble voice resounds along the *Meuse*,
> And White-hall echoes—*Clean your Honour's shoes.*

Thus the orphan achieves independence. It is impossible to believe that Pope did not have this passage in mind when he came to write his description of the Goddess Dulness, her robes and her rags; or the bawling contest, where Westminster and Hungerford 're-echo' (A.II.254) – Hungerford market stood almost exactly where the boy took his station – or the account of the Dunces who themselves 'plunge beneath the flood'. Gay's anecdote can be read as a charming fancy, along the lines of Thomas Parnell's treatment of the Pandora's box theme in 'Hesiod'. But there is more to it than that. The myth of Cloacina articulates a strand of thought otherwise present in the poem only inchoately. The episode, in brief, suggests that there is something energetic and life-giving about the currents of filth that course beneath the streets of London (or beside them). Gay makes something almost pretty out of the showers of mud that bespatter citizens; the dirt can perhaps be identified with the lower segments of society – it has certainly become part of the moving stream of the city, a kind of urban hormone which sets the activity of the whole town in motion.[124]

Pope approaches similar ideas in a very different way. Nevertheless there are enough points of connection to make the transition a fairly easy one. The events of *The Dunciad* are even more accurately placed than those of *Trivia*:

> This labour past, by Bridewell all descend,
> (As morning pray'r, and flagellation end)
> To where Fleet-ditch with disemboguing streams
> Rolls the large tribute of dead dogs to Thames,
> The King of dykes! than whom no sluice of mud
> With deeper sable blots the silver flood. (B.II.269)

The Fleet is king of dykes in the sense that Cibber is king of poets. Behind the last line we can discern a host of earlier lines, celebrating such tributaries of the Thames as 'The blue, transparent Vandalis'.[125] It is in this carefully defined location that the venal bookmakers compete to discover 'him who dives the best'. There is a culminating example here of Pope's ability to make the facts of geography body forth a degrading critique of the ways of the Dunces. To take the first to hand, there is (in the second version) the miscellaneous compiler Oldmixon, who would turn his hand to scandalous memoirs, secret history, court tales or whatever the booksellers would buy:

> He said, and clim'd a stranded lighter's height,
> Shot to the black abyss, and plung'd down-right.
> The Senior's judgement all the crowd admire,
> Who but to sink the deeper, rose the higher. (B.II.287)

I hope it is not too pedantic to add that a number of coal-barges actually *were* stranded periodically in the canal.

The next diver is Smedley, round whom 'the quaking mud' closes. He is given up for lost, but significantly the contest goes on – hacks are always dispensable. However, the disreputable clergyman reappears after a succession of plunging prelates and precipitately dull scribblers have made their attempt. Smedley relates 'the wonders of the deep' in a parody of a time-honoured literary device, the vision of the underworld:[126]

> First he relates, how sinking to the chin,
> Smit with his mien, the Mud-nymphs suck'd him in:
> How young Lutetia, softer than the down,
> Nigrina black, and Merdamante brown,
> Vy'd for his love in jetty bow'rs below,
> As Hylas fair was ravish'd long ago.
> Then sung, how shown him by the Nut-brown maids
> A branch of Styx here rises from the Shades,
> That tinctur'd as it runs with Lethe's streams,
> And wafting Vapours from the Land of dreams,
> (As under seas Alphaus' secret sluice
> Bears Pisa's off'rings to his Arethuse)
> Pours into Thames: and hence the mingled wave
> Intoxicates the pert, and lulls the grave:
> Here brisker vapours o'er the Temple creep,
> There, all from Paul's to Aldgate drink and sleep. (B.II.331)

This is the authentic Popian effect. A brutal and jolting contrast is set up between the pleasant endowments of myth (including even the mellifluous proper names) and the jagged asperities of London reality, summed up in the glottal Saxon sounds of 'Aldgate'. Eternal sleep is the ultimate condition of Dulness, its Nirvana and its ideology. Shortly the entire gathering of Dunces will be reduced to a drugged trance by the tedium of the final contest – appropriately held between academics, that new breed of non-literary literary men whom Pope so presciently feared. With deft economy, the poet has related this circumstance to the fetid air around Blackfriars. The 'pert' will not survive for long; it is the irremediably Dull who will feel the breath from Lethe and spread their influence over London and then the whole nation. That is what Settle prophesies in the next book; that is what happens in the final book. The Fleet Ditch, agency of disease, harbinger of poverty, home of both crime and punishment – this is, too, the great artery of Dulness through London and the first place to give itself up to that everlasting sleep which the Dunces so earnestly crave.

This unfortunate quarter witnessed, then, every plague that beset men and women of the time, both literal and metaphorical. As such, it was fit domicile for the forces of Dulness: for that condition is but a literary rephrasing of the experience of a London slum-dweller in the eighteenth century. Pope's myth of social disorder consigns his victims to a world of darkness, poverty, squalor, idleness, vice and ignorance. The rise of a scribbling gentry, indigenous to garrets such as the ramshackle lath-and-plaster tenements of Grub Street afforded, was a circumstance Pope knew well how to utilise. He collaborates imaginatively with history. And for this purpose, it was ideally suitable that his controlling metaphor should remain – as it was before the poem was ever conceived – a real part of real London. Not Aeneas, but Rome, is the final, unstated subject of *The Aeneid*; and it is not Queen Dulness, but her Grub Street realm, whose epic destiny Pope recounts to us.

Epigraphs (*i*) 'They' refers to the ancients, 'our' to modern worthies. Phlegeton, or Phlegethon, was of course a river of liquid fire in Hades. Quoted from *Poems of Ben Jonson*, ed. G. B. Johnston (London, 1954), p. 69.

(*ii*) See note 44 below.

1. I have used for general reference three serviceable books by W. G. Bell: *The Great Plague of London in 1665* (London, ed. 1924); *The Great Fire of London in 1666* (London, ed. 1923); and *Fleet Street in Seven Centuries* (London, 1912). Other specialised sources are referred to in the notes below.

2. Hart, 'Some Reflections on Johnson as Hero', *Johnsonian Studies*, ed. M. Wahba (Cairo, 1962), pp. 28–9.
3. Quoted from the Penguin edition of *Roget's Thesaurus* (Harmondsworth, 1953), pp. 221–2.
4. W. K. Wimsatt, jr., *The Verbal Icon* (New York, 1958), p. 124.
5. Penfield Roberts called his study of the diplomatic events in Europe *The Quest for Security 1715–1740* (New York, 1963). This phrase could be transferred from the sphere of foreign policy and international alignments to that of personal psychology.
6. Pope's concern is evidenced by his own letters during 1715 (e.g. that to the retired diplomat Trumbull, on 16 December – 'Fire and sword, and fire and faggot, are equally my aversion . . .'), and also by those addressed to the poet by his closest friends (notably that of Blount on 11 November). See Pope, *Correspondence*, I, 307–24 especially. Among the better known Dunces, Defoe and Cibber were active followers of William III on his arrival; Oldmixon witnessed the events at Sedgmoor.
7. This aspect of the Jacobite risings has been stressed by several modern historians. See for example C. B. Realey, *The Early Opposition to Sir Robert Walpole 1720–1727* (Lawrence, Kansas, 1931), p. 53.
8. *The Crowd in History* (New York, 1964), pp. 47–65. In eighteenth-century usage, 'crowd' meant a bustling, pressing concourse – one could say 'there were many people present but no crowd' (=crowding). See Susie I. Tucker, *Protean Shape* (London, 1967), p. 160.
9. Rudé, p. 4; British Museum, *Catalogue of Prints and Drawings*, III, 302.
10. On the difficulties of maintaining the peace in the eighteenth century, see Radzinowicz, IV, 105–57 ('The Control of Crowds').
11. Rudé, p. 9.
12. During the Gordon riots there were rumours that lions had been let loose from the Tower and that lunatics were to be released from Bedlam. This is analogous to the fictional riot of *The Dunciad*, where (in the first version) the menagerie of Dunces are set free from their 'čell' near the Tower; and where (in the second version) the lunatic corps engulf the city from their 'cell' near Bedlam.
13. Dulness 'includes . . . Labour, Industry, and some degree of Activity and Boldness: a ruling principle not inert, but turning topsy-turvy the Understanding, and inducing an Anarchy or confused State of Mind' (note to B.I.15). The turbulent, anarchic forces of Dulness seek to overturn the due order of things, much as a mob of levellers would subvert the rule of law. Yet, for all their momentum and massiness, there is a sort of drugged or stupefied quality in the band of Dunces, such as crowd psychologists have detected.

14. Williams, pp. 131–58.
15. Rudé, pp. 7n. 217, 233; Williams, p. 143.
16. Rudé, pp. 51, 225, 54, 72, 61, and cf. p. 204; George, p. 125.
17. Rudé, pp. 198, 62, 59. The same writer observes (pp. 59–60) that the rioting bands (a noun Pope uses of his Dunces) 'were frequently "captained" by men enjoying temporary authority.' Now in one sense Cibber's elevation is permanent; but in another, his authority derives from the Settle succession, i.e. the City Poet whose term of office is confined to the single occasion of the Lord Mayor's Show. (Though a re-election could be made each year in practice.) More generally, Pope contrives, by linking Cibber's apotheosis to the specific post of laureate which he had obtained, to suggest that his kingship had as short a term as his own poetic works.
18. Swift, *Correspondence*, IV, 62: cf. II, 12n, 15n. Pope had dealings with Barber at least as early as 1714: Pope, *Correspondence*, I, 444.
19. On the procession see for example Malcolm, II, 15–18; Thornbury, I, 26–7. Both accounts probably incorporate fable as well as fact. See also the poem to Francis Child, in the *Grub-street Journal*, reproduced as Appendix C. Swift refers to the procession in his *Journal* on 17 November 1711.
20. For an account of the procession in 1679, attended by an alleged 200,000 persons, and of the activities of the mob, see David Ogg, *England in the Reign of Charles II* (Oxford, 1963), II, 595–6.
21. *The Tatler*, ed. G. A. Aitken (London 1898–9), I, 333–5. It may be pertinent to add that the Artillery Ground was the venue for another stirring contest at arms in the year of Pope's death, just after the revised *Dunciad* made its appearance. This was the celebrated match between Kent and All England, on 18 June 1744: the first representative game of cricket, and the first for which detailed scores were preserved. It even stimulated a mock-heroic poem by James Love. See H. S. Altham, E. W. Swanton, *A History of Cricket* (London, 1947), pp. 34–6. For Pope's reference to the ground, see above, p. 104. Jokes at the expense of the 'Cripplegate Grenadiers' were common: e.g. Read's *Weekly Journal*, 16 January 1720.
22. TE, V, 260.
23. TE, V, 263.
24. Cf. Ian Brownlie, *The Law Relating to Public Order* (London, 1968), pp. 201, 37–59; Radzinowicz, II, 164; Holdsworth, X, 705–6.
25. Rudé, *Wilkes and Liberty* (Oxford, ed. 1965), esp. pp. 17, 58–73, 153.
26. Rudé, *Wilkes*, pp. 76, 173, 220–1.
27. *Diary and Letters of Madame D'Arblay*, ed. A. Dobson (London, 1904), I, 438. According to Austin Dobson, Johnson never did *afterwards* visit Grub Street. The letter is dated about 15 July 1780; cf. *Dr. Johnson and Mrs. Thrale*, ed. C. B. Tinker (London, 1912), pp. 118–19. It might perhaps be a day or two earlier.

28. *The Letters of Samuel Johnson*, ed. R. W. Chapman (Oxford, 1952), II, 368–71.
29. *The Yale Edition of Horace Walpole's Correspondence*, ed. W. S. Lewis et al. (London, 1967), XXIII, 39: cf. p. 221. Similarly the Duchess of Devonshire speaks of 'a violent mob in Moorfields' at the start of the Gordon riot: Iris Leveson Gower, *The Face Without a Frown* (London, 1944), p. 55. Gibbon writes of the mob in a letter of 6 June 1780, the 'tumult' caused by the 'scum' on the surface of 'this huge Cauldron (London) . . . every Gentleman . . . must extinguish the flame . . . Col. H. was all last night in Holborn, among the flares . . .' *The Letters of Edward Gibbon*, ed. E. J. Norton (London, 1956), II, 243–4.
30. *The Complete Poetical Works of William Cowper*, ed. H. Milford (London, 1907), p. 306.
31. Hibbert, *King Mob* (London, 1958), esp. pp. 27, 32, 34, 39, 44, 45, 48; see also J. P. de Castro, *The Gordon Riots* (London, 1926), p. 140.
32. Hibbert, pp. 56ff: de Castro, p. 105: Denton, pp. 176–8.
33. Hibbert, pp. 98, 102–3, 109, 117, 122, 125.
34. *The Works of Samuel Johnson, Ll.D.*, ed. A. Murphy (London, 1824), I, ii, 4.
35. Brian Gibbons, *Jacobean City Comedy* (London, 1968), p. 155. According to Gibbons, the London setting in one representative play 'is accurately achieved with many placing references to streets and district names, to attract local interest' (p. 23). Again, he contends that '. . . the detailed setting of Cony-Catching episodes in specific parts of London was similarly intended to give sensational interest to otherwise very commonplace material' (p. 140). As is, I hope, apparent from the text, I believe that the topographic basis of Augustan satire is far from being confined to questions of mere 'local colour': it is a device for moral insight and revelation.
36. Defoe, *Tour*, I, 351; cf. pp. 326–7, 341.
37. See R. H. Barker, *Mr. Cibber of Drury Lane* (New York, 1939), pp. 127–8, 140. Riots at Drury Lane were common throughout the century; there was a bad outbreak in 1744, and a curious step was then taken. 'In order that grievances might have expression and that excesses might be avoided, a spokesman for the public was appointed in or about 1744, and regularly attended the pit on all important occasions.': W. J. Lawrence, 'The Theatre', in Turberville, II, 178. There could scarcely be a clearer demonstration of the tumultuous and divisive nature of eighteenth-century society than the recurrent party squabbles in places of entertainment, or than the need to appoint a kind of industrial conciliation officer in the theatre. Spikes even had to be placed across the proscenium arch, leaving the theatre almost in the condition of a South American football ground. See Marshall, p. 183, where details of a riot at Drury Lane in 1737 are supplied.

38. TE, V, 287.
39. Sutherland's note (TE, V, 288–9) is particularly helpful at this point.
40. See also B.III. 253 ff, and B.III.315–6. The evocation of 'one wide conflagration' occurs at B.III.240.
41. Cudworth, *A Sermon preached before the Honourable the House of Commons* . . . (Cambridge, 1647), pp. 63–4. To cite a modern instance, Dorothy Marshall (pp. 236–7) speaks repeatedly of 'the spark that lit the flame', 'inflamatory pamphlets', a populace 'inflamed' by 'fiery' gin.
42. J. L. and Barbara Hammond, *The Skilled Labourer 1760–1832* (London, 1927), pp. 206, 209.
43. Hammond, p. 205, where the writers also record the fact that the weavers donned masks and other disguises prior to wreaking violence.
44. *The Eighteenth-Century Constitution 1688–1715*, ed. E. N. Williams (Cambridge, 1965), pp. 414–7. For Mansfield's speech in the Lords on the application of the Act during the Gordon riots, see pp. 417–20. See also *English Historical Documents 1714–1783*, ed. D. B. Horn, M. Ransome (London, 1957), pp. 271–9.
45. Rudé, *The Crowd in History*, p. 54.
46. Cf. Radzinowicz, I, 8–9: 'Few other offences induce the same degree of public alarm' as arson. See also the quotation from Pollock and Maitland, p. 8.
47. On the predominance of property considerations, cf. the quotation from Basil Williams in Radzinowicz, I, 34.
48. J. J. Baddeley, *An Account of the Church and Parish of St Giles, without Cripplegate* (London, 1888), p. 24.
49. See Denton, pp. 122–34.
50. Defoe's *Journal* mentions the heavy inflictions of the plague on the parish of St Giles' Cripplegate: e.g. (Harmondsworth, 1966), p. 36. See also his 'Due Preparations for the Plague', in *Romances and Narratives*, XV, 59ff.
51. *A Trip through London* (8th ed., 1728), pp. 1, 52–3.
52. *The Poems of John Dryden* (London, 1910), p. 39.
53. Hitchen, *A True Discovery* (1718), p. 7, quoted by Radzinowicz, II, 1; cf. F. J. Lyons, *Jonathan Wild, Prince of Robbers* (London, 1936), p. 225.
54. *The Dispensary* (ed. 1718), pp. 28–9, 36.
55. *Jonathan Wild* (New York, 1962), p. 28: cf. *Romances and Narratives*, XVI, 241–2.
56. Butt, p. 696 ('Epilogue to the Satires', II, 38).
57. Butt, pp. 577, 598, 676, 681–2.
58. Butt, pp. 232–3.
59. Butt, p. 233.
60. J. H. Plumb, *England in the Eighteenth Century* (Harmondsworth, 1950), p. 13.

61. Bell, *Plague*, pp. 275-6. Another report by the Commissioners, in 1653, alluded to the practice of keeping swine in the Fleet River: T. F. Reddaway, *The Rebuilding of London after the Great Fire* (London, 1940,) p. 202.

62. "Is there not as much skill in making Dikes, as in raising Mounts?", asks Martinus Scriblerus in Ch. IV of *Peri Bathous* (Steeves, p. 15). For Swift's use of the motif of ditches, see Ch. III below.

63. Watt, 'Publishers and Sinners: The Augustan View', *Studies in Bibliography*, XII (1959), 14.

64. Faber, p. 68.

65. TE, V, 108.

66. *The History of the Rebellion* (Oxford, 1702), I, 158. Cf. Valerie Pearl, *London at the Outbreak of the Puritan Revolution* (Oxford, 1961), p. 1, and Marshall, p. 11.

67. Nigel Barton, *The Lost Rivers of London* (London, 1962), Ch. IX ('The Uses of the Lost Rivers'), pp. 65–100, is of help here. See also Ch. X ('Disasters, Diseases and Drains'), pp. 101–126. Not surprisingly the Fleet figures prominently in this latter.

68. George, p. 94.

69. Bell, *Plague*, p. 276.

70. Stow, pp. 9–10: Reddaway, p. 201, says 1502 and 1606.

71. Reddaway, pp. 201-2.

72. Reddaway, pp. 202-15.

73. Reddaway, pp. 220-1; Barton, p. 77.

74. Defoe, *Tour*, I, 355-6.

75. The notorious Saffron Hill district, infamous into the time of Dickens, adjoined Smithfield proper. The liberty lay in the parish of St Andrew's Holborn. It was associated with prostitutes, with poor Irish immigrants, with disease (e.g. typhus) and with crime: see George, pp. 91, 92, 121, 130, 351; E. B. Chancellor, *The Pleasure Haunts of London* (London, 1925), p. 176.

76. Further north still the Ditch ran near Hockley in the Hole, famous for boisterous sport, and mentioned in *Trivia* as well as in the *Dunciad* (B.I. 222, 326). Clerkenwell sprawled on the slopes of the Fleet Valley, 'a district of innumerable twisting lanes and alleys': O. H. K. Spate, 'The Growth of London A.D. 1660–1800', *A Historical Geography of England*, ed. H. C. Darby (Cambridge, 1963), p. 534.

77. On Lincoln's Inn Fields, see George, pp. 106–7, 342 (a particularly telling instance), 350. Just by the Fields lay Whetstone Park, a leading feature of London night-life for those who were not particular with whom they slept. Prior writes of 'that hallow'd Ground/Of *Temple-Walks*, or Whetstone's Park' as haunts of the prostitute: 'The Antiquated Coquet', in his *Poems on Several Occasions* (London, '5th' ed., 1767), II, 332.

78. A convenient guide is *New Remarks of London . . . Collected by the Company of Parish Clerks* (1732), which sets out the streets and alleys in each parish. It is to be feared that the parish of St Dunstan's was not always very scrupulously managed; at least, the scandal of holding an expensive feast when the officers met to settle the poor book suggests as much: see Dorothy Marshall, *The English Poor in the Eighteenth Century* (London, 1926), p. 64. A century before St Bride's had already been 'scarred with pestilential slum dwellings' which the Fire, unfortunately, could not reach: Pearl, p. 13.

79. Opposite lay Blackfriars, a scarcely more salubrious district. It was described in 1756 as filled with 'laystalls and bawdy houses, obscure pawn-brokers, gin-shops and ale-houses; the haunts of strolling prostitutes, thieves and beggars . . .' (George, p. 339).

80. T. B. Macaulay, *The History of England* (London, 1906), I, 290–1.

81. Cf. Wheatley, p. 398.

82. Stanley Morison, *The English Newspaper* (Cambridge, 1932), p. 93n; W. M. Sale, *Samuel Richardson Master Printer* (Ithaca, 1950), esp. pp. 10, 61; Chancellor, *Pleasure Haunts*, pp. 64, 76ff; Dobson, *Samuel Richardson* (London, 1902), pp. 174–6; Pope, *Correspondence*, IV, 338; see also R. J. Blackham, *The Story of the Temple Gray's and Lincoln's Inn* (London, n.d.), pp. 54–9.

83. Webb, VI, 12ff. In a characteristic 'Preface' to this work, Bernard Shaw wrote, 'If the prison does not underbid the slum in human misery, the slum will empty and the prison will fill' (p. xi). This is a particularly suggestive statement with regard to the Fleet (debtors') Prison and its environs.

84. Reproduced by Barton, opp. p. 80. Perhaps this shows some authorial backing for this location, though Aubrey Williams (pp. 38–9) seems to be following the text when he places the games at the very outlet of the Fleet into the Thames.

85. De Castro, p. 268: E. G. O'Donoghue, *Bridewell Hospital* (London, 1929), passim.

86. Pope, *Correspondence*, IV, 233–4. It was said that one in six of those who passed Temple Bar was a writer by profession: Thornbury, I, 45ff. But it cannot have been true.

87. Radzinowicz, I, 300; Wheatley, p. 395, places this execution of 1733 at the Fetter Lane end of the street, opposite Mitre Court.

88. Christopher Hibbert, *The Roots of Evil*, (London, 1963), p. 48.

89. See Lyons, pp. 270, 273, etc. For Shenstone's comments to Richard Jago on the prevalence of armed footpads in the region of Fleet Street around 1744, see Hibbert, *Roots*, p. 50.

90. O'Donoghue, II, 188.

91. Bell, *Plague*, p. 276.

92. Barton, p. 75.

93. Wheatley, pp. 388–92; Webb, VI, 8, 26.

94. Wheatley, pp. 392–3.

95. J. T. Boulton (ed.), *Daniel Defoe* (London, 1965), p. 237.

96. Moore, *Citizen*, p. 47.

97. For a gruesome story set in a garret in Stonecutter Street, see Bayne-Powell, p. 81.

98. Butt, p. 695.

99. Webb, VI, 30–1, mention the famous occasion in 1750 when judges, aldermen and counsel perished along with prisoners from the disease. For Boswell's visit to Newgate's 'dark mansions' and dismal cells in 1763, see his *London Journal*, ed. F. A. Pottle (London, 1950), pp. 251–2. Savage and Wycherley were confined there.

100. Radzinowicz, I, 168ff, gives a great deal of interesting evidence on the subject; see also Dorothy George, in Turberville, I, 175. The biblical parallel is my own.

101. Wheatley, pp. 402–3.

102. Boswell, *Journal*, p. 214.

103. Pope, *Correspondence*, II, 29, 34, is the authority.

104. Cf. George, pp. 106–7, 342–3, 350; as well as Macaulay, *History*, I, 277, for a description of Lincoln's Inn Fields, with its rubbish, its beggars and its rough sports.

105. Cf. Lyons, p. 279; F. A. Mumby, *Publishing and Bookselling* (London, 1949), p. 154ff.

106. *DNB*, s.v. Savage.

107. On Shoe Lane, see Irving, pp. 139, 259; George, p. 93. For the large number of alehouses in Holborn, see Radzinowicz, I, 400; for rioting there, see Dorothy George in Turberville, I, 193. It should be recalled that Dr. Johnson, in his young and far from affluent days, lived twice in Holborn as well as in Fetter Lane, Bow Street and other streets in the vicinity long before he came to relative comfort in Gough Square.

108. Radzinowicz, II, 310.

109. Irving, p. 260.

110. Quoted by Radzinowicz, II, 23. Some time earlier (see p. 255) John Oldham had linked Tyburn with Grub Street; one could almost set the imaginative connection out in the form of a syllogism or proportion sum:

Smithfield : Tyburn
Grub Street : Tyburn
thus Smithfield : Grub Street.

111. Defoe stood in the pillory for the third and last time by Temple Bar. For the extent of the parish of St Dunstan's (which contained Whitefriars as an 'extraparochial' district), see *New Remarks*, pp. 159–62.

112. Other unfortunate connections, of a more or less serious kind, were a wax-work show near St Dunstan's Church, for which see A. J. Sambrook (ed.), *The Scribleriad* (Los Angeles, 1967), p. ix; the legacy of the theatre which had stood in Dorset Gardens in Restoration times (theatres nearly always sent down the tone of a neighbourhood, for reasons that are only partly intelligible today); and the noxious Bugg Alley, alias Harp Alley.

113. M. D. George, *Hogarth to Cruickshank* (London, 1967), pp. 33–4.

114. Carey was buried in St James' church in 1743: *The Poems of Henry Carey*, ed. F. T. Wood (London, n.d. (? 1930)), p. 12.

115. Clifford, p. 180.

116. Morison, p. 324.

117. E. B. Chancellor, *The Literary Ghosts of London* (London, 1933), p. 171.

118. Sale, p. 26.

119. Defoe, *Romances and Narratives*, XVI, 179. The House of Correction was in Clerkenwell Close, next to the New Prison in Clerkenwell Green (*New Remarks*, p. 215).

120. Clifford, p. 180; Barton, p. 88; *DNB*, s.v. Cave; Ralph, *A Critical Review* (1734), p. 23.

121. *Poems of Ben Jonson*, pp. 69–75.

122. *The Dispensary* (ed. 1718), p. 29; Bell, *Fleet Street*, p. 417.

123. James Miller, 'Art of Life' (1739), quoted by Irving, p. 86.

124. Faber, pp. 69–70.

125. Butt, p. 207. The poem is 'Windsor Forest'.

126. Among other connotations of 'hell' at this period, it may be worth mentioning, were gambling dens (regularly so described: see for instance the Newgate *Calendar*, III, 179ff) and, in legend if not in reality, the underground lairs of such disreputable groups as the Medmenham 'monks'. It is not necessary to give credence to stories such as the one that there was at Medmenham 'a marble outhouse, beautifully designed, called "The Temple of Cloacina" . . .' – thus retailed by Daniel P. Mannix, *The Hell-Fire Club* (London, 1961), p. 24. It remains a clear fact that people of the time *did* refer in a shocked sort of way to various 'Hell-Fire Clubs', real or imaginary, whether those putatively established by Dashwood, by Philip Wharton or by others. Black magic rites and illicit sexual dealings were frequently located on the linguistic map in close proximity to Hades. However apocryphal the tales, it can hardly be gainsaid that satanic cults were identified in the popular imagination with subterranean caves which, more often than not, were described as 'hells'. In addition, 'Hell' seems to have been used in prostitutes' argot for the female pudenda – another useful connotation as far as the iconography of the Fleet was concerned. See Tom Brown, quoted by Pinkus, p. 45.

III

Swift and the Scribbler

A regiment is a corporation which consists of individuals detached
from Bridewell, the Queen's Bench, Fleet, Newgate and the Counters.

Ned Ward, Mars stripped of his Armour

———◆◆◆◆———

Writers at all times have been conscious of the Grub Street fraternity.
That is, major authors – satirists especially – have been aware of a
horde of disgruntled literary aspirants baying at their heels: men of
slender talent or none at all, racked by envy and embittered by failure. At certain periods this insistent murmur becomes louder, till it
almost drowns the voice of the major writer. The early eighteenth
century was one such period. We *need* to know something of the
lesser fry if we are to understand the procedures or appreciate the
rhetoric of the great Augustans. They were all taken up, at a deep
level, with the activities of their emulators and detractors. The
legend of Grub Street which they did so much to create testifies to
the importance that the scribblers had in their mind. Parody, para-
phrase, burlesque, mock-encomia, tongue-in-cheek 'answers' – these
are the weapons of the Scriblerians. They might also be seen as a
kind of devious tribute to Grub Street.

So much is true in general outline; but Swift remains unique. No
other great writer, surely, can have made his name by producing a
deliberately bad book: a work whose content, structure and style
alike reproduced the worst features of contemporary Grub Street
writing. *A Tale of a Tub* is not, of course, a faithful transcript of
Grubean composition in every single detail. As with all effective
parody, the *Tale* distorts, heightens, extends, telescopes. Nevertheless, the book does, by its form and matter, provide us with a sharp
insight into the eighteenth-century hack: his motivation, his personal

and literary goals, his foibles and his pathos. It took a modern critic to designate the narrator of the *Tale*, with clipped finality, *the* Hack, as though there were no other. But Ronald Paulson was right, as the widespread currency of his term has shown; the Hack *is* an archetypal figure, Everyman under the Grub Street aspect.

Let us think for a moment what the term connotes. Johnson's *Dictionary* entry for 'hackney' moves from the sense of a hired horse (with an example from *Hudibras*) to that of a prostitute to 'any thing let out for hire' (both the latter illustrated from Pope) to 'much used or common'. 'To hack' is defined as 'to turn hackney or prostitute'. We notice at once the sexual innuendo in the word and its derivatives: something lost, I believe, to most present-day readers. To be a hack, then, was to traffic commercially in something fundamentally admirable, and thus to sully it. It was to do for literature what prostitution did for sex. Hence the great advantage to the satirist in being able to suggest that the scribbling profession lived cheek by jowl with the whores. Needless to say, whores abounded in eighteenth-century London; and they abound in Swift's work, too. The facts of the language were such that Swift could convincingly present Grub Street as a brothel; as Pope had done, with his secluded 'cave' presided over by that awesome madam, Dulness.

In certain respects Swift's response to the seething world of actuality was even more immediate than that of Pope; and his compulsion to manufacture fiction of power and sometimes beauty from this unlovely reality was quite as marked. To think of the Dean's entire corpus of writings is to call up pictures of sturdy beggars, of rainstorms in the City, of litter in the streets, of quacks at Bartholomew Fair and servants below stairs. And his climactic figure of folly, outside the pages of *Gulliver's Travels* at least, is a nakedly human personage. Pope embodies the ultimate stage of folly in a quasi-mythological symbol, Queen Dulness; even if he does provide her with a closely observed social milieu for her domain. But with Swift the casting is brutal and unavoidable. The great exemplar of literary iniquity is the hack in his garret; the setting is a London as real and unmistakable as if John Rocque had drawn a map for frontispiece to the *Tale*.[1]

Likewise, Swift's poetry is rich in allusions to Curll, Lintot, Temple Bar, Ludgate, Duck Lane, cellars and attics, sponging-houses and pastry-cooks, doggerel and the *Craftsman*. It is not, of course, mere reportage; its social brightness and topicality are not those of the gossip column, and its realism is not to be confused with straight naturalism. Despite that reservation, it would be fair to say that Swift makes more *poetic* capital out of the raw material offered him by real life than any other writer of his time. If we take 'real life' to mean, for the moment, the daily round of eighteenth-century urban dwellers, then Swift, far more than Prior or Gay, is the poet of real life. His poems reflect the same power of eager observation as his portrait of the Grub Street Hack; the same power to make of the temporary a solid vehicle for the permanent.

Grubean Spokesman

A Tale of a Tub is a revelation of the complex fate of Duncehood.[2] The modern scribbler is anatomised both through direct reference and through self-betrayal on the part of the putative author. Before we have left the very title-page, a strain of megalomania has appeared: a bibliographical formula conveys this literary vainglory nicely – / / / A / TALE / OF A / TUB. / Written for the Universal Im- / provement of Mankind. / / And so on. Opposite the title-page in early editions was found a list of 'Treatises wrote by the same Author, most of them mentioned in the following Discourses [oh dear, yes!]; which will be speedily published.' These classic works of the un-learned include 'A Character of the present set of *Wits* in this Island' along with (what is much the same thing) 'A Dissertation upon the principal Productions of *Grub-Street*.' Thus early is the haunt of folly identified. Later in the list occurs 'A Description of the Kingdom of *Absurdities*', and it is already plain that the capital of this realm of nonsense is to be London. A few years afterwards, a tract was to appear – possibly, as we shall see, by Swift; if not, certainly inspired by him – in which the absence of a Grub Street in Dublin was lamented. Only London was so privileged; and, to move from metaphor to history, it could be said that in 1700 only London had reached the condition of modern urbanism. The person of quality from '*Terra Australis incognita*' who is to make a voyage into England (another tome advertised in the list) will find in its capital city an unparalleled degree of crime, turbulence and overcrowding. He will also find Dulness in its finest expression.

The elaborate preliminaries to the *Tale* are led off by the author's 'Apology' from the fifth edition of 1710. There is, of course, plenty of disagreement as to the intent of this section. For the present I shall remark only that the literary meanings of the book are emphasised quite as sharply as the religious. The writer singles out 'those heavy, illiterate Scriblers, prostitute in their Reputations, vicious in their Lives, and ruin'd in their Fortunes, who to the shame of good Sense as well as Piety' write against religion and morality. The books of these men are condemned as exhibiting 'Errors, Ignorance, Dullness and Villany'. The first writers mentioned by name, who are inevitably connected by the reader with this general condemnation, turn out to be Dryden, and L'Estrange – 'who having spent their Lives in Faction, and Apostacies, and all manner of Vice, pretended to be Sufferers for Loyalty and Religion.' His style in the Introduction, he explains, parodies such writing.

Another form of parody appears in the dedication to Lord Somers. Unlike some satirists, Swift did not choose to supply a comic invocation to the man in the moon or some such figure of myth. He chooses to write in the person of the bookseller to the great patron and bibliophile Somers. And although the writer is presented as both foolish and ignorant, he is at least allowed to make this eminently sane decision to inscribe the book to Somers. Instead of the hack's own absurd Prince Posterity, the dedication is really to go to the worthiest recipient. That is the point of the joke. Despite the bookseller's fawning, his pathetic civic ambition 'to grow an Alderman' (the verb nicely suggesting a sort of unhaltable bourgeois progression, something fundamentally *unearned*), and despite his niggardly commercial caution, he has at least more sense than the allegedly 'professional' hack whose work he is vending. He knows who collects books and encourages literature. Swift's recourse to Somers, then, is no back-handed compliment: the parody of a very bad dedication to a very good patron is the most effective satire he could have devised.

The bookseller, like many writers of dedications in this age, remarks on the tired conventions of the genre – it *was* a minor literary genre of some interest: 'I should now, in right of a Dedicator, give your Lordship a List of your own Virtues, and at the same time, be very unwilling to offend your Modesty . . .' Most people mention such conventions in the course of explaining that they will avoid such falsities. The bookseller, however, proudly continues that he really was going to to 'peruse a hundred or two of Dedications, and transscribe an Abstract, to be applied to your Lordship . . .' He was sidetracked only by the mysterious words *'Detur dignissimo'*. None of his authors can, of course, understand the Latin phrase – although, as the bookseller ruefully observes, 'I have them often in pay, to translate out of that Language' – and he has to go to a curate. Having established the sense of the words, the bookseller calls at 'a Poet's Chamber (who works for my Shop) in an Alley hard by'. The poet names himself as the likeliest candidate, with Somers as second choice; and a similar result ensues after visits to other wits 'with no small Hazard and Weariness to my Person, from a prodigious Number of dark, winding Stairs'. 'Poor authors', runs a note in the 1720 edition, 'generally lodge in Garrets.' The bookseller concludes that Somers must be the intended dedicatee. But, 'being very unacquainted in the Style and Form of Dedications', he is forced to return to the scribblers for a panegyric on Somers. Predictably, the authors bring him a standard encomium, so blatantly plagiarised that even he can see it. 'So that I look upon my self, as fifty Shillings out of Pocket, to no manner of Purpose,' the bookseller adds with intended pathos. He despairs of changing the name and using the panegyric again on another occasion, since its terms fit only the matchless Somers. A genuinely delicate compliment is fashioned out of this graceless narrative. Moreover, the dedication shows us Swift aligning commercial motives with ignorance, impudence and fraud. The environment, needless to say, is that of the garret in the back-alley. We are in the purlieu of Grub Street, ecologically and morally.

In the absurd Epistle Dedicatory which follows, the first piece of the putative author's own handiwork, Swift introduces the central idea of his satire. The writer explains how Time has intervened to forestall any sight by Posterity (who is the recipient of the letter) of the numerous 'Studies' by contemporary hacks. Time, indeed, has insolently thinned the ranks of 'our vast flourishing Body' of authors, on account of 'a peculiar Malice' he bears against this class. In a splendidly funny passage, the hack-figure creates a vision of thousands of fugitive writings condemned to an early grave, stifled in their cradles or frightened into convulsions. Then he shifts to a more businesslike vein:

> But the Concern I have most at Heart, is for our Corporation of *Poets*, from whom I am preparing a Petition to *Your Highness*, to be subscribed with the Names of one hundred and thirty six of the first Rate, but whose immortal Productions are never likely to reach your Eyes, tho' each of them is now an humble and an earnest Appellant for the Laurel, and has large comely Volumes ready to shew a Support to his Pretensions. The *never-dying* Works of these illustrious Persons, Your *Governour* [Time], Sir, has devoted to unavoidable Death . . .

There is a pomposity here ('an humble and an earnest'), a quasi-legal air at times, an impression of not having quite learnt what some words exactly mean: it all suggests the trade unionist satirised by Peter Sellers. Nor is this inappropriate: since the poets are leagued together in a mutual-protection organisation. Like the Dunces, who coalesce in a seething mass of corrupt humanity (B.IV.77), the poets have incorporated themselves to disguise their individual frailty. They are, in the Webbs' sense, an association of producers:[3] another proof of the professionalisation of letters, that movement towards a scribbling bureaucracy which the Tory humanists so much feared. One element of the whole Grub Street fiction, indeed, is that poor writers are now banded together as an institutionalised estate of the realm; they operate in contemporary culture as a perversely anti-educative and anti-literary force. They resemble the least enlightened City companies; they form a *corporation*.

The dedicator goes on to speak of a list of (duncely) 'Titles' which were 'posted fresh upon all Gates and Corners of Streets.' In a few hours these were all torn down: all trace of the existence of these works had been lost. The question naturally arises, 'What is then become of those immense Bales of Paper, which must needs have been employ'd in such Numbers of Books? Can these also be wholly annihilate . . .?' The answer, though the writer professes some hesitation about revealing the details to so high a potentate as Posterity, is that the sheets have been allocated a use in a jakes, an oven, in 'the Windows of a *Bawdy-house*, or . . . a sordid *Lanthorn*. Books, like Men their Authors, have no more than one Way of coming into the World, but there are ten Thousand to go out of it, and return no more.' The quality of the wit here is distinctly seventeenth-century and metaphysical. The conceit, it need hardly be added, serves to ally literary production with the dark corners of life: scribblers are waste-makers above all.

The next passage incorporates a roll-call of the deserving moderns. They are, in order: Dryden; Nahum Tate; Tom Durfey; the critics Rymer and Dennis; 'a Person styl'd Dr *B*[en]*tl*[e]*y*'; and William Wotton, who played such a major part in the Ancient and Moderns controversy. All these writers have produced works which the world unaccountably disregards. To remedy this situation, the author plans to write 'a Character of the present Set of *Wits* in our Nation.' Meanwhile, he is content to put before Prince Posterity a 'faithful Abstract' of modern learning – the *Tale of a Tub* itself.

There follows yet another in the series of preliminary puffs. This one is called a preface, though it serves the same naïvely self-advertising function as the others. The 'Design . . . [of] the Treatise' is soon announced, in a passage central to the understanding of Tory satire in this era.

It is intended that a large Academy be erected, capable of containing nine thousand seven hundred forty and three Persons; which by modest Computation is reckoned to be pretty near the current Number of *Wits* in this Island. These are to be disposed into the several Schools of this Academy, and there pursue those Studies to which their Genius most inclines them. The Undertaker himself will publish his Proposals with all convenient speed, to which I shall refer the curious Reader for a more particular Account, mentioning at present only a few of the

Principal Schools. . . . No Person to be admitted Member into any of these Schools, without an Attestation under two sufficient Persons Hands, certifying him to be a *Wit*.

Here is the germ of the Grand Academy of Lagado, of the intellectual enquiries of Martinus Scriblerus, of the 'regular Institutes' of the lowlands of Parnassus, set out in *Peri Bathous*. The idea of an academy is perhaps so dominant because of the impression made by the Royal Society on men's minds. But whatever the source of the concept, and however we try to locate these Scriblerian fancies in the tradition of learned wit, the fact remains it was a small group of writers – Swift, Arbuthnot, Pope – who saw the potential in this idea. The exact term used varies: college, seminary, lyceum, even hospital, are among the descriptions encountered. In each case, however, the sense is of folly institutionalised. Dulness, once a matter of individual quirks and personal inadequacies, has now organised itself into union militancy. Moreover, the aspirant writer is bred up by a distorted *alma mater*, supplying the place occupied in the Renaissance dream of learning by the university. The success of the Grubean academy is, amongst other things, an indictment of the ancient English universities, given over to pedantry, faction and soft living.

It might also be noted that the writer describes himself as an 'Undertaker', a word then carrying suggestions of graft – a City magnate such as Sir Henry Furnese, who amassed great wealth after engrossing the contracts for paying the army abroad during Marlborough's campaigns, would be a representative figure of this kind. And we know that Swift's circle had no high opinion of Furnese.[4] After this, the author utters his apothegmatic statement on the 'Walks and Purlieus' of wit, quoted as an epigraph to the Introduction. It is, of course, further proof of the connection between topographic and literary matters. Far from being a global village, London was then a kind of rustic metropolis: its cultural life curiously atomised by modern standards.

Finally, in this preface of garrulous non-progression, the author lets slip that 'the shrewdest Pieces of this Treatise, were conceived in Bed, in a Garret: At other times (for a Reason best known to my self) I thought fit to sharpen my Invention with Hunger; and in general, the whole Work was begun, continued, and ended, under a long Course of Physick, and a great want of Money.' This explicit admission that the *Tale* was composed in a garret under needy circumstances should not be overlooked. The book is a product of indigence, and that fact colours its entire artistic and moral identity. By the end of these introductory sections, then, we have already been alerted to the status of the author, and the nature of his 'undertaking'.

It is not possible, or necessary, to make a detailed survey of the *Tale* proper. Rather, we may isolate the themes already noticed as they make their reappearance. In the introductory chapter, the scribbler describes various kinds of oratorial machine, including the stage-itinerant. This last serves as 'the great seminary' for the pulpit and the execution-ladder: that is, 'the Mountebank's Stage, whose Orators the Author determines either to the Gallows or a Conventicle.' It can be shown that dissenting houses were concentrated most thickly in the haunts of Dulness; whilst dissenting academies thronged the Grub Street/Moorfields area. Swift goes on to explain the 'physico-logical' scheme of oratorical machines as conveying an analogy 'to the spacious Commonwealth of Writers, and to those Methods by which they must exalt themselves to a certain Eminency above the inferiour World.' The pseudo-mysticism of the hack author is thus converted to the ends of direct literary satire.

A paragraph or two later, the subject is revealed in a still more explicit manner:

> Under the *Stage-Itinerant* are couched those Productions designed for the Pleasure and Delight of Mortal Man; such as *Six-peny-worth of Wit*, Westminster *Drolleries*, *Delightful Tales*, *Compleat Jesters*, and the like; by which the Writers of and for *GRUB-STREET*, have in these latter Ages so nobly triumph'd over *Time*; have clipt his Wings, pared his Nails, filed his Teeth, turn'd back his Hour-Glass, blunted his Scythe, and drawn the Hob-Nails out of his Shoes. It is under this *Classis*, I have presumed to list my present Treatise, being just come from having the Honor conferred upon me, to be adopted a Member of that Illustrious Fraternity.

The writer has just been admitted to the fraternity of Grub Street, as one would be admitted to the freedom of the City. His treatise is a kind of commemorative offering: the gift one bestows in some pagan *rite de passage*. Yet his pride is mixed with a certain apprehension:

> Now, I am not unaware, how the Productions of the *Grub-street* Brotherhood, have of late Years fallen under many Prejudices, nor how it has been the perpetual Employment of two *Junior* start-up Societies, to ridicule them and their Authors, as unworthy their established Post in the Commonwelath of Wit and Learning.

(Note the epithet 'established'). These upstarts are the Royal Society and Will's coffee-house, the leading place of resort for literary and theatrical men at this time. The scribbler has more than one ground for resentment against these 'Societies', not least their manifest ingratitude:

> For, how can it be forgot by the World or themselves, (to say nothing of our own Records, which are full and clear in the Point) that they both are Seminaries, not only of our *Planting*, but our *Watering* too?

If the respective contributions of Grub Street and the new societies are compared, as to both weight and number of their books, Grub Street will easily carry the day – always provided that an impartial judge shall decide 'which Society each Book, Treatise or Pamphlet do most properly belong to . . . For, We are ready to produce a Catalogue of some Thousands, which in all common Justice ought to be entitled to our Fraternity, but by the revolted and new-fangled Writers, most perfidiously ascribe to the others.' Such has been the scale of the intrigue among the new academies that a huge defection has been induced from Grub Street to its rivals: 'the greatest part of our Society hath already deserted to them, and our nearest Friends begin to stand aloof, as if they were half-ashamed to own us.'

This section is usually read, and correctly, as a satire directed against Will's and the Royal Society. It is certain that these historical gatherings of intellectual London form the principal target at this point. But, semi-fictional as it may have been, Grub Street is more than simply the vehicle of a satiric metaphor. The insult to the Royal Society is as cutting as it is because Swift could rely on a ready assent to the identity of the Grub Street fraternity.

The word 'seminary' has occured two or three times. It may be recalled that in the *Memoirs of a Woman of Pleasure* Fanny Hill refers to the brothel in which she was lodged as an 'academy', with cognate usages such as 'professors of pleasure'. This mode of speech may have been connected with the mock-solemn rites of Medmenham and Crazy Castle. At all events, it is apparent that words to do with educational establishments could be applied, without much of a semantic leap, to places of immoral behaviour. 'Seminary' today has a rather neutral air to it. In the eighteenth century, it was poised ready to form combinations like 'seminary of vice'. When Arbuthnot, then, gave vent to his exclamation, '*O Grubstreet!* thou fruitful Nursery of tow'ring Genius's!' he, was taking advantage of an image already partly degraded. Others apart from the persona who masks Arbuthnot's identity in *John Bull* had the 'good Fortune to receive [their] Education there' – Grub Street was a sort of extension college.[5] It was all the better that many hacks turned out, in the 1720's and 1730's, to have attended John Eames's academy in Moorfields (Ch.I).

The narrative now moves to a celebrated passage in which the writer describes the indirect methods adopted by 'the *Grubean* Sages' (a Swiftian coinage) to convey their deep ideas. The scribbler puts foremost among the reasons for the bad press which 'the Writings of our Society have formerly received' the unwillingness of the reading public to delve into the hidden meaning of things. The only remedy for this lack of comprehension is 'a compleat and laborious Dissertation upon the Prime Productions of our Society, which besides their beautiful Externals for the Gratification of superficial Readers, have darkly and deeply couched under them, the most finished and refined Systems of all Sciences and Arts . . .' The language here is alive with innuendo and veiled malice. 'Beautiful externals' perhaps hits at the ugly chapbooks, wretchedly printed with crude woodcuts as illustration, which formed a considerable part of the Grub Street output. The word 'couched' manages to hint slily that the deep systems are after all *sleeping* in their subterranean hideout. The dissertation will of course be 'laborious' to read as well as to compile. And so on.

Not surprisingly the works of vast erudition to be studied in this critical survey prove to be on the level of *Reynard the Fox*, *Whitting-*

ton and his Cat and *Tom Thumb*. With an extra touch of scorn, Swift adds *The Hind and the Panther*, 'the Master-piece of a famous Writer now living, intended for a compleat Abstract of sixteen thousand Schoolmen from *Scotus* to *Bellarmin*.' Scotus, of course, was the primal Dunce. Additionally, William Wotton is indicated as a leading member of the scribbling fraternity. Otherwise the drift is general rather than particular. It is necessary, however, for the hack author himself to make clear his credentials for the job. He mentions his 'unfortunate Life', with 'a Quill worn to the Pith in the Service of the State', i.e. in controversial pamphlets on the Popish Plot and similar events. As a (would-be) climax, he launches into a self-pitying autobiography:

> From an Understanding and a Conscience, thread-bare and ragged with perpetual turning; From a Head broken in a hundred places, by the Malignants of the opposite Factions, and from a Body spent with Poxes ill cured, by trusting to Bawds and Surgeons, who (as it afterwards appeared) were profess'd Enemies to me and the Government, and revenged their Party's Quarrel upon my Nose and Shins . . . four-score and eleven Pamphlets have I written under three Reigns, and for the Service of six and thirty Factions.

There are elements of this account which fit Dryden, and something of his occasional self-justificatory vein. Yet the main satiric energy works in a different direction. This is Scriblerus Everyman, turn-coat, opportunist, loose liver, but always industrious. The task most suited to such a writer is the archetypal duncely endeavour of compiling an abstract. Grub Street abstracts and dissects: hence its cousinhood to the anatomy hall at the College of Physicians.

This appears most clearly in the 'Digression in the Modern Kind', with the scheme to make a kind of balsam from the works of modern learning, which would then be inhaled every morning. As a result 'you immediately perceive in your Head an infinite Number of *Abstracts, Summaries, Compendiums, Extracts, Collections, Medulla's, Excerpta quaedam's, Florilegia's* and the like, all disposed into great Order, and reducible upon Paper.' You will be, in other words, qualified to take up residence in Grub Street.

To return to the society itself: at the opening of the Digression in Praise of Digressions, we hear of the 'Commonwealth of Learning' whose taste for literary medleys and '*Ollio's*' Grub Street, her seat of government, has done so much to promote. The 'Society of Writers' is mentioned shortly afterwards, and later on the 'Corporation of Authors' busy producing their collections and commentaries and lexicons. In this section, as well as in the Digression on Criticks, Swift takes no pain to conceal his scorn for the literary middle-men of his age. Humanist ideology revered the scholar when he was about his true business of enlightenment and clarification. This was something very different from the modern pedant, 'by some called the *Sieves* and *Boulters* of Learning', whose commonplace-book is more in evidence than their wisdom or taste. Their tools are 'large *Indexes*, and little *Compendiums*'; '*Systems* and *Abstracts*', a modern labour-saving device; and other short ways of becoming scholars or wits 'without the Fatigue of *Reading* or of *Thinking*'.

The famous eighth section of the *Tale* concerns 'the learned *Aeolists*'. The sect has predictably instituted 'certain refined Colleges'. There follows the most intensely debated section of the *Tale*, the Digression on Madness. At this time of day I would not wish to intervene in a discussion which often seems to leave the humdrum topic of Augustan satire far behind. My concern is with a particular literary genre in a given historical period, and the wider ranges of the debate surrounding this Digression are not germane to my purpose. But it should be noted that the central locale of the chapter is 'the *Academy* of *Modern Bedlam*'. A proposal is made for a group of high-flying Tory politiciams to act as Commissioners of Lunacy, and to inspect the merits and qualifications of 'every Student and Professor' in Bedlam. Guthkelch and Nichol Smith reproduce an illustration from the early editions which graphically underlines the immediacy and contemporanity of the satire. In the last section of this Digression, the author recommends a madman who feeds on his own ordure as a worthy 'Professor' for 'the Society of *Warwick-Lane*' – that College of Physicians whose scientific enterprises formed an exact equivalent of the literary mud-raking of Grub Street, and whose dissection of corrupt flesh so deeply perturbed Swift, a man of particularly marked sensitivity in this area of life.

Section X of the *Tale* spells out at its outset a primary meaning of the entire fiction. In accordance with established literary custom, thanks are liberally bestowed by the author. They go first of all to the sovereign and parliament, the Privy Council and every other body of remote eminence who could not possibly form any contact with so lowly a Dunce. 'But in a more especial manner' they go 'to my worthy Brethren and Friends at *Will's Coffee-House*, and *Gresham-College*, and *Warwick-Lane*, and *Moor-Fields*, and *Scotland-Yard*, and *Westminster-Hall*, and *Guild-Hall*; In short, to all Inhabitants and Retainers whatsoever, either in Court, or Church, or Camp, or City, or Country . . .' Why Scotland Yard is there is a bit of a mystery: the police, of course, had not yet claimed the locality. For the rest, however, we have the City, the law, coffee-house society, the new experimental science of the Royal Society, the College of Physicians and Bedlam all linked by one over-arching metaphor.[6] To be a resident of such a place was to be a retainer. The appeal to 'Brethren', with its aggressive mateyness, gives the game away. These are the new estates of the realm – if Westminster Hall was ancient, organised lawyers weren't to any degree. They are topographic sites, but more crucially interest-groups to which one belongs. One name is missing. Grub Street need not be thanked since its presence is everywhere. It presides over the conception of the book, it forms a good deal of the subject-matter, and its dictates govern the material throughout. The 'Republick of *dark* Authors', Wotton's 'Brother Modernists', will be placated by the very existence of the ill-made, garrulous, creaking carcase of a book. *Their* ready acceptance of the work can be taken for granted. One need no more thank them than one thanks a detergent firm for permitting its commercial to appear on television.

I said just now that Grub Street forms much of the subject-matter of the *Tale*. Some brief justification of this remark may be in place. No major work of English literature, excluding *The Dunciad*, contains more direct reference to contemporary writers and their situation. Apart from the individuals already mentioned, there is a comment on the 'faithful and painful Collection' of criminals' dying speeches, to be made in twelve folio volumes by 'that worthy Citizen and Bookseller, Mr *John Dunton*'. There is simulated rage at the activities of 'a certain paultry *Scribbler*' dealing in second parts, i.e. compiling continuation volumes to any popular book, a lucrative activity not uncommon at this time. It is interesting to note that in the *Miscellaneous Works* of 1720, where certain ancillary material appeared for the first time, the *Tale* is allotted a separate title-page on which the author is given as 'A Member of the Illustrious Fraternity of Grubstreet'. The Miscellanies that form the second part of this volume are attributed to 'a certain paultry Scribler, commonly called, The Author of the first'.[7]

As it happens, the authors named as having suffered from this pernicious habit are themselves the veriest Dunces imaginable: Blackmore, L'Estrange, and by implication Bentley. A few years later Swift might have mentioned Defoe, who suffered from this deceit at the hands of others, but who was also believed to have practised it on occasion.

The Conclusion of the shapeless *Tale*, of course, concludes nothing. The writer evinces some anxiety lest his 'treatise' should miss its due acclaim through appearing at the wrong moment. Luckily the bookseller who bought the copy is an expert in such matters; with the help of an almanac he is able to set the most propitious date for publication. The writer, '*considering* [his] *urgent Necessities*', is keen to have more immediate prospects of a good return. So that a characteristic expedient is devised:

> That when a Customer comes for one of these [copies of the *Tale*], and desires in Confidence to know the Author; he will tell him very privately, as a Friend, naming which ever of the Wits shall happen to be that Week in the Vogue; and if *Durfy*'s last Play should be in Course, I had as lieve he may be the Person as *Congreve*.

This is exactly the same stratagem as that dramatised by Pope, in which Dulness decks out 'Three wicked imps, of her own Grubstreet choir' like Congreve, Addison and Prior (B.II.123). Here the bookseller acts the part of Dulness, as one of her principal sublunary agents.

That is not the complete register of personal allusions (Dryden is brought in on several other occasions, for example as the great exponent of the pull by way of preface). The great line of critics, from Momus down to Rymer, Bentley and Dennis, figures prominently, too. But the constant play of literary comment is not wholly dependent on the introduction of individual names. 'The mutual Felicity of *Booksellers* and *Authors*' arises from their solemn league and convenant to defraud the public. The bargain is a crooked one on either side. As the scribbler complacently notes, books are produced for a variety of reasons, ranging from ill health, bad luck at the gaming table, and a long tailor's bill to 'Want of Books, and a just Contempt of Learning'. It is yet another way of expressing an idea central to the whole critique of Dulness – that the Moderns make books for extrinsic, casual or mercenary reasons, and not from the love of literature or wisdom.

In this gallimaufry of pedantry, insolence and plain stupidity, the character of the man of letters emerges in no very favourable light. The satire even infects portions of the religious allegory, which nominally concerns abuses in the Church. Thus Lord Peter is described as 'the Original Author of *Puppets* and *Raree-Shows*; the great Usefulness whereof being so generally known, I shall not enlarge further upon this Particular.' A footnote to the word 'Puppets' reads: 'I believe are the Monkeries and ridiculous Processions, &c. among the Papists.' In the light of what has been said earlier, the force of this passage should be 'generally known' enough to warrant no further particulars. The Smithfield muse is here conflated with the rites of the Catholic church, in a manner that Pope would not have countenanced. But for Swift as for Pope, puppet-shows were emblems of tawdry pseudo-drama. In modern terms, one might say that such shows are what the media make of literature; entertainments in which the display function quite overwhelms any serious inward purpose. Puppeteers are one more variety of the genus 'Smatterers', who have taken over the cultural lead in 'this Polite and Learned Age'. The freshest modern would be certain to pitch his stall at Bartholomew Fair every year.[8]

One other aspect of the work demands notice. It would be easy to get the impression from most of the extant criticism, that the *Tale* is set in some never-never land, closer to Lagado perhaps than

Illyria. In fact the narrative buzzes with direct allusion to contemporary London. There can be no doubt at all that the corruptions in learning anatomised have their headquarters in the metropolis. Swift employs, indeed, precisely the same moral gazetteer which we have seen in the case of Pope. I have already drawn attention to the use made of such conspicuous landmarks as Moorfields, the College of Physicians, Westminster Hall and Bedlam. To these we must add such lists as the author compiles to indicate the various styles of preaching, in Covent Garden, Whitehall, the Inns of Court and the City. Or the derivation of the word 'banter' from its currency among 'the Bullies in *White-Fryars*', that recurrent symbol of low-life London. Or Peter's indulgences towards 'any Rogue of *Newgate*', one of several indications that the religious narrative, too, is acted out in a sort of imaginatively recast version of the capital. Jack, one recalls from Section XI, was cured of a strange aversion to the sound of music, by 'taking two or three Turns in *Westminster-Hall*, or *Billingsgate* or in a *Boarding-School*, or the *Royal-Exchange*, or a *State Coffee-House*'. It must be confessed that the drift of this passage is not altogether clear. The point seems to be that the dissenters' hatred of church music was forgotten when they returned to their true religion of making money in the City, pleading casuistically in the courts, indulging in political intrigue, or setting up factious 'academies'. Incidentally, Westminster Hall crops up again at the beginning of *The Mechanical Operation of the Spirit*, where it is aligned with St Paul's churchyard and Fleet Street as a centre of the bookselling trade.[9]

As a portrait of the sordid fringe of the profession of letters, the *Tale* has never been excelled. Its vigour, raciness and wealth of comic absurdity remain unimpaired to this day. And while its range of allusion may to some extent confine its appeal to the modern reader, it survives as an achievement no less striking in its way than *Gulliver's Travels*. From our present vantage point, the *Tale* is particularly notable as combining so many of the satiric *topoi* of the age into an intelligible case against the scribbling fraternity. Unlike *The Battle of the Books*, the *Tale* is not explicitly set in London. But a mass of concrete references, supplemented by easily identifiable subject-matter in the illustrations (Bedlam; the Lord Mayor on his procession through the City; a mountebanks' stage set up against Tyburn), serve to fix the action in the metropolis. Swift, like Pope, was drawn towards mythological subjects in a good deal of his work; like Pope again, he drew on the classical store of timeless landscapes and sanctified dramatic locales. Yet these men, in the ultimate intensity of their vision, abjure, the bland remoteness of Olympus or Arcadia. In *The Dunciad*, the fall of Troy is a distant theatrical spectacle, which we observe through opera glasses at the instance of a superannuated City bard, whose spiritual home had been Smithfield and whose final home on earth had been in the Charterhouse. Just so Swift disposes his archetypal Peter, Jack and Martin about a modern Vanity Fair, with its sponging-houses, it raree-shows, its filthy kennels (or gutters), its shoplifters at the Exchange, its beaux and bawds. Only London would serve to catch up all the dispersed elements of a modern myth of Folly, since only London comprehended modern urban living in its developed form.[10] The supreme fiction requires the appropriate fictive venue: the great treatise on Grub Street learning can only bear a London imprint.

'Respublica Grubstreetaria'

With the metaphoric, uncapitalised 'grub street', Swift had much to do all his days. However, it was only around the time of his relatively brief stay in London, while he was in his middle forties, that he dabbled with Grub Street as such.[11] Four of the five references *eo nomine* which occur in his correspondence date from the years 1709 to 1712. The concentration is even more marked with the *Journal to Stella*. In the first half of the *Journal*, there are only two allusions, scattered through the major part of 1711. Between November of that year and December of the following year, Grub Street is mentioned no less than sixteen times. It should be noted that these occurrences run across the break in the text caused by the loss of those manuscripts which Deane Swift printed; 'Grub Street' is an authentic Swiftian phrase (as 'Presto', for instance, is not), and appears several times in the manuscript portion.

The concept, then, was most present to Swift's mind during his actual residence in London. You could be aware of the scribbling fraternity in Dublin or Letcombe Bassett – Swift obviously was. But it took direct contact with the everyday realities of the metropolis to slip, naturally and continuously, into the milieu of Grub Street, or into its idiom. Fielding was to argue that the extent of its dominions had been enlarged, and this is perhaps a proof that the term had lost symbolic identity when it shed topographical precision. The currency of the phrase in the first quarter of the century had preserved the London connection. After Pope's fantasy of Grub Street doings, blending so damagingly the *outré* and the down-to-earth, there was little room for fresh invention.

After his *Tale*, Swift seems to have left the idea dormant until March 1709. In that month he wrote from London to Robert Hunter, then a prisoner in French hands, and later Governor of New York: 'I could send you a great deal of news from the *Republica Grubstreetaria*, [*sic*] which was never in greater Altitude, though I have been of late but a small Contributor.' Swift, one observes, is thinking of himself as a citizen of the Grub Street realm. The language parodies the uninformative diplomatic intelligence of eighteenth-century newspapers. And once again the sphere of mercenary writing is allocated a posturing dignity, in this case a statehood of its own. In the following year Swift writes to his bookseller on the publication by Curll of *A Complete Key to the Tale of the Tub*: 'I believe it is so perfect a Grub-street-piece, it will be forgotten in a week.'[12] The locality is used here as an ordinary descriptive epithet, that is to characterise a shoddy and semi-piratical enterprise. In later years Swift would simply have written 'Curllian'. It did not take much in Scriblerian grammar to make a common noun from a proper.

As remarked, Swift appears to have grown more fond of the trope in 1711 and 1712. On 1 August 1712, or about then, he wrote to Vanessa, 'I will come as early on Monday as I can find Opportunity; and will take a little Grubstreet Lodging; pretty near where I did before; and dine with you thrice a week; and will tell You a thousand

Secrets provided You will have no Quarrells to me . . .' The letter is brisk, playful, relaxed. Its syntax tends to be staccato, conveying at once urgency and a certain determined orderliness. In the *Journal* he speaks of 'a hedge Lodging', address unknown, somewhere in the capital. Swift was obviously in no doubt that Vanessa would pick up the tone of his message. His accommodation will not be sumptuous, particularly after Windsor, but he will make do with it; it will be a reasonably convenient *pied-à-terre* from which to flirt with Vanessa, and anyway isn't it a suitable home for one who traffics in pamphlets and the public prints? A 'Grubstreet Lodging' is thus any old garret – you called it that because hacks infested such places and because there were plenty to let in the shacks of Cripplegate.[13]

In his very next surviving letter, Swift employs the expression twice in a couple of lines. He is writing to Jack Hill, soldier and *eminence grise*:

> Mrs Hill says, it was a very idle thing in you to send such a present to a man who can neither punish nor reward you, since Grub-street is no more: For the Parliament has killed all the Muses of Grub-street, who yet, in their last moments, cried out nothing but Dunkirk.

The allusion is to the imposition of stamp duty as from 1 August, a matter more fully dealt with in the *Journal*. One notes in passing that Swift cannot resist mythologising even in this perfunctory context. The mourning muses are a characteristic fancy by which he embellishes a piece of repressive legislation. After this date, Swift wrote several hundred more letters that have survived, not to speak of those which must have perished. But there is only one slight reference to 'the lowest Grub-street' in all these, and that relates to the Drapier's controversy in 1724. When Swift left London, he ceded Grub Street to his friends.[14]

It is the *Journal* which supplies most of the relevant material. Nor is that surprising. During the period of its composition, Swift was domiciled in London, deeply involved in public affairs, widely active in journalism. He moved amongst great men, but also among the underlings of the world of letters. As *Examiner* he combated stoutly with the Whig press, wielding their own chosen weapons in fierce and frontal assault. He was, some might say, himself an habitué of

Grub Street in these years.[15] Perhaps for that very reason, he eschews
the phrase in his published works. He speaks regularly of '*Wit-
starved* Writers, who have no other visible Support' (than attacking
him). He adopts an air of mincing irony, recalling the *Tale*, when
describing the 'Taste' of certain 'judicious Criticks'. He uses the
terms 'Answerers', 'merciless Pens', 'malicious Papers', and the
rest. But he abstains from the direct label 'Grub Street'.[16] Curiously,
he was in this only reflecting all the more faithfully the manners of
Grub Street itself.

On many of the occasions in which the trope occurs in the *Journal
to Stella*, Swift makes little play with it. Often the term figures simply
as a convenient shorthand. The first mention is on 31 January 1711;
Swift had been to see St John, as he then was, the Secretary of State.
'They are here intending', he informs Stella, 'to tax all printed penny
papers a half-penny every half-sheet, which will utterly ruin Grub-
street, and I am endeavouring to prevent it.' If Swift is serious, and I
think he is, his attitude is worthy of note. But the expression of his
views looks careless enough. There is perhaps a more indulgent touch
to the phrase than there would be later, but that is all. The metaphor
might be as dead as it is today. So too with the heedless phrase
'Grubstreet paper' which turns up on 21 August of that year: 'We
have only a Grubstreet paper of it, but I believe it is true.' Delicious
but![17]

Towards the end of the year, Swift's imagination seems to have
been caught in a more vivid and inward fashion by the possibilities
of the conceit. Of course, we still hear of Grub-street papers, Grub-
street accounts, and Grub-street speeches – though the latter (18
December) is noteworthy because Swift is protectively calling his
own poem about the Earl of Nottingham by this deprecatory title,
a trick he was to develop further.[18] Sometimes Swift hovers on the
edge of half-hearted personification: 'Do you know, that Grub-
street is dead and gone last Week,' he writes after the Stamp Act on 7
August 1712, 'No more Ghosts or Murders now for Love for Money.'
Or on 17 January 1712, when the act was being considered, and
Swift reported the Queen's desire to see 'some law to prevent libels
against the government; so farewel to Grub-street.' At other times

the phrase becomes one of straightforward opprobium: 'these devils of Grubstreet rogues . . . will not be quiet' (28 October 1712). In a more picturesque style, shortly afterwards: 'she [the Duchess of Hamilton] must have been tortured with the noise of the Grubstreet Screamers, mention her Husbands murder to her Ears.' The elliptical syntax obscures neither the sense nor Swift's indignation. Another linguistic stratagem was to use a Grubstreet as a noun, meaning a hack effusion – a more or less kindly usage, depending on the origin of the paper. Thus, Stella is briskly addressed on 12 December 1712: 'So you read one of the Grubstreets about the Bandbox . . .' On one occasion this is truncated to 'Grub', and combined with a muted prosopoeic figure: 'To day there will be anothr Grub; a Letter from the Pretendr to a Whig Ld. Grubstreet has but ten days to live, then an Act of Parlmt takes place, that ruins it . . .' (19 July 1712).[19]

The most conspicuous of these references form a separate class. In these, Swift is using the term as an evaluative or defining expression rather than just as a statement of source. For instance, Swift comments on his friend Arbuthnot's satire (17 June 1712): 'Well but John Bull is not writt by the Person you imagine, as I hope – It is too good for anothr to own, had it been Grubstreet, I would have let People think as they please . . .' In a letter already quoted, and with reference to the alleged bandbox plot, Swift writes, 'There was a pure Grubstreet of it full of Lyes and Inconsistencyes.' The two best examples of this class occur at the end of the previous year. In one, Swift describes his making a ballad 'two degrees above Grubstreet' (6 December 1711). The day before, he had written this significant sentence: 'I have got an under spur-leather [William Oldisworth] to write an *Examiner* again, and the secretary [St John] and I will now and then send hints; but we would have it a little upon the Grub-street, to be a match for their writers.' There is no clearer revelation of Swift's attitude than this. Grub Street is a fact of life, not something from which one averts one's eyes with horror. The battle has to be carried on, and if the terrain is Grub Street then the engines of war must be those fitted to such a mire-laden venue.[20]

On 17 July 1712 Swift told Stella, 'Since Dunkirk has been in our

Hands, Grubstreet has been very fruitfull: pdfr has writt 5 or 6 Grubstreet papers this last week.'[21] Swift himself was never so fruitful again, though he did not cease to turn out squibs, ballads, mock-petitions and anything else that topical events called for. With his departure from London and the full heat of publicist squabbles, he largely abandoned a concept which had been most prominent in his familiar writing around 1712. Of course, his *Journal* could not give added currency to the phrase, because it remained unpublished for over half a century. Yet Swift's reliance on the term is itself an indication of the part Grub Street played in early Scriblerian thinking. Moreover, Swift returned the expression to his vocabulary in his poems of the 1730's. On one momentous occasion, indeed, he capitalised on the situation which Pope had set up with *his* decisive mythmaking in the Grubean kind. And at least once he managed to turn one small plot of Irish land into a place that was forever Grub Street – a form of colonialism in fantasy that he must have relished more than the sterner forms it took in reality.

It may well be more than coincidence that Pope only draws on the expression twice in his extant correspondence, both in early years. In 1716 he writes to Caryll of 'a most ridiculous quarrel with a bookseller', that is the famous episode of Curll and the emetic, 'the history whereof has been transmitted to posterity by a late Grub-street author', namely Pope himself. At this stage of his career, Pope (like Swift in his *Journal*) unashamedly labels his polemical squibs in this fashion; later, he was to present himself as above the din of battle. Possibly his own removal to the then rural locality of Twickenham, distant from the clamorous suburbs of Dulness, helps to explain the change. Three years earlier, Pope had written to Gay a celebrated account of the new Scriblerian 'design', entered into by Swift, Parnell and himself:

Dr *Swift* much approves what I proposed even to the very title, which I design shall be, *The Works of the Unlearned*, published monthly, in which whatever Book appears that deserves praise, shall be depreciated Ironically, and in the same manner that modern Critics take to undervalue Works of Value, and to commend the high Productions of *Grubstreet*.

The phrase recalls that earlier title promised in the *Tale*, namely 'A Dissertation upon the principal Productions of *Grub-street*', In the formative years of Scriblerian satire, it was Swift whose idiom and even phraseology dominated the club. Literary trash is imaged as 'high Productions' with obvious irony; it may also derive from the garret (as in the *Epistle to Arbuthnot*, where the rhymer dwells 'high in *Drury-lane*' (41)), and like a ramshackle Grub Street hovel its lofty port is no guarantee of security or permanence.[22]

I have just said that Swift took up the conceit again in his poetry of the 1730's. Actually there are a couple of brief mentions earlier. One comes in a broadside aimed against William Wood in the course of the Drapier's controversy, entitled 'Prometheus'. The author supplies an aptly turned version of the Prometheus myth, in which 'this *Thief* and *Black-Smith*' substitutes a chain of brass for 'that *Chain* of *Gold*, | Which links the *Subject* to the *King*'. Probably the real target of the satire is Walpole, for whom '*brass* and *brazen* had become the standard nicknames.' In a poem of 75 lines, the word 'brass' occurs four times, and 'brazen' no less than five. However, the official reading of the allegory is more politic:

> Ye Pow'rs of *Grub-street* make me able,
> Discreetly to apply this *Fable*.
> Say, who is to be understood,
> By that old Thief *Prometheus?* WOOD
> For *Jove*, it is not hard to guess him,
> I mean *His Majesty, God bless him.*

The muse who presides over ballads and broadsides has no name in the classical pantheon, but Swift knew where to find her. Similarly 'The Progress of Poetry' (1720) shows us the needy hack in his garret, 'while from below all *Grub-street* rings.'[23]

After *The Dunciad*, references crowd in. The splendidly vivacious poem 'To Doctor Delany, on the Libels writ against him' (1730) provides a good example. Early on, Swift advises Delany to compose panegyrics upon the Irish parliament – the public spirit and honesty of its members, especially. Then, he will find,

> Thus grown a Member of the Club,
> No longer dread the Rage of *Grub*.

Later in the poem comes a contemptuous vignette of the hack author's ambience:

> Yet, what avails it to complain:
> You try to take Revenge in vain.
> A Rat your utmost Rage defyes
> That safe behind the Wainscoat lyes.
> Say, did you ever know by Sight
> In Cheese an individual Mite?
> Shew me the same numerick Flea,
> That bit your Neck but Yesterday,
> You then may boldly go in Quest
> To find the Grub-Street Poet's Nest,
> What Spunging-House in dread of Jayl
> Receives them while they wait for Bayl?
> What Ally are they nestled in,
> To flourish o'er a Cup of Ginn?
> Find the last Garret where they lay,
> Or Cellar, where they starve to Day . . .

One notes how, consciously or unconsciously, Swift takes up the idea of a grub or bug, the form of insect life which might be encountered in a dirty garret and which (imaginatively, anyway) might serve as eponym for the hacks' quarter. In an early work Pope had noted the transmogrification of 'Grubs obscene' into 'wriggling Worms,/Then painted Butterflies.' The horror of Swift's vermin is that they lack even this life-history; they are indistinguishable, myriad, swarming and pullulating in their fetid hole. Moreover, Delany cannot even be sure that he *has* been libelled by this obnoxious brood. The print-seller may be lying in order to whip up sales:

> Whate'er the noisy Scoundrel says
> It might be something in your Praise:
> And, Praise bestow'd in Grub-Street Rimes,
> Would vex one more a thousand Times . . .
> On me, when Dunces are satyrick,
> I take it for a Panegyrick.

Thus a vehement poem moves to its breezily unworried close. The libellers of Delany have been made small in a number of ways. Imagery, open contumely, inserted fable, have played their part. Not the least telling section, however, is that in which the anonymous and waspish assailants are consigned to a wretched habitat, combining Gin Lane, the debtor's prison and abject living quarters. Is it too literal-minded to recall that Grub Street was 'scarred with pestilential slum dwellings', with mean 'Courts and Alleys'; that its alehouses and dramshops were legion; or that the district had its places of confinement even before the White Cross Street debtors' gaol opened?[24]

A year later Swift returned briefly to the theme in his best-known poem, 'Verses on the Death of Dr Swift'.[25] It is a casual usage:

> Now Grub-Street Wits are all employ'd;
> With Elegies, the Town is cloy'd:
> Some Paragraph in ev'ry Paper,
> To *curse* the *Dean*, or *bless* the *Drapier*.

But in his other great creation of these years, 'On Poetry: A Rapsody', the idea looms much more prominently. This work might be regarded as Swift's final review of the Grub Street cohorts, whose puny yet belligerent antics he had observed ever since the *Tale* and *The Battle of the Books*. Among the many miseries which Swift describes as incident to the scribbler's career, he notes the annexation of former hack territory by a licensed invader, the poet laureate:

> Your Portion, taking *Britain* round,
> Was just one annual Hundred Pound.
> Now not so much as in Remainder
> Since *Cibber* brought in an Attainder;
> For ever fixt by Right Divine,
> (A Monarch's Right) on *Grubstreet* Line.
> Poor starvling Bard, how small thy Gains!

Again one sees the emphasis on the hereditary succession of Dulness, in this case given the dynastic power of George II – a King among Dunces (as Pope depicted him) and kingmaker into the bargain. One stratagem which Swift recommends, to help the unfortunate scribbler out of this fix, is to make sure that his work comes out anonymously: for 'Criticks have no partial Views,/Except they know whom they abuse.' But if the hack reveals his identity:

> You lose your Credit all at once;
> The Town will mark you for a Dunce:
> The vilest Doggrel *Grubstreet* sends,
> Will pass for yours with Foes and Friends.

Finally, after the celebrated passage in which Swift images the literary world in terms of vermin, fleas preyed on by smaller fleas, comes a masterly change of key into pretended lament:

> Thus ev'ry Poet in his Kind,
> Is bit by him that comes behind;
> Who, tho' too little to be seen,
> Can teaze, and gall, and give the Spleen;
> Call Dunces, Fools, and Sons of Whores,
> Lay *Grubstreet* at each others Doors:
> Extol the *Greek* and *Roman* Masters,
> And curse our modern Poetasters.
> Complain, as many an ancient Bard did,
> How Genius is no more rewarded . . .
> And all their Brother Dunces lash,
> Who crowd the Press with hourly Trash.

> O, *Grubstreet*! how do I bemoan thee,
> Whose graceless Children scorn to own thee!
> This filial Piety forgot,
> Deny their Country like a SCOT:
> Tho' by their Idiom and Grimace
> They soon betray their native Place:
> Yet *thou* hast greater Cause to be
> Asham'd of them, than they of thee.
> Degenerate from their ancient Brood,
> Since first the Court allow'd them Food.

This is a climactic moment in the evolution of Grub Street mythology, characteristically handled (almost slurred over, indeed) by Swift, with his easy vernacular of scorn.[26]

In these lines a number of the principal elements in the myth are brought together. The image of parasitic insects carries with it the usual idea of internecine struggle, the relentless competitive urge of men on the make. Similarly, the scribblers emerge as ungrateful, groundlessly vain of their place in literary history, *arrivistes* whose low origins are only too clear. On this occasion, Grub Street is explicitly call a territory, in the comparison with Scotland. Elsewhere in the poem more is said of the 'Idiom', that is not just the argot but the whole life-style of hacks, and the 'Grimace', the unlovely postures they strike at the behest of any well-heeled patron. Like his friend Pope, Swift draws attention to the municipal organisation of the Dunces:

> But these are not a thousandth Part
> Of Jobbers in the Poets Art,
> Attending each his proper Station,
> And all in due Subordination;
> Thro' ev'ry Alley to be found,
> In Garrets high, or under Ground . . .

'Jobbers' because they are middlemen, ingrafters, men who profit out of warmongering. And Swift, too, has noticed the way in which urban civilisation mirrors the spread of Dulness:

> For Poets (you can never want 'em,
> Spread thro' *Augusta Trinobantum*)
> Computing by their Pecks of Coals,
> Amount to just Nine thousand Souls.
> These o'er their proper Districts govern,
> Of Wit and Humour, Judges sov'reign.
> In ev'ry Street a City-bard
> Rules, like an Alderman his Ward.
> His indisputed Rights extend
> Thro' all the Lane, from End to End.
> The Neighbours round admit his *Shrewdness*,
> For songs of *Loyalty* and *Lewdness*.

And further, the contention between 'two bordering Wits':

> Some famed for Numbers soft and smooth,
> By Lovers spoke in *Punch*'s Booth.
> And some as justly Fame extols
> For lofty Lines in *Smithfield* Drols.
> *Bavius* in *Wapping* gains Renown,
> And *Maevius* reigns o'er *Kentish-Town*:
> *Tigellius* plac'd in *Phoebus*' Car,
> From *Ludgate* shines to *Temple-bar*.

After Tigellius, the bard of Fleet Street, comes Cibber, court laureate. The point is exactly the same as Pope's – just as the civic hierarchy has broken down, with city men invading the West End, so cultural order has been shattered. Dulness spills over from Drury Lane to St James's.[27]

There could be no clearer demonstration of the impress of the first *Dunciad* upon Swift's mind. He had been out of England for almost twenty years, excluding two brief periods in the mid-twenties. He lived in the comparatively un-metropolitan Dublin, where city fathers counted for less and where the 'suburban muse' had no chartered home. Yet he writes in the familiar 'idiom' of Grub Street: the 'lofty Lines in *Smithfield* Drols' is a choice expression, holding much of *The Dunciad* in little. Elsewhere in the 'Rapsody', we encounter other ingredients of earlier Scriblerian satire. There is the stress on duncely heritage, with the rollcall of bad poets such as Flecknoe and Blackmore; the usual easy reference to topicalities, and to the passing London scene ('Sir *Bob*', 'A *Wills*', 'A *Statesman*, or a South-Sea *Jobber*', and so on); the familiar quest for the Bathos:

> For instance; When you rashly think,
> No Rhymer can like *Welsted* sink.
> His Merits ballanc'd you shall find,
> The Laureat leaves him far behind.
> *Concannen*, more aspiring Bard,
> Climbs downwards, deeper by a Yard:
> Smart JEMMY MOOR with Vigor drops,
> The Rest pursue as thick as Hope:
> With Heads to Points the Gulph they enter,
> Linkt perpendicular to the Centre:
> And as their Heels elated rise,
> Their Heads attempt the nether Skies.

There is the customary reference to a bookseller, here Lintot, whose offences against Swift must have been marginal and second-hand. There is a verse compounded of loathing, whose very utterance requires a sort of contemptuous expectoration: 'The Spawn of *Bridewell*, or the *Stews*'. Most striking of all, perhaps, following a reference to 'A Duchess, or a Suburb-Wench', this bit of poetic townscaping:

> Or oft when Epithets you link,
> In gaping Lines to fill a Chink;
> Like stepping Stones to save a Stride,
> In Streets where Kennels are too wide:
> Or like a Heel-piece to support
> A Cripple with one Foot too short:
> Or like a Bridge that joins a Marish
> To Moorlands of a diff'rent Parish.

This is like some Hogarthian nightmare, with its crowd of infected, tumultuous, irrevocably *urban* visions. It would be fanciful to read into the lines a conscious reference to the marsh of Moorfields, abutting on the parish of Cripplegate. One need not even assert that Swift drew subliminally on such recollections of the London scene. It is quite enough to remark that, unfailingly, the topography and nomenclature of London's ghetto suburbs come to the aid of the poetry. When the Augustan satirists think of foul conditions, they never stray far from the map of London.[28]

I have not pointed out these elements in order to impugn the 'Rapsody' on the score of originality. On the contrary, it is full of the flavour and race of Swift. The interesting fact remains: it was written in 1733, the last of its author's major poems. (I exclude 'The Legion Club', where the undeniable power is in some degree a function of distortion or imbalance.) The 'Rapsody' is controlled, assured, precise in aim. If it lacks the dramatic conviction and engagement of the *Epistle to Arbuthnot*, the 'Rapsody' does exhibit abundant imaginative life. All in all, it constitutes Swift's most complete enquiry into the present state of Dulness, once the *Tale* was behind him. By contrast 'The Legion Club' offers sustained invective. Only the opening description of the 'large and lofty' building which houses Parliament can be seen to allude to the themes we have been considering.[29]

In the poems considered, a few references to the fraternity of 'Dunces' may have been observed. These also are concentrated in the later poems. Apart from the instances quoted, the expression is found in 'A Libel on Doctor Delany' (1730) and, in a less specialised sense than usual, in 'A Panegyric on Dr Swift' (1730). This is, of course, a further sign of the ways in which Swift's poetic vocabulary was modified after the appearance of *The Dunciad*.[30]

If Grub Street itself is not conspicuous in the correspondence of Swift, then the full panoply of ugliness which the term stood for is much more prominent. Both in letters to Swift and in his own communications to friends, the plagues of Dulness occupy a good deal of space. London correspondents, predictably, furnish apt examples. As remarked in Ch.I, the doughty City alderman, John Barber, wrote to Swift, in 1732 describing 'a raree-show (or pageant)' with a satirical poem 'thrown from the press to the mob, in public view'. This cavalcade had been briefly foreshadowed by Anthony Henley, in a letter of twenty years earlier. Swift himself writes to Barber of the riots occasioned by the Excise Crisis, with all the intense concern of an expatriate. The doings of the 'mob' and the 'rabble' figure largely in the letters of the Harley ministry era – as witness the index to Sir Harold Williams' edition, *sub voce* 'mob'. Events retailed to Swift in his isolation include a fire on Tower Hill, described by Charles Ford. Another time a correspondent mentions the sights of the town as they were then conceived: '[we] made the tour of the city: we saw *Bedlam*, the lions, and what not . . .' When Swift himself is in London, his topics range from the Mohocks to scurrilous 'Scribblers'. In short, the separate strands that went into the symbolic drama of Grub Street can be plucked from the journal of everyday doings that go into the correspondence. What was physically oppressive becomes no less painful when ritualised in art. The harsh lineaments of eighteenth-century London take on an aspect of grotesque comedy in the mask of satire; but the face still fits.[31]

The Road to Tyburn

It is hard to think of any major artist so possessed by one quarter of the town as was Swift by Newgate and its environs. Two aspects of the social character of this district were overlaid on one another to produce this striking impress. As outlined earlier, there came together in this quarter two potent currents of myth – Smithfield, with its tradition of fairs and boisterous showbiz junketings, and Newgate, the epicentre of crime and punishment. Thus geography locked in symbolic embrace the centre of the entertainment industry – a moddern, but not inappropiate, phrase – and the setting for that drama of guilt and retribution which acted out the same penal ethos as did Augustan satire. Clearly, physical proximity went with other bases of comparison. The Fleet ran across this tract of land, bringing in its sluggish wake the usual flotsam of squalor. In addition, since the procession to Tyburn set off from Newgate up Holborn, the abundant files of the malefactors' register supplied a ready-made Newgate literature, to match the productions of the Smithfield muse. When Pope wrote of 'hymning Tyburn's elegiac lay' (B.I.41), he was helping to forge this link. And when journalists of the time spoke of the court at Old Bailey as a 'scene' or 'theatre', they were likewise suggesting a parallel with the elaborately staged shows at Bartholomew Fair. Defoe, for example, relating the end of Jonathan Wild, speaks of 'the last scene of his Life at the Gallows' and adds 'the Scene was then short'. He refers to the 'Tragedy' enacted. Of course, the semantic facts follow the historical facts. Tyburn executions *were* staged as theatrical set-pieces.[32]

All this, every writer of the age inherited. Swift is unique in the pressure exerted on him, not in the nature of the influence. It was he who, in a suggestive aside, originally set out the idea of 'a Newgate pastoral, among the whores and thieves there', over a decade before *The Beggar's Opera*. Long before, in the *Journal*, he had spoken of 'a Smithfield bargain', the proverbial phrase for a sharp deal. He writes to Pope of 'deal[ing] in the Smithfield way.' His letters include references to Newgate and the Press Yard.[33] Throughout his life, he seems to have used Smithfield and Newgate as synonomous with quackery, crooked business and wrongdoing of every kind. It was he rather than Pope (or so the evidence suggests) who first seized the literary and lexical potentialities that were lurking beneath the London gazetteer with its offhand listing of familiar place-names. Swift, with his oddly literal-minded genius, leapt from the most commonplace reality to fancy.

In 1709–10 Swift wrote two famous poems for *The Tatler*. These comparatively short works have attracted a large amount of attention, perhaps because of a misleading 'realism' which causes them to be read as engaging travesties of classical originals, in which heroic idiom is risibly applied to squalid objects. That their effect is more complex than this, recent criticism has begun to establish. Roger Savage, in a perceptive essay on 'A Description of the Morning', has shown some of the other contributory elements in the poem. He argues:

> The *Description of the Morning* has often been seen as a piece of un-complicated realism, vivid and assured or barren and pointless, according to the taste of the critic; but its realism is not simply the result of a walk through London at dawn with a camera. It is determined and moulded by what Swift has learned from the masters of the descriptive tradition and by the attitude to them he had come to adopt. The poem is basically mock-*descriptio*, a comic imitation of the classical ideal; and on this level it reads like a parody of the dawn-scene in Bysshe's *Parnassus* . . . The mythology is adapted daringly and wittily from the classical tradition, and the result is rich burlesque. . . . Swift here is not simply putting a moustache on the *Mona Lisa*, reducing outward tradition to mere grotesque. . . . [Whereas] his journalist contemporary, Tom Brown . . . has a journalist's camera: Swift is working on a canvas prepared for formal *descriptio*. . . . Where [other writers of burlesque see] realism as one device among many useful to the parodist, Swift seems to be using burlesque of the formal *descriptio* just so that he can draw attention to the real, to common city nature. There is no place in his strategy for conceits *or* whimsies.

After devoting some attention to the companion piece on 'A City Shower', Mr Savage concludes:

> traditional ideal art . . . is at once a yard-stick and a dead letter, while the crude actual is both a source of vitality and a target for neo-classic irony. . . . The classics embody a just and beautiful nature; the contemporary realities of a sordid Queen Anne London are no more than a travesty of true nature; so to copy these apparent realities . . . is to travesty the classics.

In the light of this clinching analysis, it would obviously be a mistake to regard these poems as simply rendering the 'crude actual' in a comically high-falutin' style. The high and the low interact on one another. They form (to adapt one of Mr Savage's expressions) a chemical compound.[34]

Some valuable insights are provided by another recent critic, Brendan O Hehir. In assessing the meaning of the 'Shower' poem, Mr O Hehir observes that 'the two named well springs of the Flood have each stronger associations with moral than with physical corruption.' He mentions such Smithfield attributes as the profligacy of Bartholomew Fair, and notes the attempts to suppress the fair around this time. Settle's presence there in 1707 is also brought into account. Mr O Hehir stresses the notorious connotations of Newgate, ranging from the Tyburn procession to the offal which was left near the meat emporium. His analysis neatly relates such phenomena as the Fleet Ditch, 'the notorious cloaca of eighteenth-century London', and the 'abuse of moral and civil laws' of which the indecorous, deliberately mangled conclusion is emblematic. In fact, though he makes no claim along these lines, Mr O Hehir's eassay could be viewed as a pioneering attempt to uncover the topographic strata in Augustan satiric vocabulary.[35]

With these studies behind us, it is possible to speak more briefly of Swift's two 'Description' poems. In particular, the 'Morning' assembles standard *topoi* of the critique of Dulness – dirt, shrill noise, the lascivious maid and the slipshod prentice, bailiffs crowding the doorstep, the ill-made road, and

> The Turnkey now his Flock returning sees,
> Duly let out a Nights to Steal for Fees.

Yet these elements are left as separate motifs in a posed landscape – what Mr Savage recognises as the *descriptio* framework. Later on, both Pope and Swift himself will energise this scene, and by dissolving physical squalor, poverty and crime in one supreme metaphor they will achieve a symbolic rather than an allegoric truth – a fictional rather than a scenic vividness – a mythic rather than a journalistic entity.

The 'City Shower' is more elaborate, but something of the same process can be discerned. Briefly Swift introduces a lay figure of the type Pope utilises in his Horatian poems:

> Sauntring in Coffee-house is *Dulman* seen;
> He damns the Climate, and complains of Spleen.

But the character is dropped straight away, and the kind of spectator through whom Gay focusses the London sights in *Trivia* is dismissed from the carefully managed tableau. The setting is representative rather than detailed; the method one of graphic portraiture instead of real dramatisation. In Mr Savage's terms, the poem displays 'the ludicrous attempt of an imperfect, trivial London to live up to classical dialects and situations.'[36] The first epithet is important. What would be sinister in other contexts – an offensive stink, spleen, the feuds of 'Triumphant Tories, and desponding Whigs', drunkards, bullies, 'frightful Din' – remain on the level of amiable vignettes. There is more than one reason for this state of affairs. It has a good deal to do with Swift's uninvolved, sharply dismissive tone. But another major factor is the absence of a controlling metaphor. In the 'Shower' there is a single momentary entrance by the 'needy Poet'. Not until the idea of Dulness, with its more than spiritual home in the suburbs, was developed, would the satirists manage to turn the impressionistic photomontage into a literary fiction embodying genuine understanding. The discovery of Grub Street opened a new imaginative continent. The satire moved from social, pictorial, emblematic observation towards poetic and cultural insight. Once the myth was evolved, the writers had a basis for imagery, an explanation along with a symbol, a story-line to go with a location.

Nevertheless, when we come to the famous closing passage, it does, I think, acquire a new reverberation in the light of the argument presented in this book:

> Now from all Parts the swelling Kennels flow,
> And bear their Trophies with them as they go:
> Filth of all Hues and Odours seem to tell
> What Streets they sail'd from, by the Sight and Smell.
> They, as each Torrent drives, with rapid Force
> From *Smithfield*, or St. *Pulchre*'s shape their Course,
> And in huge Confluent join at *Snow-Hill* Ridge,
> Fall from the *Conduit* prone to *Holborn*-Bridge.
> Sweepings from Butchers Stalls, Dung, Guts, and Blood,
> Drown'd Puppies, stinking Sprats, all drench'd in Mud,
> Dead Cats and Turnip-Tops come tumbling down the Flood.

Lengthy analysis would be redundant. The torrents of Dulness concentrate into the noisome 'Flood' (ironic, of course) which is the ditch. This confluence of all that is most physically oppressive and fetid reveals the modern capital in its full glory. Humanist lore had pictured the city as the repository of civilised values. Instead of this rounded, polished, refined nucleus of the best in communal living ('urbanity', in the old sense) there is the new urbanism. Mortality instead of the timeless perfection of the great city: 'Trophies' won not in heroic combat but dredged from the lowest haunts of men. Many commentators have argued that Swift, in *Gulliver* and elsewhere, achieves his almost unbearable power through a repeated contrast he draws between the more-than-human aspirations of humanity and the sub-human physicality of life as it is actually lived. At the end of the 'Shower', he makes the same point; a vision of animalism as modern city experience make us live it. And all this in a single, precisely plotted corner of London.[37]

Swift reminds us that London was not only the great mart, but also a major productive centre. Yet, paradoxically, its landscape remained in part agrarian, with livestock commonplace in the streets. Nor was there anything paranoid or peculiar about Swift's view of Newgate. As noted, the *British Journal* compared 'the Droves that are carried to Tyburn' with those that are sent to Smithfield for the same purpose – thus linking the slaughter of beasts with that of criminals.[38] What was dubbed in *Bartholomew Fair* (II, iii) 'the heavy hill of Holborn' was ominous chiefly on account of the human carnage; but this was also the route of the last journey for countless animals bound for the abattoir. The Augustans tended to be unsentimental about such things, but they were well aware of the atmosphere of sudden death which clung to Smithfield.

Nevertheless, the district was in the entertainment business. Apart from the fairground drolls, the executions were themselves among the biggest free shows in town. Rudé expresses it thus:

> The greatest sport of all was to watch the hangings at 'Tyburn Fair' [note the expression] or to toast the victims in beer or gin as they were carried along Holborn, St Giles's and Oxford Street to the place of execution. 'Within my recollection,' wrote [Francis] Place, 'a *hanging day* was to all intents and purposes a fair day. The streets from Newgate to

Tyburn were thronged with people, and all the windows were filled.'
The onlookers on such 'brutalizing occasions' were, added Place with
pardonable exaggeration, composed of 'the whole vagabond population
of London, all the thieves, and all the prostitutes, and all those who
were evil-minded, and some, comparatively few, curious people'.

This concourse of Dulness went on till public executions ceased in
1783, in the teeth of Samuel Johnson and others. At intervals of
about six weeks, the grisly charade would go on. It is worth recalling
that in the period 1688–1718 over fifty per cent of those convicted on capital charges actually went to the gallows. More rarely
burnings went on at Tyburn, generally for that inveterate Cripplegate practice, coining. Barbara Spencer, born in the parish and resident in a Moorfields alehouse, went to the stake at Tyburn in 1721.
Others such as Mary Berry, who lodged in Grub Street itself and
then in Moorfields, and who was found guilty of coining in 1732,
no doubt followed her. But more commonly the cart would halt before St Sepulchre's, the principal as likely as not dressed in his best
clothes, while the other supporting actors wore mourning, and the
cortege would wend its way to Tyburn.[39]

It was this performance which drove so deep into the eighteenth-
century mind. The literature of the time is full of allusions, bleak or
flippant, direct or indirect. Thus, Sir Sampson Legend – apposite
surname – of his son Valentine in Congreve's *Love for Love*:

Sirrah, you'll be hanged; I shall live to see you go up Holborn Hill.
Has he not a rogue's face? Speak, brother, you understand physio-
gnomy; a hanging look to me – of all my boys the most unlike me. He
has a damned Tyburn face, without the benefit of the clergy.

Naturally, literary men were not immune from the widespread interest in these regular displays. When Boswell first came up to London,
he succumbed to the popular feeling:

My curiosity to see the melancholy spectacle of the executions was so
strong that I could not resist it, although I was sensible that I would
suffer much from it. In my younger years I had read in the *Lives of
the Convicts* so much about Tyburn that I had a sort of horrid eagerness
to be there. I also wished to see the last behaviour of Paul Lewis, the
handsome fellow whom I had seen the day before [on a visit to New-
gate]. Accordingly I took Captain Temple with me, and he and I got

upon a scaffold very near the fatal tree, so that we could clearly see all the dismal scene. There was a most prodigious crowd of spectators. I was most terribly shocked, and thrown into a very deep melancholy.

This dates from 1763, and it is filtered through Boswell's highly idiosyncratic sensibility. Yet the passage comes close to the heart of that fascinated disgust which permeates Augustan satire. Boswell's 'horrid eagerness' corresponds to the blend of emotions with which society regarded glamorous criminals, and with which Pope obsessively recorded the annals of a segment of the population whose doings he held in abhorrence.[40] The 'grotesqueries sublimed into loveliness' within his poems derive from this mixture of repulsion and creative infatuation.

Undoubtedly the publication of a huge Newgate literature contributed to the state of affairs I have outlined. The 'Lives of the Convicts' were important literary documents, if only on account of their popularity. Moreover, the one Dunce of genius chances to have forged a major imaginative vehicle (the novel) to no inconsiderable degree out of the materials of rogues' tales. This is a matter for separate attention elsewhere. However, we may note at this point that John Oldham had already noted how the suburban muse was active in the composition of the malefactors' register. His lines 'Upon a Printer' contain the following:

> May'st thou ne'er rise to History, but what
> Poor *Grubstreet* Penny Chronicles relate,
> Memoirs of *Tyburn* and the mournful State
> Of Cut-purses in *Holborn* Cavalcade . . .

On another occasion, Oldham had called up another local association:

> Till urg'd by Want, like broken Scriblers, thou
> Turn Poet to a Booth, a *Smithfield* Show,
> And write Heroick Verse for *Barthol'mew*.[41]

For most of his life Swift was unable to follow this 'cavalcade' himself, though he did take a close interest in a rather similar phenomenon, the anti-popery procession of 1711.[42] However, 'Memoirs of *Tyburn*' were always in his line: witness a poem such as 'Clever *Tom Clinch* going to be hanged' (1726). This opens,

As clever *Tom Clinch*, while the Rabble was bawling,
Rode stately through *Holbourn*, to die in his Calling;
He stopt at the *George* for a Bottle of Sack . . .

and passes on via reference to Jonathan Wild to a resolute conclusion: 'Then follow the Practice of clever *Tom Clinch*, / Who hung
like a Hero, and never would flinch.'[43] Again, there is 'Blue-skin's
Ballad', variously attributed to Swift and to Gay, a sort of *Beggar's
Opera* writ small, with the ostensible setting named as Newgate
gaol and the Old Bailey, but the animus obviously directed against
Walpole, the Court and its placemen. ('Honest *Wild*' figures once
more.)[44] These, and there are others like them, are not poems of high
merit. Their interest derives from the fact that Swift, in exile, still
turns to the criminal ecology of London to develop his moral and
political critique of the age. There were criminals and desperados
in Dublin; there was the full array of judicial pomp. But the
authentic Tyburn imagery could not be translated to Ireland; it
flourished only in its native soil, where the grisly 'tree' thrust its
roots deep into the English imagination.

Swift's links with Bedlam and Bridewell have been noted in
previous chapters. More interesting in some ways is his special in-
volvement with the bookselling quarter of Little Britain. In fact the
stretch of the road formerly known as Duck Lane, running out of
Smithfield, was the part that interested him. In Stow's description,
'*Duck-lane* cometh out of *Little Brittain*, and falls into *Smithfield*,
a Place early inhabited by Booksellers, that sell second-hand Books.'
According to some authorities Little Britain was already losing
ground to the area about St Paul's; this is what John Macky, usually
a reliable witness, implies in 1724. Certainly in the reports of Robert
Harley's press spy around 1705, printers were still numerous in
Little Britain: at least one leading music publisher set up there in the
1730's. A number of figures in the newspaper business were located
there well into the century. The unfortunate John Matthews lived
in the street, where the family printing works stood. According to
the eminent antiquarian Sir Henry Ellis, the Ballards 'were the last
of the old race of booksellers who inhabited Little Britain.' Probably
the high point in the history of the area had been the late seventeenth

century. It was then that John Oldham wrote of the archetypal Dunces Ogilby and Quarles,

> Who after shalt in *Duck-Lane* Shops be thrown,
> To mould with *Silvester*, and *Shirley* there,
> And truck for pots of Ale next *Stourbridg-Fair*.

Samuel Buckley, the printer turned Gazetteer and government liaison man, lived in Little Britain in later years. It was through contacts such as these that Pope and Swift must have come to know the place. For Moll Flanders it had been simply an avenue of escape; for the Scriblerian group, it became a ready and affectionate topic. The unusual name of the street occasioned some byplay. The author of *A Trip through London* (1728) thinks it proper to remind the inhabitants that 'the same is a Part of his Majesty's Dominions', although the inhabitants act as if it weren't. And similarly Swift to Alderman Barber in 1738: 'pox on the modern phrase *Great Britain*, which is only to distinguish it from Little Britain, where old cloaths and books are to be bought and sold'. In a pamphlet of five years earlier, Swift makes mention of rummaging about in Duck Lane. If the 'Shower' devises an *ur*-Grub Street in the Newgate area, Duck Lane formed a sort of equivalent to Moorfields and Rag Fair – likewise the resting place of the second-hand and the unwanted.[45]

Some of the associations trapped within the orbit of Smithfield may be gauged from this passage of Andrew Marvell's *Rehearsal Transpros'd*, the first satire to develop the Grub Street conceit (Ch. VI).

> The Duke of Muscovy indeed declared war against Poland because he and his nation had been vilifyed by a Polish poet: but the author of the Ecclesiastical Politie [Samuel Parker] would, it seems, disturb the peace of Christendom for the good old cause of a superannuated chanter of Saffron-Hill and Pye-Corner. But though indeed he doth not write his books in the Smithfield metre, yet they are all blank ballad . . .[46]

Pope was equally to associate 'superannuated' bards like Settle with Smithfield, on account both of the Fair and of his Charterhouse lodging. Swift assuredly knew *The Rehearsal Transpros'd*.[47] Though he never took this hint farther into a full-blown Smithfield myth, as works like the 'Shower' seem to promise, he had two good excuses.

He was in close touch with Pope, and privileged to get advanced news of the progress of his friend's 'Dulness' during its composition. Secondly, and less happily, he was physically removed from the appointed shrine of Dulness.

Public Abuses

Swift often lamented his exile in Dublin. How genuine this often-expressed feeling was, we may find it hard to decide. Professor Ehrenpreis has suggested that 'there is always a first-handedness in his experience of his native country which the life in England lacked . . . Throughout his activities in Ireland one notices a zestfulness, a contact with reality, a depth of insight, which Swift often fails to exhibit in England . . .'[48] Whatever the truth on this point, it cannot be denied that Swift makes great rhetorical play with the fact of exile. A good example crops up in a splendid and too little considered poem, 'To Charles Ford Esqr on his Birth-day' (1723). Notable for rapid, well managed transitions, this work modulates at one juncture into a passionate outburst against London. Its swarm of 'bugs and Hanoverians', its oppressive police-state régime under Townshend 'threatning the Pillory and Jayl', are presented in lurid yet explicit terms, echoing for a moment those of Pope's 'Epilogue to the Satires' of fifteen years later. How can Ford, currently on a visit to Ireland, wish to return to such a place ? Then Swift adopts a more confidential tone towards Ford; the style grows more intimate, if not chatty :

> I thought my very Spleen would burst
> When Fortune hither drove me first;
> Was full as hard to please as You,
> Nor Persons Names, nor Places knew;
> But now I act as other Folk,
> Like Pris'ners when their Gall is broke.
> If you have London still at heart
> We'll make a small one here by Art:
> The Diff'rence is not much between
> St James's Park and Stephen's Green;
> And Dawson street will serve as well
> To lead you thither, as Pell-mell . . .

And so on, for thirty sharply chiselled lines more.[49] It may look here like a desperate fiction, a wish-fulfilment perhaps. Yet there are indications that Swift may have been affected at a serious level by the notion of the mountain coming to Mahomet. At least, the goonish conceit of transplanting London 'by art' to the banks of the Liffey occurs more than once.

In this connection we must consider two works sometimes relegated to the Swiftian apocrypha. The first is the *Letter to a Young Poet*, well-known and often reprinted as Swift's. Some recent enquiries have cast doubt on this attribution and have disputed the validity of certain statististical findings. In my view the matter has not yet been established beyond doubt.[50] A fondness for certain syntactical forms is doubtless one important element in the profile of a given writer. It may be, however, that there are equally good tests, less amenable to statistical analysis. For example, the controls which an author brings into effect with relation to euphony deserve attention. It is possible to imagine, that is, the writer breaking a life-long habit and employing completely new syntactical patterns, for some particular end. Yet he might never permit a jarring hiatus – putting 'they amiably parted' for 'they parted amiably' – no matter what the overall structure of the sentence. It is also highly interesting, to return to the present case, to observe the use of Swift's favourite imagery in the *Letter to a Young Poet*. The rationale here is that critics were then largely unconscious of this element in style, or at least very little inclined to treat of it directly. Their terminology for discussing metaphoric activity of any kind was somewhat primitive, and they habitually take no account of such things as the sustained figures in Shakespeare or the controlling metaphors (as we should say today) in a work such as *Absalom and Achitophel*. One consequence of this state of affairs is that even an able parodist would be unlikely to attempt a close copy of his subject's figurative devices. When, therefore, we come on not merely the ideas of Swift, the language of Swift, and the humour of Swift in this *Letter*, but also – more tangibly – the metaphoric idiom of Swift, the case grows less easy to brush aside. I do not know if Swift did write the *Letter*, but I am sure that the evidence so far adduced against his authorship is less than conclusive.

Certain of the apparently Swiftian features might be explained as merely the product of a remarkably sedulous ape. There is a well-known section concerning the 'short and easy Method lately found out of Abstracts, Abridgments, Summaries, &c. which are admirable Expedients for being very learned with little or no Reading.' The hint for this might easily have been taken from the 'Digression in Praise of Digressions' in the *Tale*. Even here there is a surprising metaphysical wit in evidence: 'For authors are to be used like Lobsters, you must look for the best Meat in the Tails, and lay the Bodies back again in the Dish.' Perhaps a skilled paradist of Swift *could* have possessed his distinctly seventeenth-century character of mind, but one should not multiply such hypotheses beyond reason. At all events, the writer exhibits plenty of concrete life, with an easy recourse to homely analogy. Thanks to the modern editor, he says, 'every author . . . sweats under himself, being over-loaded with his own Index, and carries, like a North-Country Pedlar, all his Substance and Furniture upon his Back, and with as great Variety of Trifles'. It may not be Swift, but it really is quite magnificent.

The second half of the *Letter* is more directly relevant. The writer sets out his thoughts for the encouragement of poetry in the kingdom. Initially his topics are unmistakably Irish, with Hibernian politics and economics hovering in the background.

> . . . And withal of what great Benefit it may be to our Trade to encourage that Science here, (for it is plain our Linen-Manufacture is advanced by the great Waste of Paper made by our present Sett of Poets, not to mention other necessary Uses of the same to Shopkeepers, especially Grocers, Apothecaries, and Pastry-Cooks; and I might add, but for our Writers, the Nation wou'd be in a little time be utterly destitute of Bum-Fodder, and must of Necessity import the same from England and Holland, where they have it in great abundance, by the indefatigable Labour of their own Wits . . .

Here are several familiar ingredients in the assault on Dulness. The patriotic projector, trumpeting his 'Birth-right as a Briton'; the sanitary allusions; the hypostasised present set of wits, unnaturally leagued together; the cosy intimacy with journeymen of the town.

No surprise, consequently, when the next paragraph makes this link explicit:

Seriously then, I have many Years lamented the want of a Grub-Street in this our large and polite City [Dublin], unless the whole may be called one. . . . Every one knows Grub-Street is a Market for Small-Ware in Wit, as necessary, considering the usual Purgings of the human Brain, as the Nose is upon a Man's Face: And for the same Reasons we have here a Court, a College, a Playhouse, and beautiful Ladies, and fine Gentlemen, and good Claret, and abundance of Pens, Ink, and Paper, (clear of Taxes) and every other Circumstance to provoke Wit; and yet those whose Province it is have not yet thought fit to appoint a place for Evacuations of it. . . .

This 'Defect' has not only prejudiced the commonwealth of letters, it has even impaired the citizens' health:

I believe our corrupted Air, and frequent thick Fogs, are in a great measure owing to the common exposal of our Wit, and that with good Management our poetical Vapours might be carry'd off in a common Drain, and fall into one Quarter of the Town, without infecting the whole, as the Case is at Present, to the great Offence of our Nobility and Gentry, and others of nice Noses. When Writers of all Sizes, like Freemen of the City, are at liberty to throw out their Filth and excrementious Productions in every Street as they please, what can the Consequence be, but that the Town must be poyson'd, and become such another Jakes, as by report of our great Travellers, Edinburgh is at Night, a thing well to be consider'd in these pestilential Times.[51]

For once, the projector is opposed to the effects of Dulness; but the diagnosis itself is the customary one. Likewise with the appeal which follows to the municipal authorities, asking them to serve two ends at once, 'both to keep the Town sweet, and encourage Poetry in it'. Nor is any exception to be made for satirical poets or writers of lampoons,

for though indeed their Business is to rake into Kennels, and gather up the Filth of Streets and Families, (in which respect they may be, for aught I know, as necessary to the Town as Scavengers or Chimney sweeps) yet I have observed they too have themselves at the same Time very foul cloathes, and, like dirty Persons, leave more Filth and Nastiness than they sweep away.

If this is simulated repugnance, a careful take-off of Swift's passion for cleanliness, it is notably well carried out.

At this juncture there appears the central thesis:

> In a Word, what I would be at . . . is, That some private Street, or
> blind Alley, of this Town may be fitted up at the Charge of Publick,
> as an apartment for the Muses, (like those at Rome and Amsterdam, for
> their Female Relations) and be wholly consigned to the Uses of our
> Wits, furnish'd compleatly with all Appurtenances, such as Authors,
> Supervisors, Presses, Printers, Hawkers, Shops, and Ware-Houses,
> abundance of Garrets, and every other Implement and Circumstance
> of Wit; the Benefit of which would obviously be this, viz. That we
> should then have a safe Repository for our best Productions, which at
> present are handed about in Single Sheets or Manuscripts, and may
> altogether be lost, (which were a Pity) or at the best are subject, in that
> loose Dress, like handsome Women, to great Abuses.

I hope that this far into my argument it will be unnecessary to specify
each commonplace of the Scriblerian satiric platform. Once again
hack writing is forced to find its accomodation in the worst part of the
town; its devotees go cheek by jowl with whores, its stock of 'every
. . . Implement and Circumstance of Wit' packed into crowded
commercial premises hedged about with garrets. The location of
Little Britain in relation to Smithfield, Saffron Hill and Holborn
comes quickly to mind.

The narrator then turns to the state of the playhouse, and moves to
a proposal that if the national bank is granted a charter, so then should
poetry be accorded this privilege. And he has another scheme, taken
directly from the *Tale*:

> I believe also, it might be proper to erect a Corporation of Poets in this
> City. I have been Idle enough in my Time, to make a Computation of
> Wits here, and do find we have three hundred performing Poets and
> upwards, in and about this Town, reckoning six Score to the Hundred,
> and allowing for Demi's, like Pint Bottles; including also the several
> Denominations of Imitators, Translators, and Familiar-Letter-Writers,
> &c.

These scribblers will easily 'furnish out' a corporation. Moreover,
there are abundant poetasters (if not one 'Masterly Poet') to supply
enough 'Wardens and Beadles' – the municipal image again. This
desire to see poetry made a lackey of the civic authorities is plainly
enunciated at one point:

> I long to see the Day, when our Poets will be a regular and distinct Body, and wait upon our Lord-mayor on publick Days, like other good Citizens, in Gowns turn'd up with Green instead of lawrels; and when I myself, who make this Proposal, shall be free of their Company.

Pope was to go one better, and permit his regular troops of Dulness not only to parade on Lord Mayor's Day but to make sport and riot as they pleased.

At the end the writer brings us back to the comparison with the city where the true Grub Street lay.

> What if our Government had a Poet-Laureat here, as in England? What if our University had a Professor of Poetry here as in England? What if our Lord-Mayor had a City Bard here, as in England? And, to refine upon England, What if every Corporation, Parish, and Ward in this Town, had a Poet in Fee, as they have not in England?

This is a beautiful piece of rhetoric, though distorted by its application to so silly an end. The repeated phrase 'as in England', followed by the splendidly anticlimactic 'as they have not in England' – even the cadence is bathetic. Not even England has yet sunk to that, despite their professors who are poetasters (Joseph Trapp, say) and their Elkanah Settles. The writer has in mind that domestic poets might be instituted, along the lines of a domestic chaplain, but he seems pessimistic about this plan.[52]

All in all, the *Letter* is a striking piece of writing. Its root ideas are ordinary enough – roughly, the establishment of what Pope, in his imitation of Donne's second satire, was to refer to as 'new tenements in Hell' (42). *The Dunciad*, needless to say, gives us a more comprehensive and integrated vision of these new quarters let out to the Dull. Yet the *Letter to a Young Poet* is itself executed with brilliant imaginative zest. The persona is deployed with finesse: he both embodies literary idiocy and exposes it in others. Moreover, the idea of blaming Dublin for lacking the horrors of Grub Street opens up splendid avenues for satire. Simultaneously the writer can draw attention to the real defects of the place, mostly shared with any modern city, and re-emphasise the still-unique nightmares of the London scene. There is an underlying political innuendo, as well. Ireland is subservient, dependent, even to the provision of a Grub

Street. Her deprivations extend to the public vices she is allowed to enjoy.

Several of the tracts Swift composed in his Irish years bear on the theme of this book, under one aspect or another. His interest in criminal biography appears in a characteristic hoax, *The Last Speech and Dying Words of Ebenezer Elliston* (1722). Similarly, another pamphlet full of the flavour of Swift, entitled *An Examination of Certain Abuses, Corruptions, and Enormities in the City of Dublin* (1732), displays the author's sharp awareness of the life of the streets. In this work he deals with the urban landscape that inspired Dickens to create a poetic symbolism of city living. But Swift for his part devises no elaborate imagery of dustheaps and rivers: he speaks with a flat finality of heaped-up human excrement, of raucous cries and bellows from the hawkers, of garrets and cellars. The tone is gaily ironic, indeed almost flippant, but these are the topics of the most intense Augustan vision. In a more glancing way, a curious piece called *On Barbarous Denominations in Ireland* exhibits the real Swift. Here the writer fulminates with mock-petulance against barbarous Hibernian place-names. He cites a number of English names, among them Farn-ham, Corn-bury, Barn-elms (thus printed), as a model of sensible nomenclature, against the 'hideous words' in the Irish brogue. He even proposes certain 'appelations, proper to express the talents of the owners' of various country seats. These include '*Dunce-hill*'. This analytic approach to language is as marked in Swift as in Joyce. One can hardly suppose that the implications of the phrase 'Grub Street' could have been lost on such a mind.[53]

Perhaps the most direct approach to our theme is found in *A Serious and Useful Scheme, to make an Hospital for Incurables* (1733). This was attributed by Scott and subsequent editors to Swift. It was, however, excluded from the eighteenth-century collections of the works, and Herbert Davis suggested Matthew Pilkington as a possible author.[54] As with the *Letter to a Young Poet*, the issue is largely academic. The *Scheme* is composed with assumed gravity, its manner that of a 'reasonable' advocate – a civil servant making a case, say – rather than a demented projector. It encapsulates much of the Grub Street legend as developed by the Scriblerian group.

The writer begins by pointing to the munificent provision of hospitals in London – for 'seamen worn out in the service of their country, and others for infirm soldiers', for those deprived of their reason, for widows and orphans, etc. Only one institution is lacking: a home for incurables of all kinds. With the usual confidence of the man who has an idea, he expects his innovation to be 'universally allowed necessary'. As a principal factor, he invokes the huge number of 'absolute incurables' in every walk of life:

> For instance; let any man seriously consider what numbers there are of incurable fools, incurable knaves, incurable scolds, incurable scribblers, (besides myself), incurable coxcombs, incurable infidels, incurable liars, incurable whores, in all places of public resort . . .

to which the writer adds such categories as the incurably vain. The process is a common one in Augustan satire: we move from a technical or neutral term (here the medical word 'incurable') to a loaded, moralising sense ('incurable' meaning 'inveterate' or 'obstinate'). To this list, there is further augmentation:

> Under the denomination of incurable fools, we may reasonably expect, that such an hospital would be furnished with considerable numbers of the growth of our universities; who, at present, appear in various professions in the world, under the venerable titles of physicians, barristers, and ecclesiastics.

The seminary of Dulness, in fact, by another name. And, predictably, the very next sentence uses the word – 'those ancient seminaries have been, for some years past, accounted little better than nurseries of such sort of incurables . . .'

The author goes on to analyse in detail the recruits to be expected, were such a foundation set up. (The last noun, incidentally, is employed more than once.) So many people will need 'accomodation', the inventor of the scheme concludes, that a strict rationing or quota system will be required. The legal profession would be denuded almost entirely; the Stock Exchange and the Palace of Westminster would likewise feel the pinch. A sort of nation-wide *anomie*, such as that envisaged in the *Argument against Abolishing Christianity*, is the likely outcome. A splendidly controlled hyperbole runs through the scheme:

When I first determined to prepare this Scheme for the use and inspection of the public, I intended to examine one whole ward in this city, that my computation of the number of incurable scolds might be more perfect and exact. But I found it impossible to finish my progress through more than one street.

None the less, this public-spirited enquirer carries out something of a sample survey, starting with a wealthy Cornhill councillor. By a statistical projection familiar to modern readers, the total number of incurables in London, Westminster and Southwark is calculated.

At this point, the municipal interest shifts to the region of Cripplegate:

As to the incurable scribblers, (of which society I have the honour to be a member), they probably are innumerable; and, of consequence, it will be absolutely impossible to provide for one-tenth part of their fraternity. However, as this set of incurables are generally more plagued with poverty than any other, it will be a double charity to admit them on the foundation; a charity to the world, to whom they are a common pest and nuisance; and a charity to themselves, to relieve them from want, contempt, kicking, and several other accidents of that nature, to which they are continually liable.

Grub Street itself would then have reason to rejoice, to see so many of its half-starved manufacturers amply provided for; and the whole tribe of meagre incurables would probably shout for joy, at being delivered from the tyranny and garrets of printers, publishers, and booksellers.

What a mixed multitude of ballad-writers, ode-makers, translators, farce-compunders, opera-mongers, biographers, pamphleteers, and journalists, would appear crowding to the hospital; not unlike the brutes resorting to the ark before the deluge! And what an universal satisfaction would such a sight afford to all, except pastry-cooks, grocers, chandlers, and tobacco-retailers, to whom alone the writings of those incurables were anyway profitable!

The ideas at the start are those of 'On Poetry: A Rapsody'; the idiom generally that of Scriblerus. Pope, we recall, had thought fit to provide for 'the whole tribe of meagre incurables' by creating a Chelsea Hospital for veteran hacks;[55] whilst the innuendo in the closing sentence is often paralleled in the satirists.

The author now moves on to Simon Wagstaff's territory, the decayed beaux of St James's, here described as 'so many living burlesques of human nature'. After this he turns to infidels and liars.

Then, recollecting his 'serious' intent, he produces a sort of costing exercise, headed 'A Computation of the Daily and Annual Expenses of an Hospital, to be erected for Incurables' (observe that last verb). In style this recalls the famous Bills of Gratitude drawn up by Swift in *Examiner* no. 17. This calculation does not reach quite the same delicious pitch of absurd-looking outrage; but it has its moments: as the item, 'Incurable coxcombs, are very numerous; and, considering what numbers are annually imported from France and Italy, we cannot admit fewer than ten thousand, which will be . . . £500.' At least forty thousand incurable scribblers are to be admitted, as they are amongst those 'in greatest distress for a daily maintenance'. Overall, this finicky and apparently literal weighing of the costs involved serves the writer's ends with conspicuous success: it reinforces our sense of his muddleheaded pertinacity, and bestows on his project a lunatic air of cogency. The same attention to detail emerges from a second calculation, the precise expense incurred in each category of inmate, as well as in the specific taxes which are to be levied to disburden society of these 'inconceivable plagues' in its midst.

After exculpating himself, very much in the style of Swift's projectors, from the charge of proposing 'an unjust or oppressive Scheme', the writer suggests a measure of self-help on the part of the incurables. Naturally the body of scribblers will have to be excused, as being 'found in very bad circumstances'. But other funds should be available for the 'endowment' from the estates of the other candidates for the hospital. Lotteries are another possible source of revenue. Finally, £6000 is to be obtained from the estate of Richard Norton, Esq, whose memory is to be fitly commemorated by a statue in the first apartment of the hospital. Now the footnote by the publisher (George Faulkner, Swift's main outlet) tells us that Norton was a man of fortune, who left his wealth to the poor of England. Now in fact Norton was a great crony of Anthony Henley, who had been a particularly good friend of Swift's over twenty years earlier. It is a little surprising that the much younger Pilkington should use this instance, although we know that he offered to the London bookseller Benjamin Motte a pamphlet on the subject, 'which he pretended came from an eminent hand' (doubtless Swift). According to Motte, another bookseller issued the book on his own refusal, but lost money on the venture. It is certain that Pope and Swift knew of the Norton affair; and the references in the *Scheme* are far from ruling out Swift's own participation.[56]

After this, the writer sets out certain features of the hospital as he envisages it. The governors should have '(if such a thing were possible) some appearance of religion, and belief in God' – a visionary expectation which would interest the arguer against abolition. Then comes the real *coup*:

> And I hope, in regard to the great pains I have taken, about this Scheme, that I shall be admitted upon the foundation, as one of the scribbling incurables. But, as an additional favour, I entreat, that I may not be placed in an apartment with a poet who hath employed his genius for the stage; because he will kill me with repeating his compositions: and I need not acquaint the world, that it is extremely painful to bear any nonsense – except our own.

Thus the scheme is commended to the legislature, in the hope that the endowment will duly be made. Again we find Nonsense given, not just institutional respectability, but a physical home – a place of its own. Not surprising, then, to find the dateline at the foot of the text: 'From my Garret in Moorfields, Aug. 20, 1733.' Whether the tract is by Pilkington or not, it is a characteristic development of garret mythology: one more lively survey of Grub Street properties.[57]

A work that comes into a slightly different category, and one undoubtedly from the hand of Swift, is *A Complete Collection of Genteel and Ingenious Conversation* (1738). The portion relevant to this study is not the 'conversation' itself, that curious anthology of worn-out cliché, but the Introduction. This is attributed to 'Simon Wagstaff, Esq.', a name possibly recalling Dr William Wagstaffe. The use of this persona involves something of a departure for Swift. In the *Tale of a Tub* he had likewise adopted the manner of a conceited, incompetent scribbler. And in his party writing during the Harley ministry he had taken over the accents of the hack journalist. What is new about Simon Wagstaff may be summed up under two headings – his social pretensions, and his technical concern.

Where the standard figure of myth is the garreteer, Wagstaff has spent his life in pursuing the great. And, whatever the rebuffs, he has to some degree made it – his address is not Moorfields or Hounsditch, but lodgings 'next door to the Gloucester-head in St James's-street'. This was a West End location, appropriate to one bent on instructing the public in the *ton* and manners of polite society. It was also a region familiar to Swift. He himself had lodged in King Street, St James's, and friends such as Sir Andrew Fountaine resided there at various times.[58] Possibly this in itself represents a dry comment by Swift. By the end of his life, that is, the scribbler has quit his former humble quarters in the slums, and set up house in the fashionable area. Grub Street has crossed the city into Westminster – the very removal allegorised in *The Dunciad*.

A large proportion of Wagstaff's energy is devoted to presenting himself as 'of good reputation in the world, and well acquainted with the best families in town'. He is, of course, one more in the grisly line of projectors compassed by Swift's imagination: his life has been spent 'improving and polishing all parts of conversation between persons of quality'. To this end he has 'laboured' in the usual misapplied fashion, having concocted a fixed routine by which the greater part of his days are nights are given to 'polite' company. With the methodical habits that the Scriblerian group always attach to pedantry, Wagstaff transcribes the choicest expressions he has overheard as soon as he returns home. Naturally, this Boswellian enterprise needs time – 'this I found was a work of infinite labour, and what required the nicest judgment, and consequently could not be brought to any degree of perfection in less than sixteen years more' than the twelve he had previously spent. With the usual complacence, he describes his resolution to defer publication until he could 'present a complete system to the world'. We are back with the threats of the author of the *Tale*. This recollection is driven home further when Wagstaff passes on to congratulate his native country on having 'outdone all the nations of Europe, in advancing the whole art of conversation to the greatest heighth it is capable of reaching'. Predictably, he believes that 'the whole genius, humour, politeness, and eloquence of England are summed up' in his system. Like the earlier Grubean spokesman, he makes a virtue out of every literary necessity. He boasts of the antiquity of his collection, that is its lack of originality. He delights in its amenability to rote-learning.

The place Wagstaff holds in the pantheon of Dulness comes out most clearly when the argument passes to the cultivation of this 'science'. He fulfils every Scriblerian demand by offering a 'proposal for erecting publick schools, provided with the best and ablest masters and mistresses, at the charge of the nation' to promote the subject. As often where the satirists are envisaging the 'selling' of a project by pressure-group methods, the verb *to erect* receives a special emphasis. It is as though Pope and Swift were not content merely to dramatise the founding or establishment of a college of unreason: they had to carry the idea as far as physical building. Another reason, of course, why Grub Street served their turn.

The prefacer goes on to display his gentility, by scornful asides on 'mean and vulgar people' (luckily, 'A footman can swear, but he cannot swear like a lord') as well as by easy references to the nobility in most cases, though, to an obscure baronet or a frumpish lady. But in reality the company he keeps is different. His 'intimate friend' is Tom Brown; he has been 'particularly acquainted, with Mr Charles Gildon, Mr [Ned] Ward, Mr Dennis, that admirable critic and poet, and several others'. His habitat, obviously, is the cell of the Dunces. He boasts of the 'great assistance' he has received from the 'illustrious' translators, John Ozell and Captain Stevens. His ambition is openly declared: to imitate these 'great refiners of our language'. And the last two of his ingenious friends to earn a mention are the King Dunces themselves, Cibber and Theobald. In the light of the foolish charade to follow, we cannot mistake the drift of the satire. Swift is showing Dulness no longer as pure ignorance, illiteracy, the literature of the ghetto. Its vices are now those of brisk confidence, shallow jauntiness, or vulgar familiarity. The faults apparent in the productions of the Dull have grown to be the faults of a *parvenu* culture, which has succeeded in lifting itself out of the slum but has not achieved true gentility. Its style will be (in a favourite term of Augustan criticism) 'pert'. Its general manner will be that of the pushing social climbers in Fanny Burney or Jane Austen.[59] The new Grub Street has given itself airs.

In conformity with this milieu, Wagstaff has learnt to parrot brightly of his methods as a writer. Here we see the second main point of distinction from the earlier scribblers I have mentioned in this chapter. Wagstaff introduces a note of the self-satisfied technician; he is the would-be craftsman as well as the would-be gentleman. Contemptuous as he is of 'one Isaac Newton, an instrument-maker, formerly living near Leicester Fields, and afterwards a work-man in the mint at the Tower', proud of his 'polite' orthography (which has *in sickly pay-day* for *encyclopedia*), his boorish approach undermines the intended civility of his undertaking. At times there is almost a trade-union flavour to his proposal: his conviction, for instance, that his public spirit ought to find due reward from the state, and also his unconscious xenophobia. At times he recalls rather the scientist, in the abstract perfection he commends in his useless scheme (cf. the Academy of Lagado). But mostly it is the upstart 'educator', embattled in his johnny-come-lately London mentality:

> I have rejected all provincial or country turns of wit and fancy, because I am acquainted with very few; but indeed chiefly, because I found them so much inferior to those at court, especially among the gentlemen-ushers, the ladies of the bedchamber, and the maids of honour; I must also add the hither end of our noble metropolis.

and incurably optimistic in his visionary dreams:

> I have determined next session to deliver a petition to the House of Lords, for an act of parliament to establish my book as the standard grammar in all the principal cities of the kingdom, where this art is to be taught by able masters, who are to be approved and recommended by me. . . . Neither shall I be so far wanting to myself as not to desire a patent, granted, of course, to all useful projectors; I mean, that I may have the sole profit of giving a licence to every school to read my grammar for fourteen years.

Such refined idiocy could not be bettered. It is, as the nineteenth century would say, the quintessence of solemn pretension.[60]

Swift's concern with the separate strands that went into the Grub Street structure of ideas was lifelong. He maintained, as all the world knows, an obsessive interest in physical corruption, and he was pre-ternaturally sensitive to the blots on the urban landscape. He was alive to the doings of those who occupied lower slopes on Parnassus, even if he lacked Pope's comprehensive service of information retrieval. He hated rascally booksellers as cordially as his friend, though with rather less cause. And he developed, in the *Tale* particularly, a resonant mode of satiric placing, whereby contemporary culture could be superimposed on the map of London, and its running sores subjected to the bright light of demonstration.

Yet he never quite attained the complex symbolism of *The Dunciad*, and never found so apt a vehicle for an integral survey of Grub Street. There are many reasons for this. Pope got in first; Swift was less effective in devising (as opposed to transforming) mythology to his purpose. Finally, Swift's use of disagreeable physical detail is not the same as Pope's. Swift tends either to be seeking a deflating, contrived coarseness; or else to find his outrage subverted by a kind of affection – unwilling, ungenial, but powerfully antiseptic in the presence of that revulsion which the satirist must always profess. Pope could make beauty out of squalor. If Swift was less consistently successful in his treatment of Grub Street, that may be because he couldn't help seeing some beauty *in* squalor.[61]

Epigraph. Quoted from Trevelyan, II, 430 (the work dates from 1709).

1. Maynard Mack has recently argued that 'the England of Pope's satires, like (Johnson's) . . . London in his poem *London*, is not wholly to be discovered on any of John Rocque's maps.' – *The Garden and the City* (Toronto, 1969), p. 231. There is only an apparent contradiction here with my contention. The *Tale* clearly embraces themes remote from contemporary London, and its effective geography is by no means limited to the capital under Queen Anne. My point is that it *starts* from the data offered up by topical reality; the facts of London life (Bedlam, Grub Street, etc.) are employed not just as setting but as symbols of the author's satiric vision.

2. In this section I do not supply detailed page references to the *Tale*, since these are abundant and largely follow in a consecutive fashion the order of the text itself.

3. See for instance Webb, IV, 367–9.

4. Cf my article, 'Sir Henry Furnese, Matthew Prior and the Kit Cat Club,' *Notes & Queries* xviii (1971), 46–9.

5. John Cleland, *Memoirs of a Woman of Pleasure* (London, ed. 1970), pp. 116,

146; Arbuthnot, pp. 231, 277, 289: cf. p. 300, where Arbuthnot mentions a project to unite 'several small corporations of liars into one society'. For the idea of an academy, as well as Swift's letter to the Lord Treasurer, see *Tatler* no. 18. Cowley had described his prophets' college as a 'university', caricatured by Dryden in *MacFlecknoe* as the 'Nursery' (cf Ch.I). Horace Walpole was later to describe bear-gardens as universities: letter to Dalrymple, June 1760, quoted by P. A. Scholes, *The Life and Activities of Sir John Hawkins* (London, 1953), p. 65. The pejorative use of 'seminary' is very common in the eighteenth century. See for instance Trevelyan, I, 27, where the open commons are described by a contemporary as 'seminaries of a lazy, thieving sort of people'. Smollett is another to use the expression, with special reference to the suburbs as 'seminaries of drunkenness': Radzinowicz, I, 400.

6. For Locke's juxtaposition of Westminster Hall, the Exchange, almshouses and Bedlam, see his *Essay concerning Humane Understanding*, ed. A. C. Fraser (New York, 1959), IV, xx, 5.

7. *Tale*, p. lxx.

8. See my article, 'Swift, Walpole and the Rope-Dancers,' *Papers on Language & Literature*, VIII (1972), 159–71.

9. *Tale*, p. 262.

10. Cf. Webb, IV, 407–8: 'the overgrown and unorganised conglomeration of houses of the Metropolis was, from the beginning to the end of the eighteenth century, pre-eminent in criminality. We despair of conveying any adequate picture of the lawless violence, the barbarous licentiousness, and the almost unlimited opportunities for pilfering and robbery offered by the unpoliced London streets of that century.'

11. There are a couple of brief and unimportant references in the Partridge pamphlets. They are not by Swift himself but they do confirm the availability of the trope. See Partridge's *Account of the Proceedings of Isaac Bickerstaff, Esq*: 'There is one John Partridge can smell a Knave as far as Grubstreet.'

12. Swift, *Correspondence*, I, 133, 165.

13. Swift, *Correspondence*, I, 305; *Journal*, II, 553.

14. Swift, *Correspondence*, I, 306; III, 44.

15. See for example Trevelyan, II, 120.

16. Swift, *Prose Works*, III, passim, esp. 35–6.

17. *Journal*, I, 178, 337.

18. *Journal*, II, 416, 426, 441, 468, 511.

19. *Journal*, II, 466, 551, 553, 568, 572, 579.

20. *Journal*, II, 430, 431, 539, 573.

21. *Journal*, II, 548.

22. Pope, *Correspondence*, I, 195, 339.

23. Swift, *Poems*, pp. 179, 279; Mack, *The Garden and the City*, pp. 131–2, 157.

The motifs of the garret, ragged poets and their master Curll reappear in 'Advice to the Grub-street Verse Writers' (1726), *Poems*, p. 309. However, the expression does not occur within the text of the verses themselves.

24. Swift, pp. 438, 440–1; Butt, p. 15. For the allusions to the Cripplegate quarter, see Ch.I.
25. Swift, *Poems*, p. 501.
26. Swift, *Poems*, pp. 571, 573, 578–9.
27. Swift, *Poems*, pp. 577–8.
28. Swift, *Poems*, pp. 570, 574, 580.
29. Swift, *Poems*, p. 601.
30. Swift, *Poems*, pp. 418, 420, 434.
31. Swift, *Correspondence*, I, 148; II, 65; III, 320; IV, 62, 143, 396 and passim.
32. *Romances and Narratives*, XVI, 277–8. 'All the way from *Newgate* to *Tyburn* is one continu'd Fair', says the writer of *A Trip through the Town* (1735), quoted by Ralph Straus, *Eighteenth Century Diversions: Tricks of the Town* (London, 1927), p. 145. 'Fairground droll', one might amend the phrase.
33. Swift, *Correspondence*, I, 215; II, 215; III, 253.
34. Savage, 'Swift's Fallen City', *The World of Jonathan Swift*, ed. B. Vickers (Oxford, 1968), pp. 176–9, 180, 190.
35. O Hehir, 'The Meaning of Swift's "Description of a City Shower"', *ELH*, XXVII (1960), 204–5.
36. Vickers, p. 187.
37. Swift, *Poems*, p. 93. For a similar account of 'real' London, see Webb, IV, 236, quoted by Holdsworth, X, 214–5.
38. Radzinowicz, II, 36.
39. Information chiefly from George Rudé, *Wilkes and Liberty* (Oxford, 1962), pp. 11–12; Radzinowicz, I, 210; II, 155–6; Dorothy George in Turberville, I, 175; Marshall, pp. 250–2. For the criminals mentioned, see especially *The Proceedings at the Sessions of the Peace, and Oyer and Terminer, for the City of London, and County of Middlesex* (London, 1732–3), pp. 222–5; and *Select Trials at the Old Bailey* (London, 1742), I, 40–4.
40. Congreve, *Love for Love*, ed. E. L. Avery (London, 1967), p. 47; Boswell, *London Journal 1762–3*, ed. F. A. Pottle (London, 1950), pp. 251–2.
41. *The Works of Mr John Oldham* (London, 6th ed., 1703), pp. 261, 426: cf. Irving, pp. 33, 35.
42. *Journal*, II, 415: a typical blend of the fire/rabble/carnival cluster of ideas.
43. Swift, *Poems*, pp. 312–3.
44. Swift, *Poems*, pp. 661–3.
45. Strype, III, 284; F. A. Mumby, *Publishing and Bookselling* (London, 1949), p. 141; H. L. Snyder, 'New Bibliographical Data for the Reign of Queen Anne', *The Library*, XXII (1967), 336–7; Stanley Morison, *The English Newspaper* (Cambridge, 1932), pp. 121–3; *State Trials*, XV, 1341; Sir Henry

Ellis (ed.), *The Obituary of Richard Smyth* ([London],) 1849), p. viin; Oldham, *Works*, p. 417; Pope, *Correspondence*, III, 70; *A Trip through London* (London, 8th ed., 1928), p. 51; Swift, *Correspondence*, V, 118; Swift, *Prose Works*, XII, 264. Campkin (p. 7) speaks of the street as 'the great emporium for booksellers and publishers'. Smithfield itself was the great emporium for flesh.

46. *The Works of Andrew Marvell, Esq*, ed. Edward Thompson (London, 1776), II, 280.

47. See *Tale*, pp. lix, 10, etc.

48. Ehrenpreis, II, 93.

49. Swift, *Poems*, pp. 236–9.

50. See (for the affirmative case), Paul Fussell, 'Speaker and Style', *RES*, X (1959), 63–7, and Louis T. Milic, *A Quantitative Approach to the Style of Jonathan Swift* (The Hague, 1967), and see for the sceptical view, C. S. Matlack and W. F. Matlack, 'A Statistical Approach to Problems of Attribution: *A Letter of Advice to a Young Poet*', *College English* XXIX (1968), 627–32. See Teerinck, § 621–2, for doubts about its authenticity; as well as *Prose Works*, IX, xxiv–xxvii.

51. On Edinburgh at this time, cf. Trevelyan, II, 218–20.

52. Swift, *Prose Works*, IX, 225–45.

53. Swift, *Prose Works*, IX, 35–41; XII, 215–32; IV, 280–4.

54. See Teerinck, § 730–3, and *Prose Works*, XII, 345. My discussion is based on the edition by Temple Scott of the *Prose Works* (London, 1905), VII, 287–303.

55. *Correspondence*, II, 3.

56. Scott, (ed.), *Prose Works*, VII, 301n. Cf. Swift, *Correspondence*, IV, 254; Pope, *Correspondence*, III, 390; E/C, VII, 324.

57. It is worth noting that Motte uses the very same verb as that stressed in the *Scheme*, to erect, when writing to Swift of his 'noble . . . design' to 'erect an Hospital for Lunaticks and Idiots' (Swift, *Correspondence*, IV, 373). Of course Swift himself used an analogous expression: 'He gave the little Wealth he had, / To build a House for Fools and Mad' (*Poems*, p. 512).

58. See for example *Journal*, II, 617. The Vanhomrighs lived in Bury Street at one time: *Journal*, I, 64.

59. A representative figure in the 'pert' tradition was Sir Roger L'Estrange, hack pamphleteer turned government official and censor. His literary style is often so described: it was the idiom of upstarts.

60. Swift, *Prose Works*, IV, 97–124.

61. Relevant here is Ehrenpreis's judgement (II, 386) that the stenches and vomitings of the 'City Shower' add up not to an indictment but to a cheerful acceptance of the urban scene.' He speaks, too, of 'a humorous comprehension.'

Index

Entries have normally been restricted (1) to persons who appear in the text on more than one occasion; and (2) to streets and districts with an important literary bearing, grouped together under 'London'. Grub Street and its environs are separately covered in Index (b). The entry for 'Dunces' contains the victims, satiric targets and opponents of Pope and Swift, whether or not the individual concerned figures in *The Dunciad* itself.

233

(b) Grub Street